UNIONIST-NATI

GOVERNING URBAN SCOT

SCOTTISH HISTORICAL REVIEW
MONOGRAPHS SERIES

No. 6

UNIONIST-NATIONALISM

Governing Urban Scotland, 1830–1860

GRAEME MORTON

TUCKWELL PRESS

First published in Great Britain in 1999 by
Tuckwell Press Ltd
The Mill House, Phantassie, East Linton, East Lothian, EH40 3DG
Scotland

ISBN 1 86232 039 X

British Library Cataloguing-in-Publication Data. A catalogue
record for this book is available on request from the British Library

Typeset in 10/12 Baskerville by
Aligra Lancaster
Printed and bound in Great Britain by
Cromwell Press, Trowbridge, Wiltshire

for

SAMUEL and EVANGELINE

Contents

Illustrations

between pp. 116 and 117

Tables

Figures and Textual Illustrations

Acknowledgements

This research started out as a Ph.D. thesis at the University of Edinburgh. The substantive argument of this book remains unchanged, but the thesis contains much of the technical information on the methodology of nominal record linkage and the coding decisions behind the occupational classifications employed which, for the sake of brevity, have not been reproduced here. Moreover, this book contains a number of changes made in the light of the constructive criticism of the thesis by its examiners, T. C. Smout and Lindsay Paterson, as well as the occasional footnote or two in acknowledgement of some of the more recent literature in the ever expanding field of nationalism. This re-drafting would not have been possible without the award of a Research Fellowship (H52427005694) from the Economic and Social Research Council; their support is gratefully acknowledged.

The themes of this book have been rehearsed partially elsewhere and I would like to thank the Association for the Study of Ethnicity and Nationalism for permission to reproduce material first published in *Nations and Nationalism* , ii (2) (1996) for use in Chapter 6.

To all who contributed to my life and work over the completion of the thesis and of this book, my parents most especially, I thank you once again. I would like to acknowledge and thank Allan Morton for a number of the photographs presented here. My publisher, John Tuckwell, has been a constant source of encouragement and so justified the many long hours in front of the word-processor. To the Scottish Historical Review Trust I can only marvel and admire their support for new scholars telling their illustrious and established colleagues where they have been going wrong all these years. My wife, A. E. M., a person born on a national border and acutely aware of the intricacies of complementary identities, has supported me throughout. The greatest debt of all for this work is to my two doctoral supervisors, David McCrone and Bob Morris, whose knowledge and insights are without comparison. Their guidance has been invaluable, yet all factual and conceptual errors remain, of course, my own.

G. M.

CHAPTER ONE

Introduction: Scottish National Identity in a United Kingdom

No more the 'British nation-state'

If there is a straightforward reason to justify another story about nationalism in Scotland, it is the continued failure of a 'British' identity to find favour. Despite its appearance on the passports of legal residents of the United Kingdom of Great Britain and Northern Ireland, in a recent poll only 6% of Scots regarded themselves as singularly British rather than Scottish.[1] Such national categories remain inextricably problematic, and so inevitably beg the question of why citizens of the United Kingdom are not all 'Britons' after 460 years of union between England and Wales, nearly 300 years between England and Scotland, nearly 200 years between Britain and Ireland, plus innumerable centuries of ethnic intermixing between the four.[2] Despite the respective referendum votes in favour of a devolved Parliament and Assembly in

---

[1] Source: ICM/Rowntree Reform Trust 13; data for 1993/1994.

Think of self as	England %	Scotland %	Wales %
X not British	16	37	28
More X than British	12	27	20
Equally X & British	43	25	30
More British than X	10	4	7
British not X	15	6	14
None of these	3	2	1
Totals	5,057	1,664	656

My thanks to David McCrone for this reference. A poll produced by Richard Rose in 1979 found that 67% of Protestants, but only 15% of Catholics in Northern Ireland, declared themselves as 'British': R. Rose, *Understanding the United Kingdom: The Territorial Dimension in Government* (London, 1982).

[2] When I include Ireland as one of the four nations which share the unitary British state, I make the following assumptions: that Henry VIII was designated 'King of Ireland' in 1541; that the English and Scottish plantations in Ulster began in 1610; that the Union between Great Britain and Ireland was in 1801; and that a re-jigged United Kingdom followed the creation of Northern Ireland and the Irish Free State in 1921. Methodologically, Hugh Kearney provides a landmark approach to the interrelationships between the four nations: H. Kearney, *The British Isles: A History of Four Nations* (Cambridge, 1989).

Scotland and Wales in September 1997, the UK today remains inveterately one state and four nations.

The Union of the Crowns between Scotland and England in 1603, and the Union of their Parliaments in 1707, brought the two geographically adjacent kingdoms peacefully together, 'united into one kingdom by the name of Great Britain'.[3] The prefix 'Great' was to signify an enlargement in territorial boundaries, but came to symbolise the power of the first industrial nation and its empire during the eighteenth and nineteenth centuries. Constitutional monarchy, a bargain struck well before the 'springtime of peoples', ensured British patriotism meant strength while Europe split, annexed and seceded in the name of nationalism.

Along with France, Great Britain has frequently been regarded both in popular consciousness and in the academic literature as the leading European example of the 'unitary nation-state', where there is no ethnic or civic gap between the nation and its state.[4] Westminster, the mother of all parliaments, functioning within a British constitution so strong, so age-old, and with its built-in 'checks and balances', that it need not be written down, has been labelled the leading liberal democracy since 1688.[5]

This perception of 'nation-statehood' has masked conflict within British national identity, especially in the period before formal political nationalist parties. To claim to be British can be regarded as a claim for neutrality, denying the relevance of place of birth. It is often said that Britishness is unproblematically the wider identity of those who are English,[6] and that British is simply used as the title of Englishmen abroad.[7] The conflation stems from the tendency for high politics in Britain to flow from English constitutional history.[8] That towering

---

[3] Article I of 'The Articles of the Union', reproduced in Daniel Defoe, *The History of the Union between England and Scotland* (London, 1786 edn), p. 197.

[4] E.g., T. Zeldin, *France, 1848–1945* (Oxford, 1980), p. 4; H. Kohn, *Prophets and Peoples: Studies in Nineteenth-Century Nationalism* (New York, 1946), p. 3. Blondel notes that despite the existence of the four 'countries', 'What makes Britain appear homogeneous is the fact that the population is not uniformly spread in these four countries but highly concentrated in a small area ... over 80% of the whole British population now reside in England' (in 1841, Table I from Blondel shows the figure to be 74%): J. Blondel, *Voters, Parties and Leaders: The Social Fabric of British Politics* (London, 1963), pp. 20–1.

[5] For an analysis of the contradiction in this constitutional position, see T. Nairn, *The Enchanted Glass: Britain and its Monarchy* (London, 1988).

[6] The influence of Ernest Barker in defining popular historical notions of English/ Britishness in the early years of the twentieth century is important: see J. Stapleton, *Englishness and the Study of Politics: The Social and Political Thought of Ernest Barker* (Cambridge, 1994). See also K. Robbins, *Nineteenth-Century Britain: England, Scotland and Wales. The Making of a Nation* (Oxford, 1988), p. 98.

[7] B. Crick, 'An Englishman considers his Passport', in N. Evans (ed.), *National Identity in the British Isles* (Coleg Harlech, 1989); B. Crick, 'Essay on Britishness', *Scottish Affairs* (2) (1992), p. 73.

[8] Two classic 19th-century examples of this genre are: H. T. Buckle, *History of Civilisation in England* (London, 1857–61); and W. Stubbs, *The Constitutional History of England* (1874–8).

intellect of the Scottish Enlightenment, David Hume, wrote his history of England because it was 'the duty of every Englishman to make himself acquainted with English history that he may be aware of those causes which have made this little isle the foremost amongst nations'.[9] Macaulay wrote the history of Britain in his *History of England*.[10] Walter Bagehot had no hesitation in prioritising the *English Constitution* when writing his theory of the British state in 1867.[11]

Our unease with the nomenclature for this long-united kingdom is a powerful reminder that popular notions of Britishness play fast and loose with the formal constitutional position.[12] Indeed, wider recognition of the ambiguity in British national identity has led to an ever-flowering literature on nationalism of the periphery: of Scottish, Welsh and Irish nationalisms. Until recently this has been to the detriment of 'big' nationalisms,[13] yet in many exciting ways this gap has started to be filled, and the England/Britain problematic is moving centre stage.[14] Consider, for example, David Morse's attempt to provide an understanding of the concept of 'England' during the Victorian age. He does so by stressing the centrality of the Scottish contribution to an English understanding of itself:

It was Hume and Mackintosh who laid the foundations for a modern history of England. It was Adam Smith who elaborated an economic theory that could serve as a framework for England's destiny as a trading nation. It was James Mill who in his classic *History of British India* (1818) mapped out Britain's future as an imperial power and legislator for mankind. It was Sir Walter Scott who in *Ivanhoe* produced the definitive myth of a proud Saxon race indomitably struggling against the Norman yoke. It was Thomas Carlyle who extended and developed this into a philosophy of the English character and a critique of industrialisation, and while

[9] D. Hume and W. C. Stafford, *History of England*, vol. 1 (London, 1754–62), p. 3.

[10] T. B. Macaulay, *History of England* (London, 1855–61).

[11] W. Bagehot, *The English Constitution* (London, 1963); on the conflicts within Great Britain, see J. Osmond, *The Divided Kingdom* (London, 1988).

[12] With the need for precision in his text, Kellas produced a 'geo-political glossary' to make sense of the different parts of the UK in this (still) standard textbook: J. G. Kellas, *The Scottish Political System* (3rd edn, Cambridge, 1984), p. ix. The definitional problem of referring to the United Kingdom in official publications is explored in B. Crick, 'The English and the British', in B. Crick (ed.) *National Identities: The Constitution of the United Kingdom* (Oxford, 1992).

[13] P. J. Taylor, 'The English and their Englishness: "A curious, mysterious, elusive and little understood people"', *Scottish Geographical Magazine*, cvii (3) (1991), p. 146.

[14] P. Corrigan and D. Sayer, *The Great Arch: English State Formation as Cultural Revolution* (Oxford, 1985); R. Colls & P. Dodd, *Englishness: Politics and Culture, 1880–1920* (London, 1986); G. Newman, *The Rise of English Nationalism, 1740–1830* (London, 1987); R. Samuel (ed.), *Patriotism: The Making and Unmaking of British National Identity* (London, 1987); L. Colley, *Britons: Forging the Nation, 1707–1837* (New Haven and London, 1992); L. Greenfeld, *Nationalism: Five Roads to Modernity* (Massachusetts, 1992); R. Porter (ed.), *Myths of the English* (Oxford, 1993); Stapleton, *Englishness and the Study of Politics*.

Macaulay, who was perhaps the one single writer to produce a view of England that was more influential than Carlyle's, was not himself Scottish, but was deeply influenced by the ideals of the Scottish Enlightenment, the foremost protégé of Francis Jeffrey at the *Edinburgh Review* from 1839 to 1847, and from 1852 to 1856 MP for Edinburgh itself.[15]

The many questions which are starting to be asked about the meaning of England, and of Englishness, are re-opening the sutures of union which bind four nations to the governance of the Westminster state. That it is misleading to examine this national identity as a case of advancing British homogenisation, of straightforward Anglicisation, is increasingly obvious. The conflicts within the centre are a response to nationalism of the periphery. They are a realisation that John Stuart Mill's confidence in multi-ethnic state formations in the nineteenth century, carried into the twentieth century most eloquently by commentators such as Sir Ernest Barker, were no longer appropriate.[16] Such Whiggish principles of state formation have masked national tensions which have never yet been eradicated, and a constitution which is perceived as increasingly inappropriate.[17]

This book is a contribution to nationalism of the periphery, of Scottish national identity at the high point of British imperialism. It is a period which takes in 1848–9, the 'springtime of nationalism' in Europe. Throughout the Continent, self-determination for nations applied to those which were considered to be viable (culturally and especially economically), following Mazzini's 'threshold principle'.[18] Scottish nationalism has been regarded as no more than a side-show to these events. There was, for example, no Scottish version of Young Ireland, responsible for a failed attempt at an armed rising in August 1848 in County Tipperary.[19] In a speech in Edinburgh in 1852, the great Whig historian and politician Thomas Babington Macaulay accounted for this absence:

> We owe this singular happiness, under the blessing of God, to a wise and noble constitution, the work of many generations of great men ... And, gentlemen, pre-eminent among those pacific victories of reason and public opinion, the recollection of which chiefly, I believe, carried us safely through the year of counter-revolutions ...

15 D. Morse, *High Victorian Culture* (London, 1993), pp. 47–8.
16 J. S. Mill, *Utilitarianism, Liberty and Representative Government* (London, 1910). For two examples of Barker's thought, which is noted for its consistency over his lifetime, see E. Barker, *National Character and the Factors in its Formation* (London, 1927); and E. Barker, *Reflections on Government* (Oxford, 1945).
17 On the latter point, see the editor's introduction to Crick (ed.), *National Identities*.
18 E. J. Hobsbawm, *Nations and Nationalism since 1780: Programme, Myth and Reality* (Cambridge, 1990), p. 32.
19 H. Seton-Watson, *Nations and States: An Enquiry into the Origins of Nations and the Politics of Nationalism* (London, 1977), p. 37.

I speak of the great commercial reform of 1846, the work of Sir Robert Peel, and of the great parliamentary reform of 1832, the work of many eminent statesmen, among whom none was more conspicuous than Lord John Russell.[20]

Karl Marx referred to the British constitution as that 'antiquated compromise between the class that rule officially [the aristocracy] and the class that rule non-officially [the bourgeoisie]' and so branded it a 'failure'.[21] With quite diametric views of the social order instilled by the British constitution – with its early settlement between Parliament and Crown – both Marx and Macaulay believed that the transfer of power to the middle classes meant that the fuel of revolution was dissipated.[22] Although Quinault has recently disputed the calm in England, stressing the impetus the events of 1848 gave to the Chartist movement,[23] and despite Tory fears of reform as Doomsday,[24] the stability of the state in mid-nineteenth-century Britain has been otherwise accepted as 'England über alles'.[25]

The classical nation-state, which started to appear in late eighteenth-century Europe and came into its own in the nineteenth century, was that of one-state for one-nation within a geographically bounded territory. All classical nation-states, in contrast to traditional states, are sovereign states.[26] David Beetham points out that the classical nation-state was a suitable adaptation to the economic, military and political circumstances of this period. King's definition is of a 'more impersonal and public system of rule over territorially circumscribed societies, exercised through a complex set of institutional arrangements and offices, which is distinguished from the largely localised and particularistic forms of power which preceded it'.[27] These states were established on free market economic success, upon a unified national system of law, taxation and administration.[28] The *raison d'être* of the nation-state was one of coherence between the people ('citizens') and the

---

[20] T. B. Macaulay, *The Works of Lord Macaulay: Complete*, vol. VIII (London, 1866), pp. 418–19.

[21] K. Marx, 'The crisis in England and the British Constitution' (Mar. 1855), in K. Marx and F. Engles, *On Britain* (London, 1954), p. 410.

[22] Marx's 'marginalisation' during his time in England from the English working class as a movement, and from the bourgeois intellectuals, is explored in G. Smith, 'Karl Marx and St George', *Journal of the History of Ideas*, ii (4) (1941).

[23] R. Quinault, '1848 and parliamentary reform', *Historical Journal*, xxxi (1988), p. 835.

[24] The Duke of Wellington predicted that following the Reform Act, 'nothing will remain of England but the name and the soil', quoted in J. A. Phillips, *The Great Reform Bill in the Boroughs: English Electoral Behaviour, 1818–1841* (Oxford, 1992), p. 23.

[25] F. Bedarida, *A Social History of England, 1851–1990*, trans. A. S. Forster (London, 1990), p. 92.

[26] A. Giddens, *Sociology* (Cambridge, 1989), p. 303.

[27] R. King, *The State in Modern Society: New Directions in Political Sociology* (London, 1986), p. 31.

[28] Quoted in D. McCrone, *Understanding Scotland: The Sociology of a Stateless Nation* (London, 1992), p. 216.

state as government. Fundamental to this coherence and to citizenship rights was the electoral franchise. The term 'citizen politics' refers to the extension of voting rights to all adult men and women, an event which did not happen in Britain until the twentieth century. Indeed, with the 1832 Reform Act, it is argued, the British state side-stepped the issue by enfranchising men of property and education.[29] 'After all that we have seen of Parliaments, it would be vain fancy to imagine that representation of the people is of itself sufficient security for their rights', remarked Henry Brougham.[30] Or, alternatively, keeping the 'halo' upon the 'monarchical and aristocratic elements of the constitution' is how Engels interpreted the restriction of the House of Commons to the bourgeoisie.[31] 'Citizen politics' was purposely compressed in Britain during the nineteenth century, and it was the 1832 Act, and the reform of local government in 1833 (Scotland) and 1835 (England and Wales) which, in Macaulay's line of argument (outlined above), kept the supposed coherence in the relationship between the British people and their state.

But did it? The two largest nations, Scotland and England, came together in 1707, but as commentators are becoming acutely aware this did not result in a *British* civil society. Each of the four nations became united under one state, but there was no single British nation as a result, despite the banner 'United Kingdom'. 'Ukania' and 'Yookay' are how, respectively, Tom Nairn and Raymond Williams have highlighted the ambiguity within the supposed classical British nation-state.[32] The melting pot created by the unitary state produced many instances of Anglicisation in all the 'peripheral' kingdoms, and this was often quietly accepted as part and parcel of economic opportunity. But Anglicisation, welcomed or otherwise, intentional or not, has never homogenised four civil societies into one: its title is that of a kingdom which is united, not a nation. The Scottish 'holy trinity' of kirk, law and education have long been regarded as underpinning a separate civil society, one the unitary state has not yet been able to capture. Indeed, Scotland's distinct civil society within the British state was labelled by John P. Mackintosh as producing a 'dual nationality' – where the Scots can be British if they wish, or, if not, they can 'opt out' and their identity can return to being a Scottish one.[33]

A dual (if not multiple) identity is part and parcel of being Scottish within the United Kingdom.[34] Irishness and an Ulster identity make

---

29 Hobsbawm, *Nations and Nationalism*, pp. 81–2. The deliberate restriction of the franchise is encapsulated in the title of M. Dyer, *Men of Property and Intelligence: The Scottish Electoral System prior to 1884* (Aberdeen, 1996).

30 H. Brougham, *Contributions to the Edinburgh Review. By Henry Lord Brougham in three volumes*, vol. II (London, 1856), p. 421.

31 F. Engels, *The Condition of the Working Class in England in 1844* (London, 1950), pp. 228–9.

32 Nairn, *Enchanted Glass*; R. Williams, *The Long Revolution* (London, 1961).

33 J. P. Mackintosh, 'The new appeal of nationalism', *New Statesman*, 27 Sep. 1974, p. 409.

34 Smout has built his model of Scottish national identity on 'concentric loyalties': see T. C. Smout, 'Perspectives on the Scottish identity', *Scottish Affairs* (6) (1994), pp. 102–7.

Northern Ireland into a host of competing identities, clearly stratified by religion, where the conception of Britishness is further removed from any of the peripheral nations. Welshness too is highly ambiguous, so different culturally from the core, yet so apprehensive in its political mobilisation: witness Iolo Morganwg and the Welsh literary enlightenment at the end of the eighteenth century, the Gorsedd of the Bards, eisteddfodau and, in religion, Protestant nonconformity linked to a remarkably persistent language. Such anti-Anglicanisation failed to over-run Anglicisation, and British liberalism was for so long the preference over political nationalism,[35] yet Welshness cannot simply be charac-terised in terms of an increasing and straightforwardly all-pervasive British identity, despite formal incorporation with England stretching back to 1536.[36]

Our realisation is strong: that in the three peripheral nations, and in England also (as the quotation from Morse makes clear), the idea of 'Britishness' is distinct in each, built around a number of competing and intermixed identities. There is, of course, much commonality in the British experience, but it means something unique to each of the four nations. The falsity of the conceptualisation of Great Britain as a unitary nation-state is visible culturally as well as institutionally.

The question now is how the state maintained a semblance of coherence between itself and disparate peoples without extending the franchise to the working class (the bulk of the male population) until the second and third Reform Acts in 1867–8 and 1884, and without granting the vote to some women until 1918; the 1832 Reform Act, indeed, actually disenfranchised many artisans and workers. How did the British state – which has failed to bring civil society and the nation into line – maintain its legitimacy? Political citizenship was absent for the majority; how then did the state *govern*?

Drawing upon the work of Michael Mann, David McCrone has stressed the state's 'infrastructural power' – its ability to govern by rule of law rather than by direct violence – as being central to classical nation-state formation.[37] Anthony Giddens has argued that all modern states are nation-states because they involve an apparatus of government laying claim to specific territories, possess formalised codes of law, and are backed by the control of military force.[38] Infrastructural power is about governing from a distance, it is about maintaining social cohesion

---

35 See, e.g., P. Morgan, *The Eighteenth-Century Renaissance* (Dyfed, 1981); D. Smith (ed.), *A People and a Proletariat: Essays in the History of Wales, 1780–1980* (London, 1980); and J. Davies, *A History of Wales* (London, 1993).

36 N. Evans, 'Cogs, cardis and hwentws: regions, nation and state in Wales, 1840–1940' (paper presented to the Social History Society Conference, 'National Identity', 4–6 Jan. 1992).

37 McCrone, *Understanding Scotland*, pp. 204–5; M. Mann, 'The autonomous power of the state', *Archives Européenes de Sociologie*, xxv (1984), p. 189.

38 Giddens, *Sociology*, pp. 301–3.

and the legitimacy of state power. The modern state embodies power, Giddens explains, not by absorbing civil society, but by guarding certain of the universal qualities upon which it is predicted. It is about enshrining the governing of civil society.[39] Sociologically, suggests Bryant, civil society can productively be defined as the 'space or arena between household and the state, other than the market, which affords possibilities of concerted action and social self-organisation'.[40] Ernest Gellner has recently explored one definition of civil society as, essentially, the structures of societal opposition to the despotic state:

> Civil society is that set of diverse non-governmental institutions, which is strong enough to counterbalance the state, and, whilst not preventing the state from fulfilling its role of keeper of the peace and arbiter between major interests, can nevertheless prevent the state from dominating and atomising the rest of society.[41]

However a definition of civil society is sharpened, its practical content – as far as contemporaries were concerned – existed in the town and city.

By underpinning and empowering civil society, the modern state maintains the balance of the nation-state. The exercise of the rule of law to structure civil society is fundamental to the governing of any bounded territory. Because the state in Great Britain enshrined more than one civil society there was no coherent British nation-state, no coherent and overwhelming sense of Britishness. In contrast, and importantly so, this disjuncture provides the sustenance for four national identities – and this is the root from which our argument grows. The axis between the state and civil society is the axis of national identity; the gap between the Scottish nation and its state is the point where it was governed.[42] This is not an issue of high politics, it is an issue of urban management by local elites. Because political citizenship was absent for so many and for so much of the nineteenth century in Britain, this axis, at this time, did not include parliamentary political nationalism. The strength or weakness of Scottish nationalism cannot be examined as a movement demanding political citizenship rights (a Scottish Parliament, say). Citizen politics was a concern of the bourgeoisie; it was contained within civil society. The everyday governing of urban Scotland is the focus of this book. This approach will re-discover Scotland's absent nineteenth-century nationalism.

[39] A. Giddens, *The Nation-State and Violence: Volume II of a Contemporary Critique of Historical Materialism* (Cambridge, 1985), pp. 11, 20–1.

[40] C. G. A. Bryant, 'Social self-organisation, civility and sociology: a comment on Kumar's "Civil Society"', *British Journal of Sociology*, xliv (3) (1993), p. 399.

[41] E. Gellner, 'The importance of being modular', in J. A. Hall (ed.), *Civil Society: Theory, History, Comparison* (Cambridge, 1995), p. 32. Gellner goes on to embellish this definition by stressing the associational ('modular') nature of human society.

[42] The idea that civil society can contain and direct nationalism is discussed in G. Morton, 'Scottish rights and "centralisation" in the mid-nineteenth century', *Nations and Nationalism*, vol. II, pt. 2 (1996), pp. 261–3.

The case of the missing nationalism: Scotland post-1707

It has been especially in the century up to the 1880s that Scottish nationalism has been regarded as weak and fragmented.[43] Indeed, the leading chronicler of the origins of early twentieth-century nationalism argues that even the Scots National League of the 1920s was 'shaped by nineteenth-century and pre-First World War ideas about Scottish nationalism, which [were] romantic, backward looking and largely apolitical'.[44] Nineteenth-century national identity has been castigated as stricken by kailyardism and seduced by Anglicisation. In the nineteenth century, so the argument goes, no-one has been more plagued by the fondness for warm cabbage, and no-one has been more tempted by the English apple, than the middle class of the Scottish Lowlands. Lured by Empire and stunted beneath the shadow of eighteenth-century Enlightenment, the Scottish middle class of the nineteenth century has been condemned. Its leaders, its writers, its thinkers, and above all else its culture, have been paraded as secondary, subservient and regressive.[45]

It was because 'Scotland the nation' did not become 'Scotland the nation-state' that Scottish civil society has been perceived as weak. The literature of the kailyard was the most obvious manifestation of a society culturally infirm through political acquiescence. However, this is an argument loaded down by the assumption, quite reasonable at first sight perhaps, that a nation must have its own state for it to become a nation-state. As the previous section made clear, the legitimacy of the modern state was achieved through the exercise of infrastructural power, a form of government which ensured stability through the institutions of civil society. The United Kingdom has persistently failed to match a unitary state with a unitary civil society, but it has enshrined the legitimacy of the 'peripheral' civil societies and so produced stability. It is argued here that Scotland's nineteenth-century nationalism has been missed, and replaced by a discourse transfixed by a culture of defeat, because the analysis has been located in the centre – the British state and its 'British' civil society – within the confines of a parliamentary political approach. But such a single relationship has never existed – Westminster was not coterminous with Scottish civil society.

---

[43] J. Brand, *The National Movement in Scotland* (London, 1978), pp. 11–17; C. Harvie, *Scotland and Nationalism* (2nd edn, London, 1994), pp. 20–2.

[44] R. J. Finlay, *Independent and Free: Scottish Politics and the Origins of the Scottish National Party, 1918–1945* (Edinburgh, 1994), p. 47.

[45] For two critiques of the kailyard myths, see I. Carter, 'Kailyard: the literature of decline in nineteenth-century Scotland', *Scottish Journal of Sociology*, i (1) (1976), p. 10; and I. Campbell, *Kailyard* (Edinburgh, 1981), pp. 8–17. For the role of kailyard and 'Unionist-history' in Scotland's 'failed' nationalism in this period, see T. Nairn, *The Break-Up of Britain* (2nd edn, London, 1981), pp. 155–63; C. Beveridge and R. Turnbull, *The Eclipse of Scottish Culture* (Edinburgh, 1989); and A. Calder, *Revolving Culture: Notes from the Scottish Republic* (London, 1994).

The governing of Scottish civil society has changed dramatically since 1707, and each change has produced a different expression of national identity. This is a study of the period from 1830 to 1860, a period of the *laissez-faire* state and the triumph of the bourgeoisie – which, it is argued here, was the high point of 'self-governing' civil society. Together the result was a form of nationalism that was only tangentially parliamentary, was strongly pro-Union, but nevertheless was explicit in its demands for the better government of Scotland. Various catch-phrases have been coined to describe Scotland's membership of the British unitary-state: 'semi-independence',[46] a 'nation within a nation',[47] or, 'independence within Britain'.[48] Each is an attempt to come to terms with this apparent, and enigmatic, contradiction: Scotland, a 'sort of nation-state', but without a state. Each is an acknowledgement of the continuing power of memories of independent sovereignty, and of the ability of the Scottish bourgeoisie to exercise government over its own territory. Yet no-one has attempted to analyse systematically the expression of Scottish nationalism in this unique mid-century period as a function of the nation/state axis, rather than of party politics in waiting.[49] This research tries to fill that gap; it seeks to re-interpret Scottish national identity between 1830 and 1860. It will demonstrate that because of the way civil society was governed in the mid-century, Scottish nationalism was loyal to the Union of 1707, but was in no way inferior as an (abstract) nationalism. To coin another phrase, this form of nationalism was 'Unionist-nationalism'.

Governing Scotland in the eighteenth century

The eighteenth century is important as a period of rebellion and quiet which did much to fix the image of Scottish society. The two defeated Jacobite rebellions, on the back of the Union of 1707, have been perceived as paving the way for a process of Anglicisation of Scottish society and the homogenisation of British society. Our understanding of nineteenth-century Scotland, and its nationalism, is rooted in the way that state/civil society axis developed out of the eighteenth century. How then was post-Union Scottish civil society governed?

---

[46] N. T. Phillipson, 'Nationalism and ideology', in J. N. Wolfe (ed.), *Government and Nationalism in Scotland* (Edinburgh, 1969), p. 168.

[47] R. J. Morris, 'Scotland, 1830–1914: the making of a nation within a nation', in W. H. Fraser and R. J. Morris (eds.), *People and Society in Scotland*, vol. II: *1830–1914* (Edinburgh, 1990), p. 5.

[48] Donald Dewar, MP, then Shadow Secretary of State for Scotland, talked of a Scottish parliament as 'independence within Britain' in the later 1980s.

[49] All accounts are heavily indebted to one piece of research by Hanham: see H. J. Hanham, 'Mid-century Scottish nationalism: romantic and radical', in R. Robson (ed.), *Ideas and Institutions of Victorian Britain: Essays in Honour of George Kitson Clark* (London, 1967); and H. J. Hanham, *Scottish Nationalism* (London, 1969).

The Union of the English and Scottish Parliaments in 1707 established the Parliament of Great Britain located at Westminster.[50] Resulting from the negotiations, the Union settlements guaranteed the maintenance of the Scottish legal system, the independence of the Scottish Church, and the autonomy of the Scottish system of education: that much is well known. These three institutions, the very backbone of potential Scottish nation-statehood, have been both the strength of the Union and its Achilles' heel. The Union possessed a strength born out of flexibility and a recognition of the history of the Scottish nation. But its weakness was to provide the framework of nationhood, and of potential statehood, and so enhance and give a practical reality to Scottish ethnic identity.

For the actual day-to-day governing of Scotland, the Union produced a mixed effect, but three themes can be identified. The first was the indefinite suspension of the Scottish Parliament. The Scottish Privy Council was replaced in 1708 by a new Privy Council of Great Britain. Although the Union allowed for two Secretaries of State in Scotland, real decisions were made in the smaller Cabinet where Scots were unrepresented and Scottish business ignored.[51] Only nine Acts relating to Scotland were passed by the London Parliament in the period from 1727 to 1745. Scotland's 'high politics' was increasingly being contested on an English playing field.

The second point of the post-Union settlement was that Scotland came under the control of political managers. From 1725 until 1761 Scottish politics was run by the duke of Argyll and his brother the earl of Islay; from 1775 it was Henry Dundas. These managers were expected to keep Scottish MPs and peers in line in the lobbies and keep Scotland itself quiet.[52] Although there was not always an incumbent, the office of a Secretary of State for Scotland had existed from 1707 until its abolition in 1746 (after the Jacobite defeat at Culloden). There followed a few piecemeal solutions, but in general Scotland's voice at Westminster was absent until Henry Dundas came on the scene first as Solicitor-General in 1766 and then as Lord Advocate in 1775.[53] It was the Lord Advocate, chosen from amongst the Edinburgh lawyers, who became the unofficial 'manager' of Scotland. In this role Dundas kept the Scottish politicians loyal to the government: no more so than when the government suppressed the Scottish radicals in the 1790s.[54] Dundas, and his son

---

50 For a fascinating commentary from a unique observer, see Defoe, *History of the Union*, originally published in 1709. For a more reflective account, see G. S. Pryde (ed.) *The Treaty of Union of Scotland and England, 1707* (London, 1950).
51 M. Lynch, *Scotland: A New History* (London, 1991), p. 320; A. Murdoch, *'The People Above': Politics and Administration in Mid-Eighteenth-Century Scotland* (Edinburgh, 1980), p. 3.
52 Lynch, *Scotland*, p. 325.
53 M. Fry, *Patronage and Principle: A Political History of Modern Scotland* (Aberdeen, 1987), p. 10.
54 T. C. Smout, *A History of the Scottish People, 1560–1830* (London, 1969), p. 202.

Robert, were fundamental in tying Scottish politics to that of West-minster and therefore maintaining Scottish loyalty to the Union.[55] In conjunction with this rule, the Scottish lairds controlled the justice system and, through the power of patronage, kept a firm reign in the counties.[56] This system of management was indeed an effective one, and the Dundas family ruled the roost in Scotland until 1828.

A third feature of the governance of Scotland post-1707 was the creation of a series of boards or commissions, based in Edinburgh, which attempted to administer Scottish affairs. The Scottish Court of the Exchequer, which discharged income and paid taxes to the Civil List; the Board of Excise and the Board of Customs; the Board of Police; and the Board of Trustees: all were created in the first decades after Union. Along with the Courts of Session and Judiciary, the Convention of Royal Burghs and the General Assembly of the Church of Scotland, they were a prime source of jobs and rewards for the Scottish bourgeoisie and its sons, as well as being a focus of 'hands-on' administration based in Edinburgh.[57]

In the memorable words of Fry, the Glorious Revolution of 1688 and the Union of Parliaments in 1707, 'allowed the Scots to dispense with the distraction of politics'.[58] Scotland was able to get by without its Parliament. Murdoch has termed this administrative framework a 'buffer' between English assumptions about Scotland (and power did reside in England) and Scottish institutions and society.[59] This was a generally successful compromise, for although Scotland no longer had a state it was in effect a relatively quiet place to govern.[60] To simplify greatly this characterisation of the period: Scotland's aristocracy was acquiescent to London's favours and they dominated in the counties until the late twentieth century;[61] the Scottish bourgeoisie was politically disenfranchised and failed to make any claims for power until the period of reform agitation immediately prior to 1832; Scotland's lower orders, equally disenfranchised, had their radicalism controlled by government spies and militia loyal to the managers of the state.[62] On the whole, it can

---

55 M. Fry, *The Dundas Despotism* (Edinburgh, 1992).
56 A. E. Morris, 'Patrimony and Power: A Study of Lairds and Landownership in the Scottish Borders' (Edinburgh University Ph.D. thesis, 1989); A. E. Whetstone, *Scottish County Government in the Eighteenth and Nineteenth Centuries* (Edinburgh, 1981).
57 Lynch, *Scotland*, p. 324. Murdoch, 'The People Above', p. 11.
58 Fry, *Patronage and Principle*, p. 6.
59 Murdoch, 'The People Above', p. 27. Indeed, Pocock has argued convincingly that because the rule of Union resided in England, it is in many ways justifiable to write Scottish History from the standpoint of England, but not of course the reverse: see J. G. A. Pocock, 'The limits and divisions of British history: in search of an unknown subject', *American Historical Review*, lxxxvii (2) (1982), pp. 311–36.
60 J. Mackinnon, *The Union of England and Scotland: A Study of International History* (London, 1896), p. 501.
61 The dominance of the aristocracy in Scottish local politics until Reform in 1974 is explained in Morris, 'Patrimony and Power'.
62 Fry, *Patronage and Principle*, p. 6, although recent literature is beginning to question

be said, for much of the eighteenth century Scotland was effectively governed on 'auto-pilot'.[63]

The two challenges to this general calm came from the Jacobites. The focus of Scottish nationhood in this period was their attempts to replace the Hanoverian monarchy with that of the Stuarts. In the eighteenth century the Jacobite claimants promised to repeal the 1707 Union and were significant for two major uprisings – and defeats – in 1715 and 1745/6. The second defeat, at Culloden in 1746, had the greatest impact on Scottish society. The retribution was such that the Scottish managers, Islay and Milton, were unable to control the legislative programme which followed.[64] Amongst the new laws imposed after Culloden were the prohibition of the wearing of tartan (except within the British army), and the requirement on Episcopalian ministers, often proponents of Jacobitism in the past, to take new oaths of allegiance and to pray publicly for the Hanoverian royal family.

Because of this suppression, Jacobitism was no longer a threat by the 1760s. Consequently these decades have been regarded as critical in the rise of Anglicisation and of romantic Highlandism – and ultimately in the formation of Britain. Although, as Pittock argues, the Jacobite songs maintained a critique of Scotland's place in the British state throughout both the eighteenth and nineteenth centuries, Scotland's integration into a common British body-politic increased apace. Joining the army was one of the few acts which could save a Jacobite man from treason, and many captured during the '45 were pardoned upon enlistment.[65] For the first time ever, the British army had been able to recruit men on a massive scale from the Scottish Highlands. From the 1760s, Scottish nationalism, as a Jacobite crusade, was tamed and turned around into a respectable element of polite English society. The eighteenth-century idea of the Highlander as 'noble savage' is particularly notable in this context – the Scottish Gael filling the role of 'primitive' in Enlightenment views upon the evolution of civilisation.[66] The Highlands and the Highlanders, increasingly the national image for the whole of Scotland, became sanitised and romanticised; no more so than the controversy over the publication by James Macpherson of the poetry of Ossian in 1760. Although many contemporaries were aware of the falsity of these newly discovered ancient texts, Scottish and English society wanted to

---

this passivity. This is discussed in C. Whatley, 'An uninflammable people?', in I. Donnachie and C. Whatley (eds.) *The Manufacture of Scottish History* (Edinburgh, 1992), pp. 53–71.

[63] This is indeed the impression conveyed in G. C. Lewis, *Essays on the Administration of Great Britain from 1783–1830. Contributed to the Edinburgh Review by the Right Hon. Sir George Cornewall Lewis, Bart.* (London, 1864).

[64] Lynch, *Scotland*, p. 339.

[65] M. G. H. Pittock, *The Invention of Scotland: The Stuart Myth and the Scottish Identity, 1638 to the Present* (London, 1991), p. 62.

[66] C. Withers, 'The historical creation of the Scottish Highlands', in Donnachie and Whatley, *Manufacture of Scottish History*, p. 147.

believe it authentic: Scotland's violent heritage, in this instance, had become a peaceful and romantic adjunct to that of England.

Not only was Scotland's Highland symbolism being appropriated, but the Scottish bourgeoisie and aristocracy found themselves in positions of power within England and within the Empire. The most famous example of Scots prospering in this way was, indeed, under the patronage of an Englishmen, Warren Hastings. As Governor of Bengal and subsequently Governor-General of India, Hastings actively encouraged the appointment of Scots within his administration. Well-born or well-educated Englishmen had the pick of jobs in government at home – so the most readily available source of opportunities for educated Scots was in the Empire.

There were, then, a number of conflicting stories of Scotland which began to crystallise in the late eighteenth century, the two most important of which were the onward march of Anglicisation and the romance of the Stuart line and of Jacobitism. Both narratives unfolded once the militaristic antagonism between England and Scotland had subsided. While there were signs of a newly emerging Britishness, Scots appeared to rely more and more on myth-history and heritage (of a Highland 'Celtic Race')[67] to maintain 'distinctiveness'. Yet remaining important to our understanding of Scottish national identity in the nineteenth century is the debate about how far, by this time, 'British' identity had come to dominate over the peripheral identities. If a British identity was increasingly and consistently the most important national identity expressed by the people of Britain, then all peripheral nationalisms should decline in relevance. The most recent, and powerful, argument in favour of the rise of a nation of 'Britons' is that of Linda Colley. War and empire, in Colley's thesis, were significant in cementing the Union between Scotland and the rest of Great Britain.[68]

Colley argues that so effective was this incorporation of Scots into prominent positions within the Empire that it resulted in an English nationalist backlash in the form of the tirades by John Wilkes.[69] Wilkes became the personification of liberty, and liberty was the hallmark of Englishness, she argues. Wilkesite opposition to the melting 'down' of the name 'England' into 'Great Britain' was one objection. John Wilkes functioned as an English nationalist administering comfort to a people in flux by ensuring Scottish differences remained as differences. Through such arguments Wilkes hoped that this was a guarantee that traditional Englishness *and* English primacy within the Union would remain intact. This, she continues, was exactly what large numbers of English men and

---

[67] R. Knox, *The Races of Men: A Philosophical Enquiry into the Influence of Race over the Destinies of Nations* (2nd edn, London, 1862), chap. VII: 'History of the Celtic race', pp. 318–38.

[68] Colley, *Britons*, pp. 128–9.

[69] Ibid., p. 111.

women wanted to hear; the extremism of Wilkesite propaganda was testimony to the fact that the barriers between England and Scotland were coming down, and proof that the Scots had gained power within Great Britain to a degree previously unknown.[70]

Colley's argument is premised on the view that not only did the Union of 1707 produce a British state, but that a British civil society followed, unified in blood upon the battlefields of France and elsewhere in the common cause of Protestantism: *Britons: Forging the Nation*, is the title of her book. That is a very problematic assumption, as the first section of this chapter has indicated. The degree of Anglicisation of Scottish civil society, and the commonality between Scottish civil society and English civil society which arguably occurred after 1760, building upon the cessation of military hostilities, is notable, but can it really be said to have formed a unitary nation inhabited by Britons? Bernard Crick has pointed out that Colley's use of the language of 'imagined political communities', relying on what she calls the 'looseness' of the concept, has led her to confuse patriotism with nationalism.[71] Crick states that:

> Patriotism could, indeed, positively adhere to the Dynasty, Parliament, the Protestant religion and the rule of law (or negatively hating and fearing Papists and the French) in both England and Scotland, but patriotism does not always imply nationalism. One can be patriotic about an adopted state or for a multinational state such as Canada, Belgium or the United Kingdom. Nationalism demands something more, if not always ethnic homogeneity certainly cultural homogeneity. And, of course, *whose* 'imagined community'? That is where the real confusion between Englishness and Britishness ... arises.[72]

Colley does warn against an unrealistically narrow definition of nationhood, pointing out correctly that 'few nations since the world began have been culturally and ethnically homogeneous'.[73] But her escape route, the notion of dual identities (in an attempt to acknowledge the potential of exceptions to a homogeneous 'British' identity from the Scots and the Welsh), flounders on the insistence that the British identity was dominant. As Crick makes clear, 'she sees the "dual" as only held together by an overarching Britishness, not as each emotionally co-equal to it (as federalists or pluralists might argue), as well as to each other'.[74] That patriotism in eighteenth-century England was used as a critique of the

---

[70] Ibid., p. 121.
[71] Benedict Anderson's notion of an imagined political community is one of the most cited in the current literature: B. Anderson, *Imagined Communities: Reflections on the Origin and Spread of Nationalism* (London, 1983).
[72] Crick, 'Essay on Britishness', p. 73.
[73] Colley, *Britons*, p. 374.
[74] Crick, 'Essay on Britishness', p. 73.

state, rather than as a homogeneous response to a 'Catholic Other',[75] and that Protestantism was as much about variation as it was of commonality, so Colley's thesis of the coherent British nation-state is over-optimistic.[76]

As a Whig interpretation of the formation of British national identity, Colley's thesis is one of the most forceful; but as a contribution to nationalism of the centre, let alone of the periphery, its deficiencies are clear. Nationalism within the United Kingdom cannot be unitary, and the idea that nationalism of the periphery can be placed aside, and downgraded, for nationalism of the centre, misses all that is unique about the unitary state and the four nations of the United Kingdom. As Smout has argued for the relationship between the Scottish nation and Great Britain in the second half of the eighteenth century, the Scots indeed possessed a dual identity, both Scottish and British, but:

> If downright anti-English, anti-Union, clearly separatist sentiments are hard to find, the opposite pole of completely integrationist sentiments where Scots show no consciousness of or will to be in any sense different from the English are much more unusual.[77]

Smout uses Anthony Smith's notion of concentric loyalties to make his point,[78] and explains that here was an eighteenth-century sense of being Scottish alongside a British identity. This is different from Colley, because there is a recognition that the British identity did not become either homogeneous or all-consuming – there was no sense of the Scots becoming Britons. This was no more apparent than in the language of the eighteenth-century Scottish *literati*, who spoke equally of being both Scottish and British. Scotland saw itself as a junior partner to England in this period, but that did not mean that its people, as Britons, became 'non-Scots'. As Alexander Wedderburn put it, in what Smout refers to as 'an oft-quoted passage' in the *Edinburgh Review* in 1756: 'If countries have their ages with respect to improvement North Britain may be considered as in a state of early youth and supported by the mature strength of her kindred country.'[79]

75 E. Evans, 'Englishness and Britishness: national identities, c.1790–c.1870', in A. Grant and K. J. Stringer (eds.), *Uniting the Kingdom? The Making of British History* (London, 1995), p. 223–4; M. Chase, 'From millennium to anniversary: the concept of jubilee in late eighteenth- and nineteenth-century England', *Past and Present*, cxxix (1990), pp. 141–2; H. Cunningham, 'The language of patriotism', in R. Samuel (ed.), *Patriotism*, vol. I, pp. 57–8.
76 K. Robbins, 'An imperial and multinational polity: the "scene from the centre, 1832–1922"', in Grant and Stringer, *Uniting the Kingdom?*, p. 252; despite this, Robbins (p. 253) is firmly of the view that, comparatively speaking, Britain's 'multinational state' was a 'nation-state', 'unified' if not 'uniform'.
77 T. C. Smout, 'Problems of nationalism, identity and improvement in later eighteenth-century Scotland' in T. M. Devine (ed.), *Improvement and Enlightenment* (Edinburgh, 1989), p. 4.
78 A. D. Smith, *The Ethnic Origin of Nations* (Oxford, 1986).
79 Quoted in Smout, 'Problems of nationalism', p. 6.

The acceptance of the unitary state is clear from Smout's evidence, but so too is the recognition of partnership between England and Scotland. The continued existence of two separate civil societies was maintained by constant negotiation between the two. For the second half of the eighteenth century, following the defeat of the '45, it appears that Scotland had accepted the role of junior partner: a view which lasted until the 1820s, when the nationalist rhetoric began to argue that Scotland was emphatically an equal partner with England.

For the intelligentsia and for the bourgeoisie, the Union provided material opportunity which they were not prepared to pass up for a few insults.[80] There were 'jobs for the boys' in the British civil service, naval and military jobs at home and abroad, and jobs with the East India Company – all served up by Islay and Dundas. It can be argued that Scottish feelings of national identity in the eighteenth century were strong and powerful, but they were not anti-English. Nicholas Phillipson refers to the 'noisy inaction' of a middle class who had accepted the economic rewards of the Union, and so throughout its agitation accepted that the Union should remain; 'semi-independence' for Scotland was how Phillipson termed much of this eighteenth-century period.[81]

At times a 'British' identity did dominate over a Scottish identity, but at times it patently did not. It is true that anxiety about a Scottish accent, or writing in Scottish idioms, was widespread among the literati and among their allies in the landed classes in the eighteenth century. These elites, if they could, sent their children to school in England to learn polite language.[82] Indeed, this has been picked up by Nairn and other authors as being symptomatic of a weakness in Scotland's self-identity.

Nevertheless it is argued here that, as Murdoch and Sher state, this view should not be taken too far:

It is ... not quite fair to accuse eighteenth-century Scots who wrote self-consciously polished English of pandering to the 'ruling classes' or assimilating themselves to a dominant English culture. As the new lingua franca of the age, English opened the door to a larger cultural world, just as it does in many non-English countries today. By the mid-eighteenth century English had become the medium of polite, urbane Scottish culture in the universities and the cities of Edinburgh, Glasgow and Aberdeen.[83]

---

[80] Ibid., p. 8.

[81] Phillipson, 'Nationalism and ideology'.

[82] Smout, 'Problems of nationalism', p. 7; S. Nenadic, 'The rise of the urban middle class', in T. M. Devine and R. Mitchison (eds.), *People and Society in Scotland*, vol. I: *1760–1830* (Edinburgh, 1988), p. 122; A. Murdoch and R. B. Sher, 'Literacy and learned culture', in Devine and Mitchison, *People and Society*, pp. 128–9.

[83] Murdoch and Sher, 'Literacy and learned culture', p. 129.

By 1750, they point out, most 'thinking Scots' were prepared to perceive of themselves as both British and Scots in a way that was positive and unproblematic. Polite society tried to rid itself of Scotticisms, but still tried to remain Scottish. The language of Scots was used informally and was frequently spoken, while English was employed when demanded for formal occasions. The path of Anglicisation was not smooth, and, despite any apparent decline in the use of Scots, there occurred in the nineteenth century a revival in its use as a literary form, which has been regarded as important to the growth of nationalist sentiment in that century.[84]

If the Scots be not Britons, but be Scots *and* Britons, then how did this manifest itself in the expression of Scottish national identity? Was nineteenth-century Scottish nationalism no more than a non-threatening component of romantic nationalism seen elsewhere in Europe?[85]

A nationalist romance?

The romantic elements in nineteenth-century Scottish national identity and nationalism stem quite clearly from the second half of the eighteenth century. From Ossian to the increasingly popular Highland tour, external romantic colouring of Jacobitism dominated popular consciousness throughout Britain.[86] Within Scotland the Jacobite critique of the Hanoverian monarchy placed the interpretation of the Stuart past in the context of the growing prosperity of Scotland in the eighteenth century. The result, Pittock argues, was that the 'propaganda war' against the Union was left with nothing more than a strong literary and antiquarian contribution.[87] This rhetoric was a celebration of the past where, for example, Wallace and Bruce (Scotland's heroes from the Wars of Independence in the fourteenth century) were attached to the destinies of the Stuarts – a past that had been lost since the Union.[88] This was an acceptance of 'junior partner' status under England and was, as we shall see in Chapters 6 and 7, a quite different symbolic use of Wallace and Bruce from that which was made in the nineteenth century, when the two martyrs symbolised Scotland's equality with England. In fact, in terms of 'positive' expressions of Scottish national identity, the

---

84 The strength and frequency of published Scots in newspapers in the Victorian period has been thoroughly documented: see W. Donaldson, *The Language of the People* (Aberdeen, 1989); and W. Donaldson, *Popular Literature in Victorian Scotland* (Aberdeen, 1986).

85 For a brief but very useful account of all instances of European nationalisms, see R. Pearson, *The Longman Companion to European Nationalism, 1789–1920* (London, 1994).

86 Two of the most influential accounts of Highland tours, and continually so since their publication, are: Samuel Johnson, *A Journey to the Western Isles of Scotland* (London, 1775); and D. Wordsworth, *Recollections of a Tour made in Scotland in AD 1803* (Edinburgh, 1974).

87 G. Donaldson *et al.*, 'Scottish devolution: the historical background', in J. N. Wolfe (ed.), *Government and Nationalism in Scotland* (Edinburgh, 1969), p. 5; Pittock, *Invention of Scotland*, p. 34.

88 Pittock, *Invention of Scotland*, p. 37.

heroic failures of the Jacobites in the '15 and the '45 had a greater cultural impact in the nineteenth and twentieth centuries than in the eighteenth century. For example, Robert Forbes's *The Lyon in Mourning*, an ambitious and comprehensive work crammed full of primary material from the second Jacobite rebellion, was written between 1745 and 1775, but its first publication in a shortened form was not until 1835. Michael Lynch states that 'the *Lyon* became part of the collective *tristesse* of a nineteenth-century industrial nation in search of a glamorous past'.[89] Similarly, as has been well documented, by the mid-nineteenth century even Queen Victoria, a Hanoverian monarch, could declare that she was a Jacobite at heart.

This use of romance in the expression of Scottish national identity became more common in the nineteenth century and remained powerful throughout the period from 1830 to 1860, although it was less the orthodoxy than has often been supposed. The kilt and Highland dress were appropriated fully by Lowlanders and turned into the 'national dress' of Scotland. The kilt's resurrection in 1782 (from the ban on its wearing which followed the '45) was emphatically clear after George IV's visit to Scotland in 1822, when the oversized monarch was stitched up in full Highland garb and pink tights.[90] Indeed, following that visit the Highland Society was overwhelmed by a flood of queries from aristocrats and Lowland notables as to details of the correct mode of Highland dress.[91]

With the 'Jacobite menace' becoming a distant memory, the process of romanticising that past could continue apace. Robert Burns had earlier made the Jacobite song respectable and accessible to the common man and woman, and Sir Walter Scott extolled the imagery of Jacobitism as the pinnacle of emotion – the heart along with his Unionist head. Scott's novels made much of Jacobitism – it really was history for the mass market. His writings revived British-wide notions of what was clearly English chivalry and the romance of medieval manners. It was no ambiguity for the earl of Eglinton, later to appear as President of the National Association for the Vindication of Scottish Rights, to celebrate English chivalry in his famed tournament in 1839.[92] In 1848, Victoria and Albert acquired Balmoral and its estate and attended their first Braemar Gathering. Victoria often exclaimed her fondness for Scotland and its lifestyle and was persuaded to buy and wear a number of Paisley

[89] Lynch, *Scotland*, p. 337.

[90] *A Full Account of King George the Fourth's Visit to Scotland in 1822; with a Collection of the Loyal Songs which appeared on that Memorable Occasion* (Edinburgh, 1838); An Old Edinburgh Citizen (Sir Walter Scott), *Hints Addressed to the Inhabitants of Edinburgh and Others, in prospect of His Majesty's Visit* (Edinburgh, 1822).

[91] Lynch, *Scotland*, p. 355.

[92] I. Anstruther, *The Knight and the Umbrella: An Account of the Eglinton Tournament, 1839* (London, 1963); M. Girouard, *The Return to Camelot: Chivalry and the English Gentleman* (New Haven, 1981).

shawls and dresses.[93] The house of Hanover had well and truly stamped out, or rather appropriated, the Stuart memory. Polite society was in love with the romance of the Highlands, as witnessed by the success of the Sobieski Stuarts – the Allen or the Hay Allen brothers – who charmed British society with their descriptions of Highland dress, based on their claim to be direct descendants of the royal Stuart line. Their literary work included *Vestiarium Scoticum* (1842); *The Costume of the Clans* (1845); *The Laes of the Century* (1847); and *Lays of the Deer Forest* (1848). Although of very doubtful authenticity, their work caught the popular spirit of the Stuart myth, and its ideological role was to spark a re-invention of the Highland dress and the Highland way of life.[94]

Stories of Scotland: a new agenda

By concentrating on Highlandism and the Anglicisation of Stuart symbolism, most completely by George IV and then Victoria, we examine the 'Scottishness of Britishness', or, in other words, the singularity of being Scottish-and-British. But this is just one story. The romance of national identity in the nineteenth century only makes sense within a process of increasingly dominant Anglicisation and the creation of Great Britain with a coterminous British state and civil society. Sociologically and politically, such a unitary British nation-state is the material underpinning of that identity; it can only be accounted for within those parameters. Yet, as was argued at the beginning of this chapter, the classical nation-state is not the proper frame of reference for either the United Kingdom or for Scottish civil society, and so its result – romantic-nationalism – cannot be a complete characterisation of national identity. There are indeed other stories of Scottish national identity in the nineteenth century. Because the state's infrastructural empowerment of civil society remains shared in Great Britain, the gaps between nation and state produce contradictory and conflicting identities which have superseded notions of romantic-nationalism.

Within those gaps mid-century nationalists developed a critique of the governance of Scotland that sits uneasily with consensual unitary identities. The story which will unfold here tells of Scottish national identity that spoke much less of clans and tartan and Bonnie Prince Charlie than might have been expected. It told of a different identity: of Wallace and Bruce, Burns and Knox, as well as majesty, the Glorious

---

93 T. Dickson and T. Clark, 'Social control: Paisley, 1841–1843', *Scottish Historical Review*, lxv (1986), p. 50.

94 McCrone, *Understanding Scotland*, pp. 183–4; Pittock, *Invention of Scotland*, pp. 104–5. In this context, see J. S. Keltie (ed.) *A History of the Scottish Highlands, Highland Clans and Highland Regiments with an account of the Gaelic language, literature and music and an essay on Highland scenery*, vol. II (Edinburgh, 1881); and *The Scotsman, The Scottish Clans and their Tartans* (Edinburgh, 1896). This remarkable publication, including a chapter on 'The highland dress and how to wear it', had reached its 40th edition in 1962.

Revolution and the Magna Carta. Despite Victoria's 'Balmoralism', mid-century Scottish patriots were less caught up in Highland romance, and were less apolitical, than the story of Britain's forging might otherwise suggest. The dialectic between political acquiescence and romantic-nationalism is a conflation of cause and effect; its initial premise (of unitary nation-statehood) is misplaced.

The 'management' of Scottish civil society was effectively ended by Canning in 1827, following Lord Melville's decision to turn down the opportunity to serve under his short-lived administration. Scottish affairs were then entrusted to the Home Office, although in practice it was the Lord Advocate who controlled matters.[95] Yet this was the start of the British state, under reform, becoming the modern state of classical theory. But there was still no unified British civil society, still no Scottish parliamentary political nationalism to challenge the British state. Indeed, romantic-nationalism appears to lose rather than gain salience at many moments of heightened national awareness. This needs explanation, which brings us to our argument here: we cannot appreciate the complexity of mid-nineteenth-century national identity without comprehending the sort of state that the Scottish bourgeoisie had, and wanted to have, to structure its citizenship rights. Before we can interpret the symbols of Scottishness we need to dissect the state/civil society axis: the first step in this process is to examine the Victorian state.

[95] G. Pottinger, *The Secretaries of State for Scotland, 1926–76: Fifty Years of the Scottish Office* (Edinburgh, 1979), pp. 6, 202.

CHAPTER TWO

An Economic and Social History of the Victorian State in Scotland

The clearest reason why it is wrong-headed to locate Scottish nationalism in Westminster politics in this period concerns that very state itself. The nineteenth-century British state was a quite distinct institution from its twentieth-century counterpart. It was different because it divested itself of many powers that it had acquired under mercantilism, and also because when it did have to intervene in society, as was increasingly the case throughout the century, its favoured route was through local government. Politically and indeed practically, Westminster's relationship to Scottish life was a tangential one, lacking real influence in the day-to-day governing of society.

What sort of state did Scotland share, and what sort of state did it want? As will be explained more fully in the following chapter, the ultimate measurement of the power and strength of nationalism and of national identity is 'self-government' – the legitimate political coherence of a 'people' and a 'government', 'a doctrine of popular freedom and sovereignty'.[1] Scottish nationalism in the mid-nineteenth century (as Chapter 1 made clear), has been marked down for its lack of such demands: Scotland at this time seems to have failed the 'test' of nation-statehood both in practice and in its aspirations. The purpose here is to explore the legitimacy of this test. We shall do so by asking why the United Kingdom has fallen short of unifying state and nation (of Britishness), yet manages to preside over dual and multiple identities with great durability. The suggestion is that perhaps we need to re-think the primacy given to legislative power in our understanding of the self-governing nation. The link to be explored is that of the Victorian state's empowerment of civil society, which implies that classical nation-state theory appears inappropriate as a tool to unearth 'Scottishness' as well as 'Britishness'. Our starting-point is a collective: the Houses of Parliament, the civil service bureaucracy popularly known as Whitehall, the legal and constitutional framework within which they operate – in other words, the British state.

---

[1] J. Hutchinson and A. D. Smith, 'Introduction', in their edited reader *Nationalism* (Oxford, 1994), p. 4.

The laissez-faire state of the nineteenth century

This conceptualisation of the nineteenth-century state as one which divested itself of many powers is pivotal to the mainstream historical literature, yet surprisingly little acknowledged by scholars investigating nationalism within Britain. Eric Hobsbawm has argued for this period that:

> The characteristic attitude of the British or other governments towards the economy before the Industrial Revolution was that they had a duty to do something about it. This is also the almost universal attitude of governments towards the economy today [1968]. But between these two eras, which might be called the norm of history, and indeed of reason, there occurred an age in which the fundamental attitude of the government was the opposite: the less it could manage to intervene in the economy, the better. Broadly speaking this era of abstention coincided with the rise, triumph and domination of industrial Britain, and it was indeed uniquely suited to the situation of this country, and perhaps one or more of those like it. The history of government economic policy and theory since the industrial revolution is essentially that of the rise and fall of *laissez-faire*.[2]

To Hobsbawm it is clear that, with reference to the international economy, the parliamentary state reduced its activities from around 1815 to 1870. Where there is much more debate for this period is in the interpretation of the state's social legislation.[3] To many the response of Parliament to the growing urbanisation and industrialisation was one of intervention, tantamount to the beginnings of the twentieth-century welfare state.[4] To others the state's response was one which empowered local government, but not one which empowered the central state.[5] This split in interpretation is explained in an example by A. J. Taylor:

> while some have regarded the concern for public health shown by local authorities in early Victorian England [*sic*] as a movement away from *laissez-faire* towards collectivism, others have viewed the resistance of these authorities to the centralising tendencies of the General Board of Health, as a no less striking manifestation of the operation of the *laissez-faire* principle.[6]

To reach an understanding of the Victorian state, and hence the state/civil society axis around which national identity hangs, our

[2] E. J. Hobsbawm, *Industry and Empire* (London, 1968), p. 225.
[3] The best summary of the then mainstream literature is still A. J. Taylor, *Laissez-faire and State Intervention in Nineteenth-Century Britain* (London, 1972).
[4] G. S. R. Kitson-Clark, *An Expanding Society: Britain, 1830–1900* (Cambridge, 1967); P. Deane, *The First Industrial Revolution* (Cambridge, 1965), p. 219.
[5] See, e.g., Hobsbawm, *Industry and Empire*, pp. 106, 203.
[6] Taylor, *Laissez-faire*, p. 12.

attention must focus on both the economic and the social role of this
state in its ideology and its actions.

Trade and economy: a minimalist state

By the end of the Napoleonic War Britain's economic position was all-
powerful. As the leading industrial nation she could undersell anyone.
As the leading colonialist, with a naval strength to protect it, Britain had
the trade routes which guaranteed prosperity. With such advantages in
access to raw materials and in the productive process, British economic
orthodoxy freed itself from the shackles of mercantilism, in which the
'zero-sum' principle that 'gains to one nation meant loss to another
nation' appeared restrictive.[7] It was accepted that the fewer strictures
there were upon the potential volume of trade, the more goods Britain
could sell, and the more powerful the country could become.[8]

Figure 2.1: *Free trade as the intelligent candidate at the hustings for the 1852
general election, as depicted by Punch*[9]

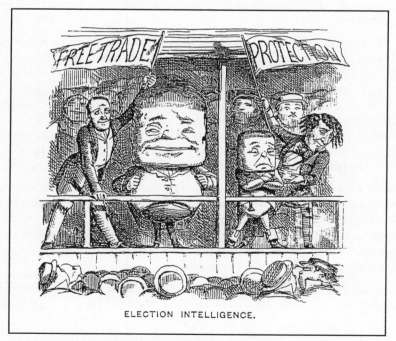

ELECTION INTELLIGENCE.

---

[7] S. L. Engerman, 'Mercantilism and overseas trade, 1700–1800', in R. Floud and
   D. McCloskey (eds.), *The Economic History of Britain since 1700*, vol. I: *1700–1860* (2nd
   edn, Cambridge, 1994), p. 197.
[8] S. G. Checkland, *The Rise of Industrial Society in England, 1815–1885* (London, 1964),
   p. 412.
[9] *Punch, or the London Charivari*, xxii (1852), p. 122.

The theories of Adam Smith were used to free world trade. John Stuart Mill's *Principles of Political Economy* (1848) argued that 'freedom of international trade would ensure peace between nations by substituting for the confrontation of sovereign states a system of mutual inter-dependence'.[10] Cobden believed that the inevitable advance of free trade would lead to 'breaking down the barriers that separate nations; those barriers behind which wrestle the feelings of pride, revenge, hatred and jealousy, which every now and then burst their bounds and deluge whole countries with blood'.[11] From 1815 onwards, and especially from the time of the Radical-influenced Whigs in 1837, via the Peel adminis-tration of 1841–6,[12] the British state was no longer to be the spur of economic growth through its protectionist policies and investment plans; instead British trade and British industry were unfettered.

Mid-century economic theory favoured the minimalist state; that is uncontroversial in the literature presented here. It is quite clear that by 1815 Britain had moved much further from the interventionist government than its main trading rivals.[13] It had started a move to limit both its tax-raising powers and its controls on the movement of trade, a philosophy which continued up until the final quarter of the century. The size and the power of the British state did not increase in this period of industrial revolution, as perhaps might have been expected. It has been estimated that between 1688 and 1815 taxation increased sixteen times (from 9% to 18% as a share of national income)[14] and at a rate far greater than that of national income (principally because of the costs of armed conflict),[15] whereas between 1830 and the 1880s the annual public expenditure per head of population in Britain remained substantially stable (and trebled in Europe).[16]

The decline of mercantilist and of protectionist tendencies saw much regulation repealed. First to be freed were the food trades, perhaps the most established set of legislative power, which were intended to protect the consumer but ultimately to safeguard the health and wealth of the British nation. By 1815 the only relic of a once elaborate system of domestic price controls was the Assize of Bread, and it was 'virtually

---

10 Checkland, *Rise of Industrial Society*, p. 413.

11 Quoted in F. R. Flournoy, 'British Liberal theories of international relations, 1848–1898', *Journal of the History of Ideas*, ii (2) (1946), p. 212.

12 M. J. Daunton, *Progress and Poverty: An Economic and Social History of Britain, 1700–1850* (Oxford, 1995), p. 552.

13 Although note that research has doubted the extent to which Britain was alone in its shift to free trade in this period: J. V. Nye, 'The myth of free trade Britain and fortress France: tariffs and trade in the nineteenth century', *The Journal of Economic History*, li (1) (1991), p. 25.

14 P. Hudson, *The Industrial Revolution* (London, 1992), p. 53.

15 P. O'Brien, 'Central government and the economy, 1688–1815', in Floud and McCloskey, *Economic History of Britain since 1700*, p. 210.

16 Hobsbawm, *Industry and Empire*, p. 233.

dead in the water'.[17] The beer trade was freed in 1830, much to the disgust of evangelical opponents who responded with a hardening of the temperance debate into one over teetotalism. Beer remained tax-free until 1880.[18] The network of Navigation Laws which were central to mercantilism were relaxed in 1849 and totally repealed in 1854. The high profile Corn Laws had gone by 1846: this talisman of economic intervention was toppled by the Manchester free-traders. Glass was freed in 1845; the brick excise was removed in 1850. Duties on colonial and foreign sugar were equalised in 1854, and gradually withdrawn thereafter. Soap and paper were freed in 1853 and 1861 respectively.

But it was not just trade that was increasingly opened up to 'fair' competition; the whole productive process was imbued with a new degree of flexibility. By the repeal of the Elizabethan labour statutes in 1813 and 1814, the state also withdrew from the wages bargain. No longer were Justices of the Peace involved in the setting of maximum and minimum wages as occasionally they were called upon to do. The Combination Laws were repealed in 1824 and 1825, enhancing the right to strike. Britain was the only country which systematically refused any fiscal protection to its industries at this time, and it was the only country in which the government avoided planning or building the railways,[19] although Parliament did impose safety regulations and exercised some control over the purchase of land and the displacement of residents.

In general the visible hand could no longer slap its invisible counterpart into line in a way it once had and would later do again. The capital market was made much more efficient by easier facilities for forming joint-stock companies, the culmination of which was the limited liability legislation of 1856. The British state also reduced its tax-raising potential. The inevitable short-term consequence of the freeing of trade was to reduce the flow of revenue into the Exchequer. Between 1825 and 1856 'a bonfire of older duties reduced indirect taxes to the minimum needed to get revenue, and the load on the citizen lightened perceptibly'.[20] This new doctrine was to be sustained by direct taxation – Robert Peel brought back income tax in 1842 for the better-off at the rate of 7d. in the pound (it had last expired in 1816); the explicit intention was to compensate for the drop in customs revenues.[21] Income tax and free trade became complementary, with the revenue from the former allowing the policy of reduced tariffs to be sustained.[22]

[17] Checkland, *Rise of Industrial Society*, p. 329.
[18] F. M. L. Thompson, *The Rise of Respectable Society: A Social History of Victorian Britain, 1830–1900* (London, 1988), p. 311.
[19] Checkland, *Rise of Industrial Society*, p. 233. However, in the north of Scotland there were a few instances of small-scale government-financed railway work.
[20] Hobsbawm, *Industry and Empire*, p. 235.
[21] C. More, *The Industrial Age: Economy and Society in Britain, 1750–1985* (London, 1989), p. 216.
[22] Daunton, *Progress and Poverty*, p. 519.

The economic policy of the Victorian state up until the final quarter of the century was therefore one of minimal intervention. It was not the story of an increasingly bureaucratic state, or an increasingly powerful state. Nor was it tying the British economy and British producers and manufacturers more tightly together in a seamless web. By unburdening trade and truncating taxation, the state was breathing new life into the free market of classical economics. This may not have directly encouraged national diversities in the four nations of the United Kingdom, but it did nothing to nourish the march of Britishness.

Urbanisation and industrialisation: a rationally interventionist state

Concomitant with becoming the leading economy in the world, British society was undergoing rapid urbanisation, effectively since around 1780. More particularly, it was urbanisation fuelled by industrialisation. This twin transformation had a well-documented impact on social life, and it was a challenge that the Victorian state could not ignore. Anthony Sutcliffe argues that it was not so much a response to 'new' problems that was needed – there was an inherited basis in power from the eighteenth century which could have been used. Rather, the main development during the period of early industrialisation was simply that a large number of communities were reaching such a size and degree of structural complexity that concerted public intervention became necessary.[23]

A greater proportion of the Scottish population was living in urban places from 1831 onwards. The 1851 census was the first to show for the whole of Great Britain that just over half the population lived in towns and cities. In Scotland one in five lived in Edinburgh, Glasgow, Aberdeen and Dundee at that point. Nineteenth-century Edinburgh experienced a fivefold growth of population between 1801 and 1911, although its earlier primacy over Glasgow had been lost (see Table 2.1, below). The rate of increase was slightly greater in the early part of the period (1801–51) while the larger absolute increment occurred during the later phase (1851–1911).[24]

In apparent contradiction of the principles of free trade which dominated economic policy, the British state introduced specific measures of social legislation to manage this urban growth. It is precisely how we interpret this intervention which is at the centre of the disagreements over characterising the years from 1815 to 1870 as the 'age of *laissez-faire*'.

[23] A. Sutcliffe, 'The growth of public intervention in the British urban environment during the nineteenth century: a structural approach', in J. H. Johnston and C. G. Pooley (eds.), *The Structure of Nineteenth-Century Cities* (London, 1982), p. 108.

[24] G. Gordon, 'The changing city', in G. Gordon (ed.), *Perspectives of the Scottish City* (Aberdeen, 1985), p. 3.

Table 2.1: *Population statistics: Edinburgh, 1801–51*

	1801	1811	1821	1831	1841	1851
County of Edinburgh	122,597	148,607	191,514	219,345	225,454	259,435
Edinburgh City	82,560	102,987	138,235	161,909	166,450	193,450

Source: PP, 1852–3, LXXXVI: *Accounts and Papers*, p. 30.

The types of social legislation introduced stemmed from a number of different causes, one of the most important of which was the Victorian sense of sympathy for the underdog, usually the child. For instance, the Factory Acts of 1833 set minimum working conditions for children and teenagers in the textile mills, and were the first real infringement of mill-owners' liberties in the interest of a group incapable of self-defence. J. S. Mill defended the principle of the state helping the child in those Acts, because 'children below a certain age *cannot* judge or act for themselves', although he regarded this legislation as mischievous for including women under its remit, who 'are as capable as men of appreciating and managing their own affairs'.[25] The Chimney Sweeps Acts of 1834, 1840, 1864 and 1875 were also designed to protect children. Women and children were no longer to be employed underground after Lord Shaftesbury's Coal Mines Act of 1842. These three sets of Acts were passed specifically to deal with the vulnerable members of society, not the able-bodied man. Ricardo and the classical economists took the view that children, not being fully rational beings, were entitled to protection as employees in factories, but adults were not: the terms upon which they laboured lay between them and their employers, and were no proper concern of the state.[26]

Only on the fringes did the state provide some help for the able-bodied workers. The Ten Hours Act of 1847, limiting the working day in the cotton industry, showed that the industrial worker was being regarded in some way as vulnerable. Gladstone's Railway Act of 1844 laid down certain minimum conditions of service, created the office of inspector of safety, and established the groundwork for government purchase of the railways after twenty-one years (although this was not carried out until the twentieth century).[27] A later Act stipulated the provision of workers' trains at affordable fares. The ordinary able-bodied man and woman did, then, benefit from a certain amount of specific legislative measures.

[25] J. S. Mill, *Principles of Political Economy with Some of their Applications to Social Philosophy*: vol. II, from the fifth London edn (New York, 1923), p. 580.

[26] Checkland, *Rise of Industrial Society*, p. 389.

[27] More, *Industrial Age*, p. 209.

So is Kitson-Clark correct to say that 'the conception of a "period of *laissez-faire*" ... is an encouragement to error'?[28] Does this evidence of social intervention mean the nineteenth century really was the precursor of the twentieth-century welfare state?[29] Of course the answer lies somewhere in between, but it is, nevertheless, a clear answer. Political economy was the dominant philosophy, but under the pressure of rapid industrialisation and urbanisation, intervention was unavoidable. As Michael Flinn makes plain:

> The political economists of the first half of the nineteenth century were, in short, too intelligent and too well informed to advocate out-and-out *laissez-faire*. They were constantly being brought up short by the realities of the economic system in which they worked and thought, and were only too conscious of the clash between the logic of pure theory and the demands of social morality.[30]

The same is equally true concerning the ideas of Jeremy Bentham and the Utilitarians. They too cannot be fitted neatly into a divide between *laissez-faire* and intervention. In their catch phrase of 'the greatest happiness for the greatest number', the Benthamites might advocate greater or less intervention, a decision dependent on circumstance. 'In practice, it urged less in the case of the Poor Law, and more in the case of Public Health', argues More.[31] The nineteenth-century state could not abdicate its role from the social costs of rapid growth as it had done over tariffs. And this was something on which the Tory paternalists seemed to be in tune with the Utilitarians more than the more likely allies amongst the Liberals.[32] Whereas Adam Smith placed his trust in a natural harmony or identity between the self-seeking impulse of the individual and the well-being of the nation, Bentham 'had no faith in a "natural order of society", divinely designed or otherwise'.[33] As Crouzet points out, the need for the state to act in the social arena was 'imposed by the

---

[28] Quoted in More, *Industrial Age*, p. 217.

[29] The direct link between the machinery of 20th-century government and Bentham's 1823 *Constitutional Code* is posited in S. and B. Webb, *English Poor Law History, Part II: The Last Hundred Years*: vol. I (London, 1929), p. 29.

[30] M. W. Flinn (ed.), 'Introduction' to *Report on the Sanitary Condition of the Labouring Population of Great Britain by Edwin Chadwick, 1842* (Edinburgh, 1965), pp. 39–40.

[31] More, *Industrial Age*, p. 211. In the matter of elementary education, e.g., John Stuart Mill argued that 'intervention of government is justifiable, because the case is not one in which the interest and judgement of the consumer are a sufficient security for the goodness of the community'. State intervention was also advocated when individuals were not in a position to decide upon their own greatest happiness. In the case of the lunatic, 'the foundation of the *laissez-faire* principle breaks down entirely. The person most interested is not the best judge of the matter, nor a competent judge at all. Insane persons are everywhere regarded as proper objects of the care of the state': Mill, *Principles of Political Economy*, ii, pp. 577–8.

[32] D. Watts, *Whigs, Radicals and Liberals, 1815–1914* (London, 1995), p. 48.

[33] Webb, *English Poor Law History*, p. 27.

urgency of the human problems caused by industrialisation and urbanisation'.[34]

The question remains, however: how do we characterise this government action? The Victorian state intervened in society when it was compelled to, but its dominant philosophy was still that of political economy. To crystallise this apparent contradiction, our attention will now turn to the two dominant social issues of the nineteenth century: poor relief and sanitary reform.

The Poor Law and local government

The 1834 Poor Law (Amendment) Act in England and Wales entrenched the principle of 'less eligibility' into the debate on the poor. The English and Welsh able-bodied poor were excluded from out-door relief with the workhouse test being introduced to identify those 'deserving' of indoor relief, to which they had a legal right of entitlement if they could not support themselves. In Scotland the reform of the Poor Law was deferred until the Amendment Act of 1845. The able-bodied in Scotland had no right to any relief unless illness prevented work or, in the case of women, the need to care for young children.[35] Neither Act was about increasing the burden on the state. Neither Act dealt with the single biggest reason for poverty, which was insufficient and irregular wages.[36] Poor Law reform in England and Wales was about reducing costs; in Scotland it was about 'better management'.

The reform of the Poor Law in England and Wales was regarded by opponents as part of the 'centralising' process, the tendency towards Westminster assuming administrative functions that contemporaries believed should rightly be local concerns. Created out of the reform in 1834 were a number of Poor Law Unions, made up of groups of 30 or so parishes, which administered relief under the auspices of the Poor Law Commission (replaced by a Poor Law Board in 1847). These unions were the first new layer of administration where previously the tendency had been to combine, divide and modify existing parishes.[37]

In Scotland the 1845 Act did not destroy the parochial administration – the Scottish Poor Law remained in the hands of 886 separate parish administrations[38] – but it was contained within the remit of the newly created Board of Supervision for the Relief of the Poor. The Parochial Boards also administered the public health laws as they existed at the time. The Board of Supervision was a semi-independent body composed of the Lord Provosts of Edinburgh and Glasgow, the Solicitor-General,

---

[34] F. Crouzet, *The Victorian Economy*, trans. A. S. Forster (London, 1982), p. 108.

[35] M. A. Crowther, 'Poverty, health and welfare', in W. H. Fraser and R. J. Morris (eds.), *People and Society in Scotland*, vol. II: *1830–1914* (Edinburgh, 1990), p. 271.

[36] See J. H. Treble, *Urban Poverty in Britain, 1830–1914* (London, 1979), pp. 7–12, 16.

[37] V. D. Lipman, *Local Government Areas, 1834–1945* (Oxford, 1949), p. 2.

[38] Crowther, 'Poverty, health and welfare', pp. 270–1.

the Sheriffs of Perth, Renfrew, Ross and Cromarty, and three members appointed by the Crown.[39]

The 1845 Act, copying the pre-reform English principle, introduced legal assessment for the first time, and the long-standing tradition of outdoor relief was also altered to follow the English model, and thus declined.[40] The parochial boards were responsible for auditing registrar's accounts (1854), enforcing vaccination (1855), dealing with lunatics (1857), public health duties (1867), licensing pawnbrokers, raising the education rate, and more besides.[41] Administrative power was clearly still vested at the parochial level. Although the Board of Supervision was the pinnacle of centralisation in Scotland, it was effectively free of parliamentary control (that is, it was ignored by the Home Office, argues Levitt), so it was centralisation based in Edinburgh.[42] The Board also had very little supervisory power over the burghs. Even after the 1867 Public Health Act, towns over 10,000 were excluded from the Board's control.[43] Relief of the poor was still effectively a parochial matter or a town or city matter. The social intervention of the British state had not seriously eroded local rate-payer responsibility for, and control over, the relief of the poor within their own administrative boundaries.

It is visible from the work of Flinn, Crowther and Levitt, that although the state was involving itself to a greater extent in society, the sharp end of its influence was administered locally. It is also apparent that following the reform of the two Poor Law Acts, the power of local parochial officials was stronger in Scotland than in England and Wales. Central inspection, as recommended by Bentham and Chadwick, was vital to the English system of poor relief; by the turn of the century England had sixty-seven inspectors for its unions, and even then the Local Government Board complained that this was scarcely adequate. In Scotland two General Inspectors were appointed in 1856 to carry out all duties (there were eventually four inspectors by the 1880s).[44] The Royal Commission of 1909 found the discrepancy between England and Scotland puzzling:

---

[39] J. E. Shaw, *Local Government in Scotland: Past, Present and Future* (Edinburgh, 1942), pp. 3–4.

[40] R. H. Campbell, *Scotland since 1707: The Rise of an Industrial Society* (2nd edn, Edinburgh, 1985), p. 160.

[41] T. C. Smout, 'Scotland, 1750–1950', in F. M. L. Thompson (ed.), *The Cambridge Social History of Britain, 1750–1950*, vol. I: *Regions and Communities* (Cambridge, 1990), p. 247.

[42] I. Levitt (ed.), *Government and Social Conditions in Scotland, 1845–1919* (Edinburgh, 1988), pp. xi–xix.

[43] *An Act to Consolidate and Amend the Law Relating to the Public Health in Scotland*, 30 & 31 Victoria, cap. 101 (1867), pt. 1, art. IV, p. 6. The figure relates to the last Census count.

[44] Crowther, 'Poverty, health and welfare', p. 272.

'Is there any reason for the number of Scottish inspectors being smaller than the number of English and Irish inspectors?', asked William Smart, the Professor of Political Economy at Glasgow. 'Only Scotland just takes what it can get', replied one of the inspectors. 'The usual neglect since the Union, in fact', commented Smart.[45]

If we ignore the nationalist gripe for the moment, then it should be understood that with its low level of administrative back-up, the Board had no more than a marginal influence over the towns in the relief of the poor. The Board had little legal clout either. For instance the Nuisance Removal Bill of 1856 and its resultant Act, an important measure of public health reform in Scotland before the 1867 Act, gave the Board only the power to decide whether the Local Authority was to be the Parochial Board or the Police Commissioners: the Local Authority was awarded the authority to enforce the Act.[46] In addition, the Board of Supervision in Scotland was based on government appointments from the landowning class and the Edinburgh advocates, and so scarcely in a position to dictate to the elected and liberal councils about how they should spend ratepayers money.[47] Despite the fact that the Board of Supervision was the first principal government department north of the Border, effective power still resided with the local elites.[48] The governing of poor relief in Scotland is one where its management was, within the town and the city, administered by the local bourgeoisie; indeed, this is a story repeated in many ways in the area of sanitary reform.

Sanitary reform and local government

With the reform of the Poor Law in 1834 and 1845 the British state was explicitly trying to juggle a reduction in the spiralling costs of poor relief with the strains of centralised administration. In the area of sanitary reform, the British state was equally explicit in the agenda it sketched out for the local authorities in order for them to respond to the excesses of *laissez-faire*.

The story of the Public Health movement is one where the state initiated social intervention, but did so through local government. Michael Lynch argues that the first steps taken towards an ordered urban society had come in the area of public health.[49] In Scotland public health reforms were left in the hands of the towns, more so than in

---

[45] I. Levitt, *Poverty and Welfare in Scotland, 1890–1948* (Edinburgh, 1988), p. 51; also quoted in Crowther, Poverty, health and welfare', p. 272.

[46] *An Act to make better Provision for the Removal of Nuisances, Regulations of Lodging Houses, and the Health of Towns in Scotland*, 19 & 20 Victoria, cap. 103 (1856), art. V, pp. 2–3.

[47] Levitt, *Poverty and Welfare in Scotland*, p. xi.

[48] Ibid., p. xvii.

[49] Lynch, *Scotland*, p. 412.

England and Wales, and actually the sanitary condition of Scotland suffered as a result. Importantly, the provisions of the 1848 Public Health Act were not extended to Scotland. This Act included the setting up the Central Board of Health (1848–58) under the chairmanship of Edwin Chadwick; it proved to be a controversial body on both sides of the Border. This Act was described as 'Un-English' (meaning unconstitutional) by the quirky Cromarty-born David Urquhart because of its establishment, in principle, of the primacy of Parliament in social intervention. The earl of Shaftesbury, focusing on the issue of public health in his address to the National Association for the Promotion of Social Science, denied that that body existed 'to promote that to which Englishmen very strongly object, a system of centralisation'.[50] It explains Urquhart's prophecy that 'Centralisation dissolves the bonds of society.'[51]

Flinn gives us three reasons for the defeat of the centralising principle in Scotland as embodied in Public Health legislation. First, because the Act of 1837 which required the civil registration of births and deaths was not extended to Scotland, there was no means of officially ascertaining which places had a death rate over 23 per 1,000 – which then triggered the setting up of a local public health board (the mechanism at the core of the 1848 Act). Secondly, the medical profession in Edinburgh was sceptical of the advantages of such a non-medical bureaucracy. Thirdly, the medical profession thought the Scottish situation was different with regard to the diffusion of disease. The upshot was that the Public Health (Scotland) Bill was rejected in 1849, and it was not until 1867 that a Public Health (Scotland) Act finally gave the Board of Supervision general supervisory powers in relation to public health in Scotland.[52] This was finally achieved, Flinn argues, because it was Scottish, not London, based:

> They [the medical profession] shared a general Scottish reluctance to submit themselves voluntarily to additional supervision from London, suggesting that, instead of submitting any future Scottish local health authorities to the jurisdiction of the central [London] Health Board, the Poor Law Board of Supervision in Edinburgh ... was the most suitable Scottish central authority for public health matters.[53]

---

50 'Address by the Right Hon. the Earl of Shaftesbury, on Public Health', *Transactions of the National Association for the Promotion of the Social Science* (1858), p. 84.

51 *Hansard*, 3rd ser., vol. XCVIII, 5 May (1848), cols. 712–13. An overview of Urquhart's parliamentary career can be found in R. Shannon, 'David Urquhart and the Foreign Affairs Committees', in P. Hollis (ed.), *Pressure from without in early Victorian England* (London, 1974).

52 Flinn, *Report on the Sanitary Condition*, p. 73; see J. H. F. Brotherston, *Observations on the Early Public Health Movement in Scotland* (Edinburgh, 1952).

53 Flinn, *Report on the Sanitary Condition*, p. 72.

The Scottish equivalents to the 1848 Public Health Act and its lineal successors were Lindsay's Police Act of 1862 and the Public Health (Scotland) Act of 1867. In was not until 1892 – the Burgh Police (Scotland) Act – that Scotland had caught up with England in terms of sanitary reform. Scotland in fact had a lot of catching up to do: not in the larger towns and cities, which had looked after their environment through private acts, but in the smaller towns which had not.[54]

From this brief discussion of poor relief and sanitary reform it has been seen that the parliamentary state did not simply legislate itself into more and more power. Centralisation of state powers was a general fear in the mid-nineteenth century. Indeed, it was one that fuelled Scottish nationalist concerns (as we shall see in Chapter 7). I have argued that Ricardian economics and the lure of free trade were attractive enough to the first industrial nation for its state to sit back and watch much economic and industrial advancement. I have also argued that, at the same time as the nineteenth-century state freed itself economically, it had to concern itself with the social and political difficulties attached to rapid industrialisation and urbanisation. What I have stressed is that over our period the state had increased governmental control over society by transferring powers to the local state, especially in the case of Scotland. Michael Flinn sums up this process when he points out that

> by authorising local government authorities – at first through the establishment of improvement commissions, and later through the Municipal Corporations Act of 1835 [*sic*] and subsequent local private acts to perform a wide range of social services – governments implicitly accepted the principle of local government intervention under the authority of the central government.[55]

The hegemony of the town and city as the fount of good government was not an easy one for the centrists to break. To return to Shaftesbury's defence of the Social Science Association, and the role of central government in public health:

> Our object ... is to stimulate inquiry, and to unite all the zeal and energy that we can in every district and individual locality, so that each separate locality should be the fountain, the centre, the alpha and the omega, of all the operations that affect that locality.[56]

---

[54] G. Best, 'The Scottish Victorian city', *Victorian Studies*, xi (3) (1968), p. 335. Tom Taylor argued that 'in our second and third-rate towns the quality of the material of local government is, I fear, deteriorating rather than improving; at all events, it is in daily danger of deterioration': T. Taylor, 'On central and local action in relation to town improvement', *Transactions of the National Association for the Promotion of the Social Science* (1857), p. 478.

[55] Flinn, *Report on the Sanitary Condition*, p. 41.

[56] Shaftesbury, 'Address', p. 84.

This constant need to counterbalance Westminster with the locality meant the relationship between the nation and the state in Britain was not a simple one. The role of the central state was to empower. The discussion of poor relief and of public health made clear that actual governing was done in part by the Boards of Control although ultimately by the local authorities and the urban elites at the municipal level.

The evolution of local government in Scotland, 1833–1900

The existence of nearly standard burgh constitutions made the reformers' task very much easier in Scotland than in England (where there was a great variety of customs and tenures). This difference explains in part the two-year delay in English burgh reform until 1835.[57] The 1833 legislation in Scotland created what was called a 'police system' of local authorities and the instigation of 'police commissioners', with the intention of producing a more comprehensive and democratically accountable system.[58] The burgh statutes allowed £10 householders in royal burghs and burghs of barony to by-pass (but not supplant) the existing councils by adopting a 'parallel police system', whereby elected magistrates and commissioners of police were given powers to raise rates.[59] Thus the 1833 reform created the rather confusing picture of urban government in Scotland, with the creation of either new councils replacing the old oligarchies, or of a parallel police system alongside an old council. This was at times an obvious hindrance to the decision-making process, although Morris has argued that by the 1840s they consisted, in practice, of the same membership.[60]

The police commissioners' main duties were: to appoint police constables to attend to watching, paving cleansing, scavenging, the water

---

[57] I. Adams, *The Making of Urban Scotland* (London, 1978), p. 131.

[58] The immediate pre-history of this structure is detailed in *Report of the Committee, appointed at the General Meeting of the Magistrates, and the different public bodies in this city, to consent measures for obtaining a more efficient SYSTEM OF POLICE* (Edinburgh, 1812). The debate in Edinburgh over corruption amongst the Police Commissioners in 1820 was notable and created extensive public debate, e.g. *Letter to the Right Honourable the Lord Provost; from Captain Brown, Superintendent of the Edinburgh Police, On the subject of the late investigation into the Police Establishment* (Edinburgh, 1820); J. C. S., 'Remarks on Captain Brown's letter to the Lord Provost of Edinburgh', *Blackwood's Edinburgh Magazine* (1820), pp. 204–7; *Reply to Captain Brown's Letter in Another Letter to the Lord Provost of Edinburgh by a Commissioner of Police* [pseud] (Edinburgh, 1820); and *A Letter to Messrs George Miller, Thomas Allan, and Peter Brown, from Captain Brown, Superintendent of the Edinburgh Police Establishment* (Edinburgh, 1821).

[59] Smout, 'Scotland, 1750–1950', p. 246.

[60] R. J. Morris, 'Urbanisation in Scotland', in Fraser and Morris, *People and Society*, p. 86. The Lord Provost, Bailies, Dean of Guild and Treasurer of the City sat alongside the Lord Justice General and local MPs, merchants, booksellers, advocates and doctors of Laws and of Physic, amongst others. See, *Copy Commission of the Peace for the City of Edinburgh and Liberties thereof, printed by order of the Lord Provost, 6 November* (Edinburgh, 1848), pp. 3–8.

supply and the prevention of infectious diseases; to name streets and number houses; to remove 'foresters' or ruinous buildings; to regulate drains, sewers and fire engines; and to license hackney coaches. They were also empowered to impose yearly assessments, to contract loans, and to receive property from tutors or curators for infants, minors, furious or fatuous persons, and married women.[61] It was an extensive list, and for rapidly changing towns it emphasised the importance of local concerns to local politics. Indeed, it can be seen that the police commissioners had responsibility over many issues which were covered by public health legislation in England. Scotland concentrated its improvements under further 'police acts' or through local acts sponsored by the individual towns and cities and passed through Parliament. The right to adopt a police system was extended in 1847 to non-royal parliamentary burghs, and in 1850 to 'populous places', certified by the Sheriff to have over 1,200 inhabitants – both these Acts (and an Act of 1856) widened the scope of the police commissioners' powers: ranging from the provision of public baths to the inspection of foodstuffs and the ordering of repairs to insanitary housing.[62] These 'police' powers were again increased in the Burgh Police (Scotland) Act – the Lindsay Act – of 1862, which enabled the police authorities to form Dean of Guild Courts to enforce building regulations. All these powers were advanced by the Police Act of 1892 and the Public Health (Scotland) Act of 1897.

The Lindsay Act was not legally enforceable, but it did serve to improve further the effectiveness of local officials in their efforts to manage their urban environment. It also dramatically extended the amount of urban government in Scotland. The Lindsay Act allowed for any locality of more than 700 in population to become a police burgh with the legal right to make building and sanitary laws of its own.[63] Yet this Act exacerbated the structural problem of overlapping government authorities and did not advance on typically inadequate drafting, whereby many statutes intended for better government of towns throughout the whole of Britain could not be imposed because they ignored Scottish law. The most quoted example of this was the Sanitary Act of 1866, which was designed to force local authorities to improve sanitary provision, but which proved unworkable in Scotland because the final means of enforcement was by appeal to the Queen's Bench, which had no jurisdiction north of the Border.[64] It was the Burgh Police Act of 1892 which ended the system of dual responsibility (so that

61 J. D. Mackie and G. S. Pryde, *Local Government in Scotland* (Dunfermline, 1932), p. 17.
62 Ibid., p. 18.
63 Morris, 'Urbanisation in Scotland', p. 86; T. C. Smout, *A Century of the Scottish People, 1830–1950* (London, 1986), p. 41; R. J. Morris *Class, Sect and Party: The Making of the British Middle Class. Leeds, 1820–1850* (Manchester, 1990), p. 88.
64 Smout, 'Scotland, 1750–1950', p. 248; Smout, *Century of the Scottish People*, p. 42; Morris, 'Urbanisation in Scotland', p. 87; Best, 'Scottish Victorian city', p. 331.

henceforth a town might be governed either by provost, bailies and councillors, or by police magistrates and commissioners, but not by both), and the Town Council (Scotland) Act of 1900 completed the process by insisting on uniform constitutions in all burghs under provost, bailies and elected councillors.[65]

The story of local government post-1833 in Scotland is one where the local state assumed ever greater powers for intervening and thus shaping the urban environment, although this duty was not always discharged proficiently. The implication for the debate over 'the age of *laissez-faire*' is that the central state did not directly alter its minimalist role because of this empowerment of the locality. This then means that there was no inconsistency in policy for a British state to embrace free trade on the one hand and to sponsor greater restrictions on the social impact of the free market on the other. Nor must we see the creation of overlapping authorities as a contradiction in the primary role so far stressed for local government. The actuality may well have been weakened effectiveness: the efficiencies of grouped resources, accumulated knowledge, national targeting of need and the avoidance of petty urban rivalries were lost. Yet it strengthened the very idea of local urban government by involving so many in its execution. Indeed, by creating so many functionaries of the local state, it inevitably questioned then need for another layer of local government, albeit one born of the centre. This leads us to ask how the resistance to centralisation lasted for so long, despite the contradictions produced by the locality's in-built inefficiencies. The ideological answer is in the theory of 'best' government; the empirical answer is the structure of civil society.

Local versus central government

Throughout the mid-century period, informed opinion warned against the evils of 'centralisation'. The virtues of local self-government had become part of the orthodox liberal creed of the 1850s. Nonconformist distrust of government had a long tradition in the philosophical foundations of economic liberalism.[66] Yet on these issues liberalism had lost the cutting edge to the Utilitarians; it was they who adapted their conception of the state not just to protect man's natural rights, but to promote general welfare.[67] The balance between the central and the local state had received widespread notoriety at this time through the campaign against Edwin Chadwick's Poor Law Commission and the General Board of Health. Perhaps the most direct exposition of the advantages of local administration of society was given by Joshua Toulmin Smith in *Local Self-Government and Centralisation* (1851):

[65] Smout, 'Scotland, 1750–1950', p. 247.
[66] H. J. Laski, *Political Thought in England: Locke to Bentham* (London, 1920), p. 185.
[67] Flournoy, 'British Liberal theories', p. 196.

LOCAL SELF-GOVERNMENT is that system of Government under
which the greatest number of minds, knowing the most, and having
the fullest opportunities of knowing it, about the special matter in
hand, and having the greatest interests, have the management of it,
or control over it.

CENTRALISATION is that system of Government under which the
smallest number of minds, and those knowing the least, and having
the fewest opportunities of knowing it, about the special matter in
hand, and having the smallest interest in its well working, have the
management of it, or control over it.[68]

Toulmin Smith's trenchant views on the value of local self-government
mirrored the Whig demand for urban government by local men. The
issue of taxation (how it was levied, who raised it, and who spent it) was
paramount to constructing the ideology of urban government by
ratepayers.[69] Hanham argues that British statesmen, scholars and
constitutional theorists were, for the most part, firmly fixed within the
Whig tradition on good government in urban society. They believed
both in the progressive evolution of institutions – of gradual refinement
– and they believed in the leadership of men of education, character and
social position.[70] This fits with the 'civic pride' movement of the 1830s
and 1840s, when there existed much inter-town rivalry between
bourgeois elites concerning 'good government' and its link to economic
prosperity. Usually this rivalry took the form of building more and more
elaborate town and trading halls, but also the building of monuments,
opera houses, bandstands and other prestige symbols. The Victorian
bourgeoisie was very conscious of displaying the trappings of wealth and
the construction of ornate buildings and street furniture was part of this
process. Inevitably this display of economic power and pride in one's
town – usually where that economic success was based – required
commensurate political power. The biggest ratepayers must have the
political control to sanction such an amount of public spending; the
number of votes being linked to a sliding scale of property ownership
was a common structure. Local self-government was, as Toulmin Smith
put it, about those with the 'greatest interest' at stake.

We have seen David Urquhart describe the 1848 Public Health Act as
unconstitutional, and the lip service that interventionists such as
Shaftesbury had to pay to the locality. To this list we can add

68 These extracts are from H. J. Hanham, *The Nineteenth-Century Constitution: Documents
    and Commentary* (Cambridge, 1969), p. 377.
69 On the importance of how revenue is raised to the central/local debate, see
    W. E. Whyte, *Local Government in Scotland, with complete statutory references* (2nd edn,
    London, 1936), p. 3.
70 Hanham, *Nineteenth-Century Constitution*, p. 1. Also note the only marginal change in
    the social class composition of local government pre- and post-reform in J. Garrard,
    Leadership and Power in Victorian Industrial Towns, 1830–80 (Manchester, 1983).

C. B. Adderley, then President of the Board of Health, who was persuaded to accept that 'he thought it was better to leave localities to settle their own affairs, than to transfer them to a central authority'.[71] *The Times* reacted to the removal of Chadwick from the Board of Health with a leader that declared:

> If there is such a thing as a political certainty among us, it is that nothing autocratic can exist in this country ... Mr Chadwick and Dr Southwood Smith, have been disposed, and we prefer to take our chance of cholera and the rest than be bullied into health.[72]

Yet such confidence in the ability of the locality to deal with its own problems, and the legitimacy of rule by local elites, was challenged. The dangers of localism structuring the political process were twofold: the first, like the North American example of 'boosterism' (where local government was a tool of entrepreneurial success), was the emergence of contradictions between economic self-interest and good government; the other danger was public apathy. The duke of Wellington warned of the latter (in an extract quoted approvingly by Toulmin Smith):

> While every one is accustomed to rely upon the Government, upon a sort of commutation for what they pay to it, personal energy goes to sleep, and the end is lost. This supineness and apathy as to public exertion will in the end ruin us.[73]

For Toulmin Smith these words were to emphasise the need for commitment in public life, and he believed this commitment was strongest in the locality. Tom Taylor, then secretary of the Board of Health, disagreed with Toulmin Smith's view that the contemporary experience was the overlaying of a suffocating system of bureaucracy. He argued that the real threat to local government was not 'ever-encroaching officialism, but ever-increasing selfishness – the result of excessive addiction to money-making'. He argued for a balance between the centre and the locality: 'I maintain that the central action may be most beneficially so called in aid of local self-government when the latter is most animated by a patriotic and unselfish spirit. It may, and should, act as an ally of real local self-government against spurious self-government.'[74]

Adding to such doubts in the 'localist' position were those who suggested that ratepayers were often too reluctant to back the necessary expenditure for addressing the demands of rapid urbanisation. This was particularly apparent over the issue of public health. Thus we find

---

[71] Hansard, 3rd ser., vol. CXLIX (1858), col. 2095.
[72] *The Times*, 1 Aug. 1854, quoted in R. M. Gutchen, 'Local improvements and centralisation in nineteenth-century England', *Historical Journal*, iv (1961), p. 85.
[73] Quoted in Taylor, 'On central and local action', p. 475.
[74] Ibid., p. 476.

Roebuck in favour of government intervention 'because it made every person having authority under it immediately responsible, not to petty local authorities, but the general authority of Parliament'.[75] Edwin Chadwick *On the Evils of Disunity* (1885), looking back at criticisms over his reforms earlier in the century, argued:

> I may here meet the exclamation apt to be raised by certain classes of politicians, 'Then you are for centralisation!' Even if it were so, it would be for you, the advocate of decentralisation and disunity, to say whether you prefer disease and premature mortality and waste with what you call local self-government, to health, and strength, and economy with centralisation. But I answer, that I am, on principle, for extensive decentralisation – actually for decentralisation to the greatest extent by well-arranged local consolidation for superior self-government over that which now exists; and that is your real choice – a true representation of the best local intelligence under unity in the place of disunity and local ignorance.[76]

This argument from Chadwick is consistent with that of John Stuart Mill in *Representative Government* (1861), that 'Power may be localised, but knowledge to be most useful, must be centralised; there must be somewhere a focus at which all its scattered rays are collected.'[77] It is fair to argue that if we are to reconcile the centralising developments in public health reform with the growth in local government – from the police commissioners to civic pride and municipal socialism – then Mill's statement strikes a cord of accuracy.

The exploitation of centralised knowledge was to the fore in sanitary reform. 'Overwhelmed by a sense of their inadequacy in the face of new problems and wants, the local rulers were often too glad to rely on the superior knowledge accumulated in the departments of central government.'[78] In particular, this was the rationale behind the appointment of the first local Medical Officer of Health by Liverpool Corporation in 1847. Edinburgh was the first authority in Scotland to appoint such an officer in 1862, Dr Littlejohn, and for similar reasons.[79] Most major local authorities followed suit before the end of the 1860s, and it became obligatory following the Public Health Act of 1872. Central state intervention was occasionally accepted; the cry of 'centralisation' was not raised against the factory acts, for instance;[80] but on the

---

75 *The Economist*, cc (1847), p. 730.
76 Reproduced in Hanham, *Nineteenth-Century Constitution*, p. 383.
77 J. S. Mill, *Considerations on Representative Government* (London, 1861), p. 281.
78 E. P. Hennock, 'Centre/local government relations in England: an outline, 1800–1950' *Urban History Yearbook*, xl (1982), p. 41.
79 H. MacDonald, 'Public Health Legislation and Problems in Victorian Edinburgh, with special reference to the work of Dr Littlejohn as Medical Officer of Health' (Edinburgh University Ph.D. thesis, 1972).
80 W. C. Lubenow, *The Politics of Government Growth: Early Victorian Attitudes towards State Intervention, 1833–1848* (Devon, 1971), p. 149.

whole it was the exception, not the rule. Charles More sums it up when
he states that:

> Benthamites, of whom the most active was Edwin Chadwick,
> disliked local autonomy because they considered it inefficient.
> Practically everyone else supported it: traditionalists because such
> welfare as existed in the past had always been locally controlled;
> rate-payers, who disliked spending local money at the dictate of
> central government; and the central government itself, who wanted
> to pay for as little as possible out of central government revenue.[81]

John Stuart Mill was against the generalisations of parliamentary
intervention, and Bentham himself, despite the social intervention of his
Panoptican and his love of codification, was essentially restrained 'by the
principle that each man was normally the best ultimate judge of his own
happiness and how to promote it'.[82] Bentham's *Leading Principles of a
Constitutional Code for any State* (1823) was to cement the primacy of
Parliament as legislator.[83] Many details of Chadwick's 1834 Poor Law
were taken from Bentham's code (Chadwick became Bentham's literary
secretary in 1830,[84] and later nursed him through his final illness).[85] Yet
within Utilitarian thought we have come across both the desire for
centralisation and the wish to safeguard the individual by making
government as near to the individual as possible. It was a fine balance:

> A government which attempts to do everything, is aptly compared
> by M. Charles de Rémusat to a schoolmaster who does all the
> pupils' tasks for them; he may be very popular with the pupils but
> he will teach them little. A government, on the other hand, which
> neither does anything itself that can possibly be done by any one
> else, nor shows any one else how to do anything, is like a school in
> which there is no schoolmaster, but only pupil teachers who have
> never themselves been taught.[86]

Particularisms and specialisms in the locality had to be traded against the
generalisations and mediocrity of the centre.

The tangential nature of Westminster government, which this
central/local axis maintained, was especially acute in Scotland where this

---

[81] More, *Industrial Age*, p. 211. For the demands of the Benthamites for the state to reassert central control over a 'chaotic system', see S. G. Checkland and E. O. A. Checkland (eds.), *The Poor Law Report of 1834* (London, 1974), p. 22.

[82] J. Dinwiddy, *Bentham* (Oxford, 1989), p. 16.

[83] J. Bentham, 'Leading principles of a constitutional code, for any state', *The Pamphleteer*, xliv (1823).

[84] M. Marston, *Sir Edwin Chadwick (1800–1890)* (London and Boston, 1925), p. 22; this link between Chadwick and Bentham is explored in S. and B. Webb, *English Poor Law History*, p. 31.

[85] R. A. Lewis, *Edwin Chadwick and the Public Health Movement, 1832–1854* (London, 1952), p. 10.

[86] Mill, *Considerations on Representative Government*, p. 284.

rule surfaced only intermittently and seemed a long way off.[87] In his phenomenally successful reminiscences, Dean Ramsay tells the story of a remote Aberdeenshire minister facing the disapproving look of a younger colleague when promising 'gude smuggled whusky' on completing the service. To his Southern guest's warning of the illegality of the action, the old minister proclaimed, 'Oh, Acts o' Parliament lose their breath before they get to Aberdeenshire.'[88]

Politics, both local and parliamentary, was dominated by issues of particular urban management. Mid-century Edinburgh voters, for example, were heavily preoccupied with the Annuity Tax, a tax peculiar to Edinburgh to raise money for the local ministers of the Established Church. Note also the important argument by Derek Fraser regarding the politicising in England of the parochial vestry, the committee associated with the maintenance of the fabric of the church and the relief of the poor. Before municipal reform, Liberal vestries counterbalanced Tory oligarchies, and after reform artisan and working-class vestries counterbalanced bourgeois dominated councils.[89] No prospective Parliamentary candidate could afford to forget that elections were won and lost on local debates.

The home-made attack on the shock urban fabric was seen in attempts at urban planning. Big towns had always relied on local acts to legislate, although this was often a slow and frustrating process.[90] In Edinburgh the building of Regent Arch to connect Calton Hill with the east end of Princes Street, and the building of the Mound and Bank Street so as to connect the Old and New Town, were achieved by Private Bills steered through Parliament by the town council early in the nineteenth century[91] – a clear example of parliamentary empowerment. Big towns, and many smaller towns too, increasingly became involved in urban service provision. Water, gas and the trams tended to be monopolies which needed permission from the local authority to use roads or land. Frequently these schemes were initially financed by the local authorities and many felt that the monopoly profits resulting from that permission and initial finance should go to the ratepayers. In 1874 Joseph Chamberlain expected that in fourteen years' time there would be a profit of £50,000 from gas municipalisation in Birmingham 'without the slightest degree increasing the cost of gas to the consumer more than

---

87 Kellas, *Scottish Political System*, pp. 29–30.
88 E. B. Ramsay, *Reminiscences of Scottish Life and Character* (26th edn, Edinburgh, 1892), p. 26.
89 D. Fraser, *Urban Politics in Victorian England: The Structure of Politics in Victorian Cities* (Leicester, 1976), pp. 9–30.
90 E.g., 'The system of local Acts stands condemned by general consent, on the ground of extravagant costliness, no less than on reasons arising from the objectionable character of the Private Bills Committee as a tribunal': Taylor, 'On central and local action', p. 478.
91 A. J. Youngson, *The Making of Classical Edinburgh* (Edinburgh, 1966), pp. 139–40, 168.

would have been the case had the corporation not taken over the concern'.[92] Throughout Britain, from the mid-1860s to the end of the century, a big authority was expected to have its own gasworks, its own waterworks, its own tramways, its own housing estates, its own electricity supply plant, and many other public utilities. Late-century municipal socialism, and municipal trading of the 1910s and 1920s, were the logical extension of the civic pride movement in the 1830s and 1840s.[93] Despite concurrent trends towards central departments, this municipal activity is perhaps the apogee of local independence at this time.

Central government always had ultimate power over the local state, of that there is no denial; the unitary state was unchallenged. Yet the legislative framework established by the centre provided the spaces whereby actual day-to-day governing of society was enacted in the locality by the enfranchised bourgeoisie. Local and central government appeared to balance each other, with the essential concern of the former being the fight to restrict the growth of the latter.[94] In this sense we can agree with Shaw that local government is a misleading title, and really these authorities administered on Parliament's behalf.[95] This should not be seen as justification for a Westminster focus to our analysis of the state and the nation, but it reminds us of the extent of decentralisation and local empowerment, and hopefully it clears the mind-block whereby 'government equals Westminster' in the literature of nationalism. It can thus be seen that throughout the nineteenth century the central state, as a substitute for extensive centralisation, sought to meet the needs for social intervention by 'passing general Acts setting out local authority powers and duties, in the belief that these statutory powers would be effectively applied without the need of coercion'.[96] The period from 1834 to 1870 saw more efficient and democratically constituted administration for these different local government functions, and its organisation varied whether it were dealing with the Poor Law, the highways or sanitary issues.[97] This very heterogeneity protected the

---

[92] A. Briggs, 'Birmingham: the making of a civic gospel', in A. Briggs, *Victorian Cities* (London, 1963), p. 222; D. Fraser, 'Joseph Chamberlain and the municipal ideal', in G. Marsden (ed.), *Victorian Values: Personalities and Perspectives in Nineteenth-Century Society* (London, 1990), p. 141.

[93] Asa Briggs explains the rationale behind the 'my town hall is bigger than your town hall' local rivalries in A. Briggs, 'Leeds: a study in civic pride', in Briggs, *Victorian Cities*, pp. 150–7. For the growth of municipal socialism, see T. Hart, 'Urban growth and municipal government: Glasgow in comparative context, 1864–1914', in A. Slaven and D. H. Aldcroft (eds.), *Business, Banking and Urban History* (Edinburgh, 1982), pp. 197–8.

[94] G. L. Gomme, *Lectures on the Principals of Local Government. Delivered to the London School of Economics, Lent Term, 1897* (London, 1897), p. 3. Gomme argued that, 'A tendency towards a local development has been stopped by the attitudes of State government, and a tendency towards a State development has been stopped by the attributes of local government.'

[95] Shaw, *Local Government in Scotland*, p. 1.

[96] Checkland, *Rise of Industrial Society*, p. 362.

[97] Lipman, *Local Government Areas*, p. 34.

ideological balance of the locality's primacy within a unitary state structure.

It was not until the early 1870s that the question of power no longer revolved primarily around the centre/local relationship. Rather it became an issue within the local authority structure itself: between the elected members and the local officials. The formation of the Local Government Board in 1871 put an end to the isolation of the Poor Law Board as the predominant agent of state centralisation,[98] and countered individual self-interest by regulating local government finance.[99] In this instance central government forged a quasi-legalistic arbitration between local interests and national needs ('with occasional inputs of policy from administrator statesmen in disguise').[100] The bewildering complexity of areas and authorities had to be rationalised if efficiency and effectiveness were to be achieved.[101] One contributor to the Cobden Club in 1875 detailed the extent of these overlapping power centres:

> It seems strange, too, in a country with a seventh of the population of England, to have such a multitude of petty parish Boards (numbering, between poor and school, nearly 1,800), each armed with the fullest powers of taxing and spending, and each limiting its views to its own diminutive bounds. Nearly every third parish in Scotland has fewer than 1,000 inhabitants; nearly every tenth parish fewer than 500. Yet these Lilliputian communities have their organised Boards, their salaried officials, their parliamentary powers to tax their neighbours and spend the money.[102]

It has been argued that as local action became more complex, so power came to be shared with national professional bodies; and as local action became more extensive, it had to be shared with the central state, the body that could raise the additional expenditure needed.[103] The cost of nineteenth-century Poor Relief in Scotland peaked in 1870 at just over £905,045, a near doubling in less than twenty years.[104] Locally raised revenue increased fivefold between 1830 and 1900; the central subsidy increased at twice that rate, and Westminster was now to demand a greater role in how that money was spent.[105] The gathering of statistics which marked the 'social science' approach to social intervention

98 Hennock, 'Centre/local government relations', p. 43.
99 R. J. Morris, 'The state, the elite and the market: the "visible hand" in the British Industrial City System' (paper for the International Group for Urban History Colloquium, Leiden, 1988), p. 22.
100 Ibid., p. 18, quoting C. Bellamy, *Administering Central-Local Relations, 1871–1919* (Manchester, 1988).
101 Lipman, *Local Government Areas*, p. 34.
102 A. McNeel-Caird, 'Local government and taxation in Scotland', in J. W. Probyn, *Local Government and Taxation, Cobden Club Essays* (London, 1875), p. 144.
103 Hennock, 'Centre/local government', p. 43.
104 McNeel-Caird, 'Local government and taxation', p. 140.
105 R. Pearce and R. Stearn, *Government and Reform, 1815–1918* (London, 1994), p. 93.

between 1820 and 1850, was thought able to obtain complete answers but rather it created many new sets of questions.[106] The weakness of workers' wages to solve the quandary of sanitary house provision at affordable rents was a classic concern where public opinion was in need of 'manipulation' if it were ever to acknowledge the case for central government intervention.[107] By the 1870s the local bourgeoisie no longer had the governmental structure which could deal with the extent of the demands made on government, although arguments in favour of more unified and all-powerful municipal authorities continued[108] (this was despite the demise of the Local Government Board in 1919,[109] and its replacement by the Scottish Board of Health).[110] The creation of the Scotch Education Department in 1872, and the creation of the Scottish Office in 1885, is part of the process of centralising government, culminating in the re-organisation of local government in 1929.[111] Mazzini's 'principle of nationality' was superseded as the twentieth century beckoned. It was supplanted by the belief that any ethnic group could and, importantly, should have a state as its form of government.[112] With the working class obtaining the vote in 1867–8, and more widely in 1884–5, it was not long before this class would demand, and receive, substantial public intervention for greater welfare. Economically, too, the British state had to abandon its hands-off approach. *Laissez-faire* as the dominant economic philosophy started to crumble after 1870, although some authors have argued for its persistence well into the twentieth century.[113] As other countries industrialised, it became evident that free trade was not enough to maintain Britain as the leading industrial power. By the final quarter of the nineteenth century, the British state and the central/local state relationship had fundamentally altered – they had begun to take on their twentieth-century features.

---

[106] O. MacDonagh, *A Pattern of Government Growth: The Passenger Acts and their Enforcement* (London, 1961), p. 345.

[107] 'Address by George Godwin on Public Health', *Transactions of the National Association for the Promotion of Social Science* (1871), pp. 106–8; J. Hole, 'Is it desirable that the state or municipality should assist in providing improved dwellings for the lower class; and, if so, to what extent and in what way?', *Transactions of the National Association for the Promotion of Social Science* (1871), pp. 523–8.

[108] E.g., the prefatory note by J. Lorne Macleod, Lord Provost of Edinburgh, in A. Grierson, *Reconstruction Problems: Local Government in Edinburgh and District. Report by the Town Clerk of Edinburgh* (Edinburgh, 1919). Grierson argued that 'The problems that await consideration are of considerable magnitude and complexity, and it would be a mistake to assume that they are such as can only be dealt with by the State', p. 5.

[109] W. C. Dundas, *Development of Local Government in Counties in Scotland* (London, 1942), p. 17.

[110] Shaw, *Local Government in Scotland*, p. 4.

[111] Whyte, *Local Government in Scotland*, p. 5.

[112] Hobsbawm, *Nations and Nationalism*, p. 102.

[113] Taylor, *Laissez-faire*, pp. 53ff. Daunton, *Progress and Poverty*, argues that 'by the early 1850s, free trade was widely accepted as the linchpin of British prosperity and it was not challenged for another half-century', p. 554.

It is between 1830 and 1860 – the pinnacle of the *laissez-faire* state –
which is so different and so misunderstood by accounts of the Scottish
nation and the British state in the nineteenth century. The state/civil
society axis for Scotland was a local relationship, and this is where
Scottish national identity was formed. The town councils were part of
the story, but they did not fully encompass 'citizen politics'. The £10
ratepayers ran local government, but importantly, they also exercised a
class and social power throughout their public life. Civil society, too, was
enshrined by the central state, and this is our final source of 'self-
governing'.

A governed civil society

In the period in British history in which town growth rapidly escalated,
why was the local level of government the focus of the response to the
ensuing urban challenge? In part this question has already been
answered – a fear of centralised bureaucracy and taxation not responsive
to each locality and to each set of ratepayers in the towns and cities. This
answer also includes the Whig philosophy expounded by Macaulay that
government should be in the hands of 'good and worthy' men, that is
the local bourgeoisie. This takes us to the remainder of the explanation.
Nineteenth-century middle-class formation – as a process – lays great
stress upon philanthropic activities in an urban environment as a means
of overcoming divisions of sect and party.[114] This activity, it is argued,
was central to the middle-class transition of class-in-itself to class-for-
itself and hence pivotal to the exercise of class power. The reform of the
parliamentary franchise in 1832 and the democratisation of local
government in 1833 and 1835, opened up the political world to the £10
householder and 'gave practical content of the idea of the town'.[115]

From a beginning in the late eighteenth century, the volume and
range of voluntary societies which were set up in the towns were
immense. Their peak was in the 1830s and 1840s. At the same time that
the town councils grew, 'the proliferation of institutions and of posts for
the making and execution of policy was at least as rapid in the voluntary
societies'.[116] There were few limits to the extent of Victorian philanthropy. The 'principle of piety' was all-important: the religious, the
moralistic, the charitable, the self-help voluntary organisation reached

---

[114] Morris, *Class, Sect and Party*; L. Davidoff and C. Hall, *Family Fortunes: Men and Women
   of the English Middle Class, 1780–1850* (London, 1987); T. Koditschek, *Class Formation
   and Urban Society: Bradford, 1750–1850* (Cambridge, 1990); O. Checkland, *Philanthropy
   in Victorian Scotland: Social Welfare and the Voluntary Principle* (Edinburgh, 1980).
[115] R. J. Morris, 'The middle class and British towns in the Industrial Revolution', in
   D. Fraser and A. Sutcliffe (eds.), *The Pursuit of Urban History* (London, 1983), p. 300.
[116] Morgan and Trainor, 'The dominant classes', in Fraser and Morris, *People and Society*,
   p. 126.

virtually every aspect of Victorian society.[117] Indeed, the very structure of the voluntary society has been seen as an expression of the whole host of competing and contradictory ideologies encompassed in the term 'Victorian values' – a vivid image encapsulating the class consciousness of the nineteenth-century bourgeoisie.[118] The scope of the voluntary society ranged from help for the sick, the fallen, the uneducated, and the disadvantaged, to expressions of cultural power and status claims (Chapters 4 and 5). For the newly enfranchised middle class, the voluntary society was the battle ground for its inter- and intra-class conflict.

It is the existence of this network of voluntary societies which explains why localism triumphed over centralism in this mid-century period. Almost any problem posed by the twin strains of rapid urbanisation and industrialisation could be met at the local level by either the local authorities empowered by Parliament or by one or other specialist voluntary societies.

> In the key period of minimalist and regulatory action by the local state in the 1830s and 1840s, these voluntary societies commanded substantial local resources. It was not until the 1860s that it was realised that they could never raise enough money and they would therefore have to work with the state.[119]

The middle decades of the nineteenth century are a distinct period in British history; the voluntary society is the final piece in the jigsaw. If a nation-state means anything, it is the power of governing over a given territory. It is government over a geographically bounded society. The towns and cities of Scotland, like the towns and cities in the rest of Britain, had all the institutions necessary to govern their urban environments. They had a local state empowered by Parliament; they had voluntary societies with a range of functions to administer the fall-out from urbanisation and industrialisation. Importantly, Scotland also had a range of voluntary societies which transcended the local environment – the norm throughout the remainder of Britain – and instead dealt with issues affecting the Scottish nation. The role of such Scottish nation-wide societies, and of those concerned solely with the urban environment, was to structure Edinburgh's civil society in the mid-nineteenth century under the will of the bourgeoisie.

The point with which to end this chapter, however, is that with its municipal direction and its nation-wide voluntary societies, Scotland did indeed have a civil society which was largely self-governed. Politics did

---

117 Checkland, *Philanthropy in Victorian Scotland.*

118 Morris, *Class, Sect and Party*; T. C. Smout (ed.), *Victorian Values: A Joint Symposium of the Royal Society of Edinburgh and the British Academy, December 1990, Proceedings of the British Academy*, lxxviii (Oxford, 1992); Marsden, *Victorian Values.*

119 Morris, 'State, elite and market', p. 20.

not begin at Westminster: for Victorians, local issues and local solutions were cardinal. The Westminster Parliament is not the shorthand state to which the British nation should immediately be connected, when one refers to nationalism in the nineteenth century. The strong, dominant and, importantly, first layer of government existed at the local level. The appropriate measurement of nineteenth-century Scottish nationalism can only be between this peculiar form of municipal self-government – a Scottish 'state' – and Scottish civil society.

The significance of understanding the structure of the decentralised Victorian parliamentary state, and the legal authority and class authority it enshrined for the bourgeoisie, which this chapter has outlined, is that it allows us to re-interpret the most influential theories of Scottish national identity in this period. It begs a more refined focus. Chapter 3 will explain how Scottish civil society has been theorised and, in so doing, will explain exactly how the empirical link can then be made from the state/civil society axis to Scottish national identity.

CHAPTER THREE

Theories and Symbols of Scottish National Identity

Compared to the European yardstick, how well can Scottish nationalism be explained by the leading theorists of the phenomenon? Their answers tend to be neither straightforward nor successful, effectively for a simple reason: the problematic of 'Britishness'. Non-parliamentary political nationalisms are downgraded in nationalist theory, often for quite legitimate and rational reasons. The essence of 'nationalism' has been variously defined as 'sentiment', 'nationalist ideology' or 'nationalist movements'. Its variations are such that there is some doubt as to whether a single manifestation of nationalism could exist (or be defined at all).[1] Still, in one influential view a synthesis of all definitions locates itself around the nationalist movement as the prime analytical tool.[2] This may be so, but for the study of national identity and nationalism in an age before mass citizen politics, and within a remarkably successful shared unitary state, it remains too narrow a definition. In Scotland we know there was a sense of 'Scottishness' in the mid-nineteenth century, but how do we explain it if it were not about self-determination in a classical sense?

Our answer to this question comes back to the fundamental determinant of nationalism in Britain: the gap between nation and state. The ambiguities buried deep within the unitary British 'nation-state' explain the existence of both nationalisms of the 'periphery' (England, Ireland, Wales, Scotland) and a nationalism of the 'centre' (Britain). It is explicit from the discussion in Chapters 1 and 2 that the nineteenth-century state was not a centralised, interventionist and bureaucratic structure so beloved of those who regard the United Kingdom as the earliest example of the European nation-state.[3] It is certainly true that Scotland did not erupt during the 'springtime of nationalism', yet the sheer variety of political mobilisation during that period should be warning enough that Scotland's apparent passivity must not be ignored as irrelevant.[4] To try to explain why Scotland has proved so difficult to

---

[1] P. Alter, *Nationalism* (2nd edn, London, 1994), p. 2.
[2] Hutchinson and Smith, 'Introduction', p. 4.
[3] See, e.g., A. Giddens, *The Nation-State and Violence* (London, 1985), p. 270; the critique of such misconceptions of nationalism of the centre is best explained in McCrone, *Understanding Scotland*, p. 207.
[4] This variety is listed in Pearson, *Longman Companion to European Nationalism*.

fit into the usual models of European nationalism requires a counter-point analysis of mainstream theory.

The work of Ernest Gellner and Benedict Anderson continues to inform our understanding of nationalism. The theoretical underpinning which they provide will allow us to explore and to reconcile some of the most important attempts to address specifically the issue of Scottish nationalism, both politically and sociologically. They will also pave the way for the empirical work of Chapters 4–7, and will help to explain the concept of national identity and the belief in historical 'continuity' and historical 'independence' so vital to it. It will be argued here that the link between the 'pre-modern past' and the construction of nations is an important contrast to strictly political definitions of nationalism. To replace such an approach – an analysis of civil society enshrined from Westminster – will unearth a national identity constructed from contemporary interpretations of the symbols of Scotland's 'past'.

Political theories of nationalism in the nineteenth century

As Chapter 1 made clear, there are problems with Scotland for any analysis of nationalism which requires a civil society to have its own state. This is especially apparent within the 'modernist' school of nationalism, those who regard nation-state formation as occurring only in the period of the late eighteenth and nineteenth centuries. In particular, tension arises when we try and apply to Scotland the theories of Gellner and Anderson, two of the most cited studies in the academic field and cornerstones of the modernist account.[5] In the definition of Gellner, nationalism is 'primarily a political principle which holds that the political and national unit should be congruent':

> Nationalism is a theory of political legitimacy which requires that ethnic boundaries should not cut across political ones, and, in particular, that ethnic boundaries within a given state ... should not separate the power holders from the rest.[6]

Anderson's premise is that nations, or rather nation-states, refer to an 'imagined political community', one that is imagined to be both inherently limited in size and over which sovereignty exists.[7] Both Gellner's 'political unit' and Anderson's 'political community' rest on the correspondence between a national territory and power to govern over it, and, of course, this has classically been the existence of one civil society and its singular state.

---

[5] E. Gellner, *Nations and Nationalism* (London, 1983); B. Anderson, *Imagined Communities: Reflections on the Origin and Spread of Nationalism* (London, 1983).

[6] Gellner, *Nations and Nationalism*, p. 1.

[7] Anderson, *Imagined Communities*, p. 14.

In Gellner's understanding of nationalism as a 'political principle', his argument necessitates the creation of common identities, producing what he calls 'one coherent world, reduced to a unitary idiom'.[8] This move to a common understanding of a wider political identity achieved on the back of modernisation is, therefore, essential for the establishment and survival of the modern nation:

> a society has emerged based on a high-powered technology and the expectancy of sustained growth, which requires both a mobile division of labour and sustained, frequent and precise communication between strangers involving a sharing of explicit meaning, transmitted in a standard idiom and in writing when required.[9]

This process is central to what he terms 'exo-socialisation', the production and reproduction of individuals outside the local intimate unit. This Gellner identifies as being the norm in industrial society. Fundamental to the common idiom is the mobilisation of 'the past' which constitutes the articulation (the publication) of shared identity – the culture of society. It is the need for exo-socialisation which, Gellner suggests, is the clearest clue as to why the nation and its state must be linked.

This argument is similar to that of Anderson, who has examined explicitly the move from local and individualistic identities to wider communal identities. Thus the first stage in the formation of adherence to the bounded nation-state was, he argues, the rise of the vernacular and its displacement of Latin. Anderson suggests that this was important both for breaking down the old religious dynasties and for replacing local by national identities amongst the mass of the population. The ability to imagine the nation-state was given the technical means by the rise of mass publication, of the newspaper and the novel, especially during the eighteenth century. This allowed the movement from the interior world of fiction to the exterior world of reality, giving 'a hypnotic confirmation of the solidity of a single community'.[10] The core of Anderson's thesis is therefore:

> that the convergence of capitalism and print technology on the fatal diversity of human language created the possibility of a new form of community, which in its basic morphology set the stage for the modern nation.[11]

From the work of both authors it can be see that as society modernised, not only did it become possible for individuals to identify themselves with the nation, but it became necessary that the nation be created as a

---

[8] Gellner, *Nations and Nationalism*, p. 21.
[9] Ibid., pp. 33–4.
[10] Anderson, *Imagined Communities*, p. 33.
[11] Ibid., p. 49

bounded political territory. Indeed, Ernest Gellner depicts nationalism as a functional necessity of modernisation, 'a theory of political legitimacy' for nations in this period. The bounded territory is important and, he argues, nationalism is a theory 'which requires that ethnic boundaries should not cut across political ones'.[12] To be of the same nation each individual must be of the same culture and recognise this to be so. Gellner argues that nationalism 'needs' the state, and, interestingly, that nationalism does not arise when there is no state.[13] Similarly, the premise of Benedict Anderson's thesis, that nationalism refers to the ability to imagine a political community which is both inherently limited in area and where sovereignty exists, is one which requires the nation to control its own state. Differently from Gellner, who stresses the falsity and the fabrication of the history which, he suggests, is often used in the (pre-planned) construction of the nation by elites, Anderson's focus is the particular form the imagination takes. Indebted to Deutsch's seminal theory, Anderson stresses the link between nationalism and 'communication'.[14] So, in answer to the question, 'what is a nation-state?', Anderson's definition comes not through an examination of the falsity or the genuineness of a claim, but 'the style in which it is imagined'.[15] For this imagination to be so, the existence of other nations must also be so: 'no nation imagines itself as coterminous with mankind', he points out. And the timing of this imagination in terms of sovereignty is, he argues, the eighteenth century, because it is in the age of Enlightenment and Revolution that the old hierarchical dynastic realms were destroyed.[16]

The theories of Gellner and Anderson have been singled out for attention because of their continuing influence on our understanding of the formation of nations and on the theories of nationalism. In trying to examine Scottish nationalism in the nineteenth century it is important that the theoretical ideal types – of official nationalisms – be understood and made plain.[17] Two essential definitional features are apparent from both Gellner and Anderson. The first is that during the eighteenth and nineteenth centuries it became, technically at least, possible to identify with a wider community termed the nation. The use of history, either 'fabricated' (Gellner) or 'imagined' (Anderson), gave credence to the nation.[18] Secondly, they argue, nationalism as a philosophy became a

---

[12] Gellner, *Nations and Nationalism*, p. 1.
[13] Ibid., p. 5. This is also the argument of Anthony Giddens in Giddens, *Nation-State and Violence*.
[14] K. Deutsch, *Nationalism and Social Communication* (2nd edn, Massachusetts, 1966).
[15] Anderson, *Imagined Communities*, p. 15.
[16] Ibid., p. 16.
[17] The different 'types' of nationalism are explained in J. G. Kellas, *The Politics of Nationalism and Ethnicity* (London, 1991), pp. 34–50.
[18] These subtle but important definition differences can be followed in greater depth in J. A. Hall, 'Nationalisms: classified and explained', *Daedalus*, cxxii (3) (1993), pp. 3–4.

necessary feature of the nation; its purpose was to tie the political and the national together.

This understanding of nation-state formation is an essential counterpoint to any study of Scotland nationalism. It is fairly uncontentious to argue that Scotland became a modern nation from the late eighteenth century onwards, along the lines Gellner and Anderson have outlined, but it failed to imagine political sovereignty over its well-established territorial boundary. The Scottish state was shared and so, in Gellner's language, the political unit and the national unit were *not* congruent. From this definition, therefore, Scotland is, to paraphrase Gellner once more, one of the very large number of potential nations on earth which fail to become nation-states.

How then does this help us to understand Scottish national identity in the nineteenth century? It is clear the Scottish nation did not become, nor did it demand to become, a nation-state (even if that were possible), so, is the only answer to the study of Scottish nationalism in this period a negative one? The following section will examine this question in the context of specific attempts to 'fit' Scotland into theories of nationalism.

Scottish civil society and its British state: the problem of Scotland

The 'problem' of nineteenth-century Scotland for theorists of nationalism is that Scottish parliamentary political nationalism did not become relevant until the 1930s with the formation of the Scottish National Party. Even then, a number of authors have dismissed Scottish nationalism before the 1960s (and the SNP by-election victory in Hamilton) as ephemeral and irrelevant.[19] Two of the more widely read accounts of nationalism, with occasional but important references to Scotland, have been John Breuilly's *Nationalism and the State* and Eric Hobsbawm's *Nations and Nationalism since 1780*.[20] Both authors place their theories of nationalism firmly in the eighteenth and nineteenth centuries and the classical period of state creation. Breuilly defines nationalism as 'modern' in the sense that he equates the *raison d'être* of any national movement with the acquisition of state power. Thus for Breuilly, nationalism is not a search for some sort of identity, instead it is primarily a form of politics, with the objective of gaining and using state power.[21] Breuilly concedes that there is some justification for looking at cultural identity, but insists that it has no political relevance in Scotland until the 1960s.[22] Hobsbawm uses the term nationalism explicitly in the sense defined by Gellner, namely to mean 'primarily a principle which

---

[19] See, e.g., K. Webb, *The Growth of Nationalism in Scotland* (Glasgow, 1977); Brand, *National Movement in Scotland*; and M. Keating, *Labour and Scottish Nationalism* (London, 1979).

[20] Both books have recently gone into second editions, so indicating their influence.

[21] J. Breuilly, *Nationalism and the State* (Manchester, 1982), pp. 1–2.

[22] Breuilly, *Nationalism and the State*, p. 282.

holds that the political and national unit should be congruent'.[23] The implication of this congruence, he argues, is that it distinguishes modern nationalism from other less demanding forms of national or group identification which existed. Thus he employs a strictly parliamentary political definition, locked into modern unitary nation-state formation:

> It [the nation] belongs exclusively to a particular, and historically recent, period. It is a social entity only insofar as it relates to a certain kind of modern territorial state, the nation-state, and it is pointless to discuss nation and nationalism except insofar as both relate to it.[24]

In neither Breuilly nor Hobsbawm's definitions is it possible to place Scotland's national identity as an example of modern nationalism in the classical period of nation-state formation. Each excludes Scotland from their analysis because Scotland remained a part of the British unitary-state, and failed to mount a political challenge for its own state. By implication, both authors accept the British nation-state as a reality, ignoring the inherent contradictions of an absent British civil society. Neither, therefore, provides us with any analytical tools with which it could be possible to measure the strength or weakness of Scottish national identity. Their strict political strait-jacket precludes any nationalism but 'official' nationalism – that of the unitary nation-state. But still, this does not advance our understanding of Scottish nationalism in the nineteenth century; that it was not parliamentary political is understood and accepted, but it is a rather superficial conclusion nevertheless.

A more sophisticated account of the development of Scottish nationalism is the collection of essays by Tom Nairn.[25] Nairn equally places the rise of nationalism in the 'age of nationhood', but he has a much greater understanding of the relationship between Scottish civil society and the unitary British state created after 1707. He follows Gellner's lead, that 'it was industrialisation which did the trick', and that 'nationalism is not a reflection, a mirror of ethnic variety. It is a set of levers (which are sometimes weapons) through which ethnos is driven into a new salience in human affairs.'[26] In particular, Nairn has contrasted the development of Scotland within the British unitary state with the European experience of nation-building during the mid-nineteenth century. Nairn has argued that the norm of European nationalism was of one political state and its society, or one distinguish-able ethnic society and its own state. But this did not happen in Scotland: 'there was a distinct civil society not married to "its" state. It is

[23] Hobsbawm, *Nations and Nationalism*, p. 9.
[24] Ibid., pp. 9–10.
[25] Nairn, *Break-Up of Britain*.
[26] T. Nairn, 'Internationalism and the second coming', *Daedalus*, cxxii (3) (1993), p. 159.

one of heterogeneity, not that relative homogeneity which became the standard of nationalist development. A foreign, much stronger state and political system was imposed on Scotland by the Union.'[27]

The point for Nairn is that this strong external state control allowed Scottish civil society the breathing space to develop free from the normal pressures of uneven capitalist development. Scotland experienced industrialisation quickly and early, in conjunction with the 'first industrial nation'. This was unusual for most small nations and was to Scotland's economic benefit. McCrone and Smout have both argued this point in their respective critiques of Michael Hechter and the underdevelopment school.[28] Clive Lee came to the same conclusion in his macro-economic hypothetical study of a Scottish economy with or without union with England.[29] Scotland was not simply the 'periphery' to England's economic 'core'. Nairn terms Scotland's economic advance and its strong external state a unique historical situation. Equally unique, he argues, was the reaction to London control by the Scottish bourgeoisie. It was because of their favourable socio-economic 'take-off' in the eighteenth century, that the Scottish manufacturing, commercial and professional elites were never forced to challenge the Union. In terms of British society, the Scottish urban middle class sought a degree of political change, but not such as to threaten their economic ascendancy.[30]

It was because Scottish civil society had advanced so far and so quickly, and it was because the new bourgeois social classes inherited a socio-economic position at a unique historical juncture vastly more favourable than that of any backward nationality, that there was no need for parliamentary nationalism. If it were not for this particular set of circumstances, the uneven spread of capitalism, which contributed to political nationalism elsewhere in Europe, would probably have occurred in Scotland. Nairn terms the result 'cultural sub-nationalism' – a sort of deformed nationalism; the result was an inferior culture and identity – a cultural neurosis.

Where Nairn is different from Breuilly and Hobsbawm is that although he sees Scottish nationalism as being weak, as having failed because it did not demand its own state, he argues it took on a cultural

---

27 Nairn, *Break-Up of Britain*, pp. 135–6; this argument is extended throughout the essay 'Old and new Scottish nationalism'.
28 McCrone, *Understanding Scotland*, pp. 61–2; M. Hechter, *Internal Colonialism: The Celtic Fringe in British National Development, 1536–1966* (London, 1975); M. Hechter, 'Internal colonialism revisited', *Cencrastus*, x (1982), pp. 8–11; T. C. Smout, 'Scotland and England: is dependency a symptom or a cause of underdevelopment?', *Review*, iii (4) (1980), pp. 601–30; T. C. Smout, 'Centre and periphery in history', *Journal of Common Market Studies*, xviii (3) (1980), pp. 256–70.
29 C. H. Lee, *Scotland and the United Kingdom: The Economy and the Union in the Twentieth Century* (Manchester, 1995).
30 Nenadic, 'Rise of the urban middle class', p. 124.

form: 'it was cultural because of course it could not be political'.[31] Nairn then launches into a major analysis of Scottish culture in the nineteenth century under the heading of cultural sub-nationalism. It was a 'pathetic nationalism' – parochial and weak because it was not demanding its own state. Tartanry and kailyard came to dominate in the nineteenth century as the symbols of Scotland, indicative, in Nairn's argument, of the failure of the Scottish bourgeoisie to challenge the British state.

Nairn's account clearly judges Scottish nationalism in terms of a nation demanding and requiring its own state. His recent critique of Paterson's 'civic' or 'bureaucratic' nationalism is that its location, civil society, was derived from Westminster, not Edinburgh.[32] As noted already, he sees nationalism in Scotland as not political, because it did not want its own state. Now, because that did not happen – and he shows that there was no material need for it to happen, Scottish nationalism, and therefore Scottish culture in the nineteenth century, is deemed to have failed, and to have been left wallowing in the parochial. But as Chapters 1 and 2 have set out, it is invalid to judge Scotland in terms of a nation-state-to-be, because that was an issue that had little relevance. The nature of the Victorian state was not a centralised one. It was anathema to contemporary thought to campaign for a Westminster-style Scottish state (that is, centralisation). Scottish nationalism, Scottish cultural sub-nationalism and Scottish culture, if they can be separated at all in the nineteenth century, must be understood in terms of a bourgeoisie that had all the power it needed to govern its own society. As has been suggested in Chapter 1, Scottish nationalism and politics could be satisfactorily combined by the Scottish bourgeoisie at the local level.

Where Nairn is most useful, however, is that he provides us with the analytical tools to understand Scottish nationalism: the axis between Scottish civil society and the British state, with the Scottish bourgeoisie as key players. But, whereas Nairn's focus is on Westminster as the means of making the nation and state congruent, the focus here is on civil society. If it can be sustained that the Scottish bourgeoisie did indeed have the power to govern their own civil society, then their material and their national aims can be said to be satisfied. If the Scottish nation can be shown to be 'self-governing', then can the argument be sustained that the resulting Scottish national identity was weak, fragmented and ephemeral, locked into the familiar images of tartanry, kailyard and self-doubt? This question is the crux of this book. The dominant discourse of nineteenth-century Scottish national identity flows from an analysis of central states and parliamentary political nationalist movements; but this story belongs to other nations, it is not the story of Scotland. Capital 'P' political nationalism will yield nothing – there is nothing to find. It is the

---

[31] Nairn, *Break-Up of Britain*, p. 156.
[32] T. Nairn, 'Upper and lower cases', *London Review of Books*, xvii (16) (1995), pp. 14–18; L. Paterson, *The Autonomy of Modern Scotland* (Edinburgh, 1994), pp. 46–72.

actions of the Scottish bourgeoisie within Scottish civil society, and the ways and means by which they governed that society, that dominate the axis of national identity.

Nairn, Anderson and Gellner all define the nation as a modern construct and the philosophy of nationalism as the product of (uneven) capitalist development. This is summed up by Gellner's paradox that 'nations can only be defined in terms of the age of nationalism and not, as you might expect, the other way round'.[33] They acknowledge the importance of the 'past' and cultural differences to the expression of nationalism, yet fundamentally in their theses the creation of the state, the homogenisation of the nation, and the joining of the two under the banner of nationalism, were an inevitable product of modernity.

Scotland, of course, does not fit these accounts. In its political experience, throughout the age of industrialisation and modernisation, a nation-state did not loom out of the primordial Scottish nation. Is the conclusion, therefore, that Scottish nationalism was absent in the nineteenth century? A strict interpretation of these theories makes this the only outcome. The Scottish nation failed to gain sovereignty over its nation; it failed to imagine a political community because it shared its state with the rest of Britain. But the argument here has been that the Scottish nation was largely 'self-governing'. How then are we to understand Scotland's nationalism? Our important route to an answer lies with the work of Anthony Smith and his adaptation of the modernist account of nationalism.

Nations and their pre-modern ethnic

In apparent contrast to the strictly modernist account is the 'ethnic continuity school', as exemplified by Anthony Smith,[34] but also including the work by John Armstrong and John Hutchinson amongst others.[35] Smith shows that any concept of the nation is wholly dependent on how the cultural attributes of that nation are shaped and mobilised. In Scotland, as elsewhere, this occurred during the age of nationalism, but in Scotland it took place within the concept of the Union. Smith tried to explore the concept of the nation as none other than 'an enlarged ethnic community'. To quote Smith:

> there can be no identity without memory (albeit selective), no collective purpose without myth, and identity and purpose are

---

[33] Gellner, *Nations and Nationalism*, p. 55.
[34] A. D. Smith, *The Ethnic Origin of Nations* (Oxford, 1986).
[35] J. A. Armstrong, *Nations before Nationalism* (North Carolina, 1982); J. Hutchinson, *The Dynamics of Cultural Nationalism* (London, 1987); J. Hutchinson, *Modern Nationalism* (London, 1994).

necessary elements of the very concept of a nation. But this is also true of the very concept of an ethnic community.[36]

Whereas the notion of political community, and the importance of a legal framework and the institutions of the state, are central to western theories of nationalism, Smith argues that for East European and Asian nationalism, the centrality of the vernacular language and of (folk) culture should be stressed.[37] The inference is that we should focus on group identities rather than upon institutional structures such as the state.[38] There is, therefore, some doubt about the universal formation of nations as argued by the modernists. Smith's work in contrast lays emphasis upon the use made, and the delimiting influence, of various types of myth in the construction of the nation. In Smith's definition the *ethnie* refers to the ethnic community 'formed through symbolism, depicting ancestry, history, common culture and solidarity, along with a common name'.[39] Heroes, celebrations and common understanding, expressed through symbols and icons, are essential to feelings of national identity. The *ethnie* is not interchangeable between nations, it is fixed to the historical past of a particular nation. But it is malleable, and as such, although the raw materials may be the same, the interpretation of the past changes over time.[40] The *ethnie* becomes the focal point in the analysis of national identity.

A problem with Smith's earlier work was his failure to acknowledge the importance of Gellner's paradox that 'nations can only be defined in terms of the age of nationalism that and not, as you might expect, the other way round'. The logical conclusion of Smith's idea of ethnic community, which played down its political dimension, was the possible theoretical existence of more nation-states than could viably exist[41] (such as that sustained within the principle of 'national self-determination').[42] More recently Smith has accepted that 'nationalism, as a doctrine and ideological movement, did arise in the modern era, in the eighteenth century to be more precise'.[43] He has accepted that nations are modern phenomena in so far as they are: (a) legally unified with the existence of

---

[36] Smith, *Ethnic Origin of Nations*, p. 2.

[37] Ibid., p. 12.

[38] Armstrong, *Nations before Nationalism*, p. 3.

[39] A. D. Smith, 'The myth of the "modern nation" and the myths of nation', *Ethnic and Racial Studies*, xi (1) (1988), p. 9.

[40] The same point is applicable equally to the anthropological literature on 'ethnicity'. See, e.g., T. H. Erikson, *Ethnicity and Nationalism: Anthropological Perspectives* (London, 1993), p. 13.

[41] Indeed, Zubiada has questioned Smith's insistence that the formation of nations is *determined* by pre-modern history: S. Zubiada, 'Nations: old and new: comments on Anthony D. Smith's "The myth of the 'Modern Nation' and the myths of nations"', *Ethnic and Racial Studies*, xii (3) (1989).

[42] C. Tilly, 'National self-determination as a problem for all of us', *Daedalus*, cxxii (3) (1993), p. 30.

[43] Smith, 'Myth of the "modern nation"', p. 5.

citizenship rights; (b) based on a single economy; (c) have a compact territory which is easily defensible; and (d) require a single 'political culture' to socialise 'citizens' of the future.[44] He has accepted that 'nations may not be immemorial, nor is nationalism primordial'. But still he maintains that 'at the same time, the long tradition of ethnic identification suggests the rootedness and functionality of ethnic and national ties in so many periods'.[45] His central argument therefore remains intact:

> Ethnic distinctiveness remains a *sine qua non* of the nation, and that means shared ancestry myths, common historical memories, unique cultural markers, and a sense of difference, if not election – all the elements that marked off ethnic communities in pre-modern eras. In the modern nation they must be preserved, indeed cultivated, if the nation is not to become invisible.[46]

No matter how modern the formation of nations and nation-states, their very form is dependent on their own pre-modern *ethnie*. Armstrong, for example, stresses the long tradition of the control of power being not just a feature of the state (the pivotal argument of modernists such as Giddens), over time and comparatively.[47] Within this ethnic continuity approach, it is the way in which the 'social construction of specific peoples and places plays a critical role in generating, refining and maintaining the social construction of the general category of the nation'.[48] This is true as much for Scotland as for all other nations, but it is our pathway to understanding the expression 'national identity'. To what extent did the Scottish *ethnie* contribute to the creation of the Scottish nation, and to what extent did the Scottish nation imagine, if not sovereignty, then 'self-governing' over its territory? How much can we read into the symbols of Scottish national identity?

The importance of these ideas is to show that although the nation-state may essentially be modern, it is not wholly a creation of the 'Age of Enlightenment' because it requires pre-modern constructs, its *ethnie*, and it is increasingly formed in the image of older ethnic symbols.[49] This is an objective which Hobsbawm, elsewhere, has termed 'invariance with the past', achieved through the '"invention of tradition": a set of practices, normally governed by overtly or tacitly accepted rules of ritual or symbolic nature, which seek to inculcate certain values and norms of

---

44 A. D. Smith, *National Identity* (London, 1991), p. 69.
45 A. D. Smith, 'The problem of national identity: ancient, medieval and modern?', *Ethnic and Racial Studies*, xvii (3) (1994), p. 394.
46 Smith, *National Identity*, p. 70.
47 Armstrong, *Nations before Nationalism*, pp. 283–99.
48 J. Penrose, 'Reification in the name of change: the impact of nationalism on social constructions of nation, people and place in Scotland and the United Kingdom', in P. Jackson and J. Penrose (eds.), *Constructions of Race, Place and Nation* (London, 1993), pp. 28–9.
49 Smith, 'Myth of the "modern nation"', p. 10.

behaviour by repetition, which automatically implies continuity with the past'.[50] Or, as Smith defines the use made of apparent continuity with the past: 'The modern nation, to become truly a "nation", requires the unifying myths, symbols and memories of the pre-modern *ethnie*',[51] the 'identity and moral regeneration of the national community'.[52] It is the lucky-dip of the historical past of a community's nationalism which determines the form that the claim to nationalism will take. Where Anthony Smith is more convincing than the strictly modernist accounts is in his treatment of the mobilisation of the symbols of the past by social groups. Rather than regarding this 'past' as being infinitely malleable, Smith stresses its limitations. The point is that there are certain symbols attached to a historical past which are used by nationalist groups in their attempts to support or create a nation-state, but that these are limited by what exists in the community or what can reasonably be 'invented'. We need to be told who we are, and that role generally falls to nationalist leaders, those 'creoles' or 'historicist intellectuals', who actively create national identity out of socio-cultural myths.[53] In so doing, they act as 'social and political archaeologists' rather than as 'social engineers'.[54] But the creation of the nation out of ethnic symbols is not a permanent construction; it is a recurrent activity which has to be reviewed periodically. This is done, Smith concludes, through the 'product of dialogues between the major social groups and institutions within the boundaries of the "nation", and it answers to their perceived ideals and interests'.[55] The question is, of course, 'who has the loudest voice of the major social groups?'.

The point to be taken from this section is that if we accept that the nation-state is a modern construct, we must also realise that its very form is limited by the materials making up its *ethnie*. To understand Scottish nationalism we must examine the ethnic materials which define 'Scotland' the concept. They are limited, but a set of symbols which can be identified as being explicitly Scottish does exist. Importantly, an examination of how the nineteenth-century bourgeoisie interpreted the symbols of Scotland's 'past' will determine the extent (if at all) to which any conception of self-government was imagined. It is this which takes us to a study of Scottish civil society, for it is there that we find the axis of state and nation and the interpretation of the symbols of Scottish nationalism.

[50] E. Hobsbawm and T. Ranger (eds.), *The Invention of Tradition* (Cambridge, 1983), pp. 1–2.

[51] Smith, 'Myth of the "modern nation"', p. 11.

[52] J. Hutchinson, 'Back from the dead? The rediscovery of cultural nationalism', *The Association for the Study of Ethnicity Bulletin*, viii (1994–5), p. 4.

[53] J. M. Lyon, 'The Herder syndrome: a comparative study of cultural nationalism', in *Ethnic and Racial Studies*, xvii (2) (1994), p. 225.

[54] A. D. Smith, 'Gastronomy or geology? The role of nationalism in the reconstruction of nations, *Nations and Nationalism*, i (1) (1995), p. 3.

[55] Smith, *Ethnic Origin of Nations*, p.206.

Civil society as container of nationalism?

'Nationality is a necessary ingredient, perhaps even pre-condition for civil society.'[56] Shils, in this statement, attempts to explain the interplay between nation, nationality, nationalism and civil society. Fundamentally, he is trying to explain how civil society is maintained as a distinct and separate entity from that of the state. His argument focuses on the production of 'spontaneous conformity' and the 'ethics of responsibility' which maintain the legitimacy of civil society. The self-consciousness he identifies is that of 'nationality'. In the argument so far presented here, much emphasis has been laid on the enshrinement of civil society by the central state through the empowerment of the urban bourgeoisie. This is a technical-legal argument as it relates to social structure. The argument of Shils is social-psychological, as it too relates to the same social structure. Both present the maintenance of civil society as being in the hands of the central state, yet we must disagree on the balance of this relationship.

In many respects Shils's argument mirrors recent thinking on the 'independence' of civil society, especially as it is manifest in the late twentieth century (taking the opportunity in some quarters for liberalism to defeat all perceived threats to 'democracy and peace' in Eastern Europe).[57] This is the clearest use of civil society as a counterbalance to a despotic state (its most common sociological definition).[58] This approach, such as the associational path trod by Gellner's 'modular man', is where civil society is conceptualised as a structure which can prevent the state from dominating and atomising the rest of society.[59] The model perceives of the state as the enemy, as an opposition from whom concessions are bargained.

Yet this is a rather idealistic view of civil society and an unhelpful characterisation of modern bureaucratic systems of power and administration. Alternatively, Hall points out, we must recognise that the state is *needed* by civil society for its protection (to 'enshrine' it is the term we have used here), and so the notion of rivalled opposition is untrue. Alternatively, it is valid to perceive of civil society being engaged in an agreed 'politics of reciprocal consent' with the state.[60] This idea gives to civil society something more than can be encompassed in notions of liberalism, democracy and citizenship, because it is itself a self-sustaining

---

[56] E. Shils, 'Nation, nationality, nationalism and civil society', *Nations and Nationalism*, i (1) (1995), p. 116.

[57] See, e.g., *The Foundation for a Civil Society* (1993–1994 Report), which, instructively, has offices in New York, the Czech Republic and Slovakia.

[58] The danger of such straightforward assumptions about the causes of the 1989 revolutions in Eastern Europe is contained in a critique of social movement modelling in J. Braithwaite, 'A sociology of modelling and the politics of empowerment', *British Journal of Sociology*, xlv (3) (1994), pp. 445–6.

[59] Gellner, 'Importance of being modular', p. 32.

[60] J. A. Hall, 'In search of civil society', in Hall, *Civil Society*, p. 16.

entity.[61] It gives a self-consciousness which allows nationalism to be located there and to legitimise it. Perhaps, as Hall speculates, civil society can even 'handle and direct nationalism' itself, rather than leave it to be a product of the state.[62] The potential of this idea to untangle Scottishness from Britishness is clear.

Shils would not go so far, arguing that in multinational examples, the core nation wins out: 'civil society exists because it is integral to the dominant nation'.[63] This is an argument in favour of unitary nation-states, where peripheral nationalism would rock the boat: 'a society in which nationality is driven into the extreme form of nationalism will set many obstacles on the path of being or remaining a civil society'.[64] Yet the notion of reciprocity between the state and civil society is important to the understanding of Scottishness in a united kingdom, because it stresses that civil society is not only enshrined by the state, but that it in turn legitimises it.[65] This, I would argue, is effective whether that civil society is of the dominant nation or of the peripheral nation or nations. The British unitary state has legitimised itself for so long because it has legitimised four civil societies, albeit by very different means. That civil society has the potential to produce and sustain its own ideology, its own nationalism, undermines our confidence in the classical test of nationalism. The encouragement is not only to look at the associations and institutions of civil society, but to warn us against regarding the modern period as some sort of Whiggish rise in a central state (and its nationalism being the only 'real' nationalism). Nationalism of the periphery in Britain is located and derived from its civil society; it is there that its *ethnie* is summoned, repackaged and contemporised.

The state/civil society axis as a research paradigm

At this juncture it is appropriate to leave the theorists and to enter the archive. We are now in a position empirically to test the nature of the state/civil society axis in nineteenth-century Scotland and then to understand the expression of Scottish national identity. Chapter 4 will explain the methodology employed in this empirical examination. It will explain the centrality of voluntaryism to intra- and inter-class relations

---

61 This is the argument of Kumar in his instructive debate with Bryant: K. Kumar, 'Civil society: an enquiry into the usefulness of an historical term', *British Journal of Sociology*, xliv (3) (1993), p. 391; Bryant, 'Social self-organisation, civility and sociology'; C. G. A. Bryant, 'A further comment on Kumar's "Civil society"', *British Journal of Sociology*, xlv (3) (1994).

62 Hall, 'In search of civil society', p. 13.

63 Shils, 'Nation, nationality, nationalism and civil society', p. 111.

64 Ibid., p. 118.

65 For two very instructive examinations of the development of the concept of civil society in the writings of Hegel and Marx, see N. Bobbio, 'Gramsci and the concept of civil society', in J. Keane (ed.), *Civil Society and the State: New European Perspectives* (London, 1988), pp. 77–82; and J. L. Cohen, *Class and Civil Society* (Oxford, 1982).

and ultimately to middle-class formation. In that chapter and Chapter 5 a detailed examination is carried out of the ways and means that the Edinburgh bourgeoisie 'governed' civil society in urban Scotland. By redefining the nation/state relationship in this way, it will firm the foundations for Chapters 6 and 7 which analyse contemporary interpretations of the symbols of Scottish national identity, free from the political strait-jacket of one-nation-one-state orthodoxy. These latter two chapters will build on the argument presented here, that a nation is made up from the particular (and changing) interpretation of its ethnic past. This mid-nineteenth-century Scottish *ethnie* was directly linked to a civil society 'governed' by its bourgeoisie.

CHAPTER FOUR

Governing Civil Society: The Public Life of the Edinburgh Bourgeoisie

The sheer strength of Scottish civil society was much more than any perceived 'difference' of church, law and education. Mid-Victorian civil society was called by contemporaries their 'public-life', and it existed in an acknowledged framework outwith the formal structures of the state. Using Bryant's definition presented earlier, civil society can be thought of as the 'space or arena between household and the state, other than the market, which affords possibilities of concerted action and social self-organisation'.[1] Its clearest manifestation was in the towns and the cities. It was the propensity of the urban middle class in nineteenth-century Britain to organise clubs, societies and associations in the 'spaces' in civil society left untouched by the central and local state which was the essential mediating structure between the two formal levels of government. It was sustained through the exercise of 'infrastructural power': the means by which the modern state maintains its legitimacy to govern by setting the limits of social order in civil society.[2] The act of subscription was pervasive and important, creating a complex web of intervention in urban society. The voluntary society's internal order and structure maintained the fine status gradation so essential to middle-class formation. By linking together the subscriber lists of many voluntary organisations, each indicative of middle-class urban action, it is proposed that civil society be mapped, its social structures delineated, and its links to 'governing' established.

Indeed, the role of voluntary activity as a vehicle for expressing economic and political power, and as points of status conflict, is central to the process of class formation.[3] The voluntary organisation was the practical means by which the middle class could engage their hegemonic grip. As Koditschek has argued, 'through the culture of voluntaryism, the bourgeoisie would finally attempt to achieve that social consensus around its values and authority that neither the work of production nor the free flows of the market had, in themselves, been able to create'.[4]

---

[1] Bryant, 'Social self-organisation, civility and sociology', p. 399.
[2] Mann, 'Autonomous power of the state', p. 189.
[3] R. J. Morris, 'Clubs, societies and associations', in F. M. L. Thompson (ed.), *The Cambridge Social History of Britain, 1750–1950*, vol. III (Cambridge 1990), pp. 410–12.
[4] Koditschek, *Class Formation in Urban Industrial Society*, p. 251.

Voluntary societies are therefore part of the process of inter-class bargaining, but, equally importantly, their internal constitutional structures were an organising principle around which the middle class's conception of itself as a coherent class was formed. It is through its construction as a social class that we are able to examine just how the Edinburgh bourgeoisie 'governed' their civil society within the framework established by the central state.

Towards an empirical framework of Edinburgh's civil society

Our question once again is: how was Scotland 'governed' in an age when Westminster was a shared state in flux over the rise of what contemporaries termed 'centralisation'? It has been argued in earlier chapters that when examined in nineteenth-century terms, the local state possessed such a degree of autonomy, and was such a loose confederation, that it forced a conceptualisation of civil society as a strong, self-sustaining entity which embodied formal and informal institutions of self-administration. The problem this then poses for analysing the state/civil society relationship, at the heart of governing one's own society, is of how to operationalise empirically such a definition.

The solution lies within the pages of two major published sources, often under-used by historians, which existed in many cities and large towns in this period: Almanacs and the Post Office Directories. Together these sources claimed to cover 'the majority of all day-to-day facts and knowledge'. Such almanacs originally included mainly religious and astronomical data but were subsequently extended to include statistics and information on topics such as the weather, political events, sporting and social events, carriage and postage rates, and anniversaries of the coming year.[5] Each almanac was an attempt at a reference to everything happening which was deemed to be important and/or relevant in a locality in one year. If we examine the structure of Oliver and Boyd's *New Edinburgh Almanac*, we are presented with what amounts to contemporaries' interpretation of British, Scottish and Edinburgh's civil society – all in just over 1,000 pages.

The *Edinburgh Almanac* functions as the most systematic and detailed guide to the institutions, organisations and associations which existed in Scotland's capital in our period: it includes such information as the office bearers and addresses of what we can assume is virtually the complete institutional structure of Edinburgh (although some exceptions are noted below). The *Almanac* was divided up into five parts: the first contains 'The Kalander, and information contained therewith'; the second presents 'Information in Commerce, Agriculture, Law, Chronology, and Statistics'; the third is entitled 'The British Empire'; the fourth 'Scotland';

[5] J. Scott, *A Matter of Record: Documentary Sources in Social Research* (Cambridge, 1990), p.156.

and the fifth 'City and County of Edinburghshire'.[6] It is especially valuable for our purposes to examine how the compilers of the *Almanac* chose to divide up and present information on Edinburgh's civil society. They delineated seven sections for data on the City of Edinburgh:

(1) 'Municipal Establishments'
(2) 'Religious Institutions'
(3) 'Educational Establishments'
(4) 'Scientific and Literary Institutions'
(5) 'Benevolent and Charitable Institutions'
(6) 'Commercial Establishments'
(7) 'Miscellaneous Lists'

The *Edinburgh and Leith Post Office Directory* (1854–5) is a guide to the (especially middle-class) residents of Edinburgh: it recorded where they lived and what they did. There were the following nine main subsections:

(1) Bank Directory
(2) Church Directory
(3) Conveyance Directory
(4) County Directory
(5) Insurance Directory
(6) Law Directory
(7) Parliamentary Directory
(8) Professions and Trade Directory
(9) Street Directory

In addition there were various lists detailing the holders of public positions such as the Parochial Board or the Magistrates and Council, and certain occupations such as accountants, writers, and Writers to the Signet, as well as information on the military, taxes, rates, steamers, stage coaches, newspapers, the postage intricacies of the time, and so on. By comparing and contrasting the *Almanac* with the *Post Office Directory* we effectively cover the range of the formal and informal institutional structures of Edinburgh's civil society. These two sources act as the reference point from which the choice of which organisations and associations are to be examined is made.

Completing our picture of Edinburgh's civil society is information gathered on the various annual and *ad hoc* subscription lists raised mid-century, but which are not included in the *Almanac* because they are not 'permanent' events (or were just missed out). For instance, the prestigious annual subscription list for contributions to the Edinburgh Royal Infirmary or the on/off subscriptions raised for the completion of the Scott Monument, fail to be picked up in either the *Almanac* or the *Directory*. Such particulars, and the range of subscriptions raised, are

---

[6] The chosen year for this example is 1856.

mined from a mixture of *The Scotsman*, the guides/histories of Edinburgh, and the biographies of prominent Edinburgh citizens.[7]

Figure 4.1: *Delivery of 1854 London Post Office Directory: its weight reflects the growing size and complexity of nearly all urban centres during this period.*[8]

Dissecting Edinburgh's civil society

With the framework of the analysis made plain, we are in a position to unearth what a governed civil society meant in reality to contemporaries. The courts and council acted as the first layer of social structure in Edinburgh's civil society – the legally required municipal institutions necessary for Edinburgh to function as a city – and they comprised the first subsection of the *Almanac* (and have been discussed in Chapter 2). To extend the concept of 'governing' the nation so far defined, our attention is concentrated on the layer of activity not legally required, but set up in all towns and cities in this period, primarily as a response to rapid urbanisation and population growth: that is, the layer of

---

[7] Problems over the representativeness of sources 'best suited' to record linkage are examined in G. Morton, 'Unionist-Nationalism: The Historical Construction of Scottish National Identity. Edinburgh, 1830–1860' (Edinburgh University Ph.D. thesis, 1993), chap. 4; problems concerning the relationship between an individual and a nominal entry are examined in G. Morton, 'Presenting the Self: record linkage and referring to ordinary historical persons', *History and Computing*, vi (1) (1994), pp. 12–20.

[8] *Punch*, xxv (1853), p. 213.

voluntaryism. This chapter will present the remaining six sections of the *Almanac* and highlight the range of activities which made up the Edinburgh bourgeoisie's 'public life'. It will explain the inter-denominational rivalry (and co-operation) between voluntary societies; it will analyse their internal structure, the tactics and the resources they mobilised to gain support, achieve their aims, and to influence class relationships; and it will examine the role of the myriad of cultural societies in the maintenance of elite exclusivity.

To this end, the analysis of the *Almanac* will be in two parts. The first will describe the structure and objectives of voluntary societies which were essentially philanthropic in nature. This will encompass 'Religious Institutions', and 'Benevolent and Charitable Institutions'. The second part will describe societies which were concerned more with 'self-help' than the help of others: societies which were part and parcel of expressions of elite status and cultural power. These latter societies come under the headings of 'Educational Establishments', 'Scientific and Literary Institutions' and 'Commercial Institutions'.[9] Together they explain the link between middle-class formation, elite intervention in urban society and self-'governing'.

I: PHILANTHROPIC VOLUNTARY ORGANISATIONS

Religious institutions

The range of voluntary activity in Scottish civil society was immense. Perhaps the greatest degree of activity by the Edinburgh bourgeoisie at this time was under the auspices of societies and organisations directly run by or, at the very least, under the behest of the religious denomin-ations. It is impossible to explain the pervasiveness and influence of voluntary action in Edinburgh's civil society without establishing the religious underpinnings of so much of the activity. In the 1830s both Edinburgh and Glasgow contained Presbyterian dissenters equal in numbers to those who attended the state church. As a result of the Disruption of the Established Church in 1843, the Church of Scotland now faced a hardening of Presbyterian dissent with the Free Church of Scotland and the United Presbyterian Church (1847). By the religious census of 1851 Edinburgh recorded only 16% of its churchgoers attending the Established Church, with 27% attending the United Presbyterian and 33% attending the Free Church. It is well known that these figures are far from rigorous and, as Brown reminds us, the Established Church was at a low point, hit by apathy, and non-returns on the Census night.[10] The Church of Scotland would gain its adherents

---

[9] A list of all the societies listed in the *Almanac* and to which analysis was attempted appears in Appendix 2.

[10] C. G. Brown, *Religion and Society in Scotland since 1707* (Edinburgh, 1997), p. 45.

again, but in our period this dramatic refocusing on theological issues as well as on issues of church governance saw all the Protestant churches, and to a lesser extent in Edinburgh the Catholic church too, use voluntary activity as a means of direct proselytising and as a means of more general, often ecumenical, evangelising.

The impetus of the Disruption upon a level of Presbyterian dissent encouraged competition amongst voluntaryists with the inevitable result being the duplication of services. To take some common examples, there was denominational competition in support for missions for the destitute and the homeless between all the major faiths in Edinburgh. The Friendly Society of Ministers in connection with the United Presbyterian Church and The Baptist Home Mission co-existed with the Edinburgh Church of England Missionary Society, while both operated alongside the Edinburgh Mission in aid of the Moravian Mission, the Edinburgh Auxiliaries to the Irish Evangelical Society, and the London Missionary Society. Similarly, both the Established Church and the Free Church had ladies' associations with the aim of advancing female education in India. Inter-denominational recruitment battles raged between the rival Sabbath School Teachers' Unions as they expanded in an effort to cope with the enormous numbers of children being enrolled into Sunday Schools in the 1850s. In Edinburgh there were the *Edinburgh Sabbath School Teachers' Union* (Free Church) and the *Edinburgh Sabbath School Teachers' Association* (Established Church), while in Glasgow all the Protestant denominations in the city were involved: Church of Scotland, Free Church, United Presbyterian, Reformed Presbyterian, United Original Seceders, the Congregational Church, the Baptists, the Wesleyan Methodists, the Primitive Methodist Church and the Episcopalian Church.[11] Duplication of service may have been the inevitable result of what today we would call 'privatised' provision, but it does indicate the degree of coverage of urban society by such 'recruitment-ready' evangelical spirit.

The structure of the voluntary society

To be successful both in their stated aims and in their ability to attract financial support and prestige, each society had to juggle the many denominational, political and status divisions which, on other occasions, established clear fissures within the middle class of this time. To impose or influence bourgeois values and teachings on the working class, without recourse to formal legislation, required much skill and negotiation. Charitable and missionary success in the voluntary sphere was no certainty, and the voluntary society had to be a resilient and flexible beast to quell the potential ruptures. An understanding of the structure

---

11 For Glasgow, see Checkland, *Philanthropy in Victorian Scotland*, p. 46.

of such societies is therefore essential in explaining their role in middle-class formation and in structuring Edinburgh's civil society.[12]

A fairly typical organisational structure to a voluntary society is that of the Edinburgh Total Abstinence Society for 1853 (Figure 4.2, below). A clear hierarchy existed: the honorary directors, president, vice-president and then treasurer and secretary – a descending hierarchy of status positions. Each position was inversely related to the incumbent's level of day-to-day activity in the society. Morris has described such a structure as a 'subscriber democracy', where the range of power positions allowed for a finely graded series of status hierarchies to be played out. One paid one's subscription and thereby agreed to abide by the aims of that society, to follow its rules, and to fit into one's place in its hierarchical constitution.[13]

The committee of management was the real centre of all organisation and decision-making. These people were the 'doers', the most active of the 'active middle class'. Not of the highest rank of the Edinburgh bourgeoisie, the management committee was often made up of the younger, aspiring parvenus. Typical also was the presence of a patron, or, as in this example a president (who was usually honorary). Davidoff and Hall note for Birmingham the symbolic importance of Lord Calthorpe, the local evangelical peer, as patron to many middle-class societies.[14] In his study of Leeds, Morris found that even a society which had little practical need of patronage (such as the Leeds Permanent Building Society), still sought for itself the public approval of the elite.[15] In Edinburgh the pinnacle of respectability was to have the Queen as patron. Frequently, however, that position or that of president was filled by either the Lord Provost or the duke of Buccleuch and Queensberry. From my survey of the *Almanac*, and of other sources, the Lord Provost was found to be an office bearer of thirty-four societies and Buccleuch of twenty-four – and these are certainly underestimates.

Notice also the 'Ladies' Visiting Committee'. It was very common that such a committee would be attached to a male-dominated organisation. Notice also that the joint secretary was a man, William Birrell. The presence of a man in the structure of a ladies' committee was also very much the norm, although, unlike this example, the position taken was usually that of treasurer, for the reason that money was involved. Men tended to address such ladies' committees – women were rarely accorded the privilege of publicly speaking to their own sex, let alone the society proper. Davidoff and Hall make the point for the Birmingham Infant School:

---

12 For an outline of the structure of welfarist voluntary societies, see P. H. J. H. Gosden, *Self-Help: Voluntary Associations in Nineteenth-Century Britain* (London, 1973), pp. 14–27.

13 R. J. Morris, 'Voluntary societies and British urban elites, 1780–1850: an analysis', *Historical Journal*, xxvi (1983), p. 101.

14 Davidoff and Hall, *Family Fortunes*, p. 422.

15 Morris, *Class, Sect and Party*, p. 293.

Women had no professional skills to offer, they were not bankers or lawyers, nor were they appealed to publicly. Rather, the committee privately solicited their wives, daughters, relatives and friends to form a ladies' committee to take on the work of visiting. Subsequently, as was usually the case with such arrangements, the men's committee had all the formal power but the ladies' committee dealt with many practical arrangements concerning the girls. Clearly much of the negotiation in such cases was done informally. A wife on the ladies' committee would mention to her husband on the gentleman's committee some matter arising, and he would attend to it.[16]

Figure 4.2: *The Edinburgh Total Abstinence Society, Office Bearers 1852–3*

Honorary Directors:
Sir Walter C. Trevalyan, Bart.
John Brown, Esq., M.D.
Thomas Knox, Esq.
William Menzies, Esq., M.D.
Rev. J. L. Aikman

Rev. Joseph Brown, D.D.
Rev. R. D. Duncan
Rev. William Reid
Rev. James Robertson
Rev. Alexander Wallace

President
John S. Marr, Bank of Scotland

Vice-Presidents:
W. F. Cuthbertson, 36 Howe Street
James Gilbert, 6 Canongate
J. Robertson, 40 N. Richmond Street
John Vallance, 22 Society

Treasurer: John Hill, 13 Blair Street
Corresponding Secretary: Roger Lawson, Pilrig Model Buildings
Secretary and Collector: W. K. Rose, 2 North Bridge
Missionary: Alexander McDonald
Committee of Management:
John Adair
Robert W. Armour
George Beddie
Dr Brodie
James Buchanan
Thomas Campbell
James Drummond
William Friend

David Little
Lauchlan Mackenzie
Ebenezer Murray
Alexander Paterson
Selby Robson
Robert Shiels
James Watson
John Wharton

Ladies' Visiting Committee:
President: Mrs Johnson
Vice-President: Mrs Homson
Treasurer: Mrs McLean
Secretaries: Mrs Armour & William Birrell
Mrs Renton
Mrs Birrell
Mrs Muir
Mrs Gordon

Mrs Irvine
Mrs Mushet
Mrs Brown
Mrs Bell

Mrs Wells
Miss Brown
Miss Dobson
Miss Mossman

Source: *The Seventeenth Annual Report of the Edinburgh Total Abstinence Society* (Edinburgh, 1853).

[16] Davidoff and Hall, *Family Fortunes*, p. 422.

The public life of women was certainly heavily curtailed in favour of men. But, as Davidoff and Hall indicate, women did find for themselves a role in carrying out the 'visit' and other practical activities around which they structured their day. A 'visiting committee' was one of the most common tactics of a 'missionary' type society such as this. It allowed for members to carry their message forth to a working-class home, or the home of the poor. This enabled the society to focus its agenda on those whom it believed needed to hear it most; it gave society members a 'hands-on' task to absolve their Christian conscience and so feel they were intervening in a problem; it also allowed the collection of case study material which could then be presented in an annual report to illustrate the society's work and to solicit subscriptions or donations. The 'visit' was thus an important resource in the armoury of such societies.

Thus not only was the structure of the voluntary organisation important to middle-class identity, but so too were the range and types of action which it undertook to fulfil its agenda. The ability of urban elites to intervene in their own society and to do so effectively is essential to an understanding of the absence of the Westminster state in the day-to-day life of Scotland's civil society. To explain this in more detail, and to begin to build up a more complete picture of the types of resources mobilised by this and similar campaigning societies, it is of value to turn our attention to the specific example of the aims and purposes of the Total Abstinence Society and the temperance movement in general.

Resources and tactics: the temperance movement

Many of the features of campaigning societies within civil society, those of a small 'p' political hue, were predominant within the temperance movement at this time. These societies are important for the argument here because they walked a tightrope between local and central government: feeding off each, resisting each, but ultimately setting their own agenda and enacting their own solutions.

The beer trade had been freed in 1830, and the wine trade in 1860. Both Acts followed a campaign to make milder and purer drinks available and thus, it was hoped, to remedy some of the dangers of alcohol abuse.[17] The opposition to these policies – before and after their enactment – came from the temperance movement. Its first society was set up in 1828, and various teetotal and abstinence societies grew up in the 1830s. This movement, although allied with the Liberal Party in the last two decades of the nineteenth century, existed outside the structure of the local government or the state. The movement tried for moderation in the consumption of drink; it tried for total abstinence – a

---

[17] D. W. Paton, 'Drink and the Temperance Movement in Nineteenth-Century Scotland' (Edinburgh University Ph.D. thesis, 1977).

'long' pledge, or even a 'short' pledge. Some supporters tried for 'education', some for 'prohibition' – a division in the movement forged in 1853 in England when the UK Alliance was formed 'to outlaw *all* trading in intoxicating liquor'.[18] In its various guises, the movement set up multifarious societies, cricket and football clubs, held lectures and organised outings and soirées. There was a conscious attempt to provide an escape route for those who wished to free themselves from a Victorian lifestyle which revolved around the consumption of alcohol. It aimed to create a counter-culture where drink was absent, unmissed. The major success of the temperance movement was the Public House (Forbes Mackenzie) Act of 1853 which developed from the controls imposed by Lord Provost Duncan McLaren in Edinburgh.[19] Apart from that parliamentary victory, however, the temperance movement at this time circumvented state legislation and tried to solve a perceived social problem by direct intervention in the public life of Victorian Britain. It was essentially a movement of evangelical dissenters, and thus the early link between religion and temperance was through the Free Church.[20]

Two of the main, or perhaps predominant, campaigning weapons of the Total Abstinence Society were the published tract and the public meeting. The tracts were often distributed during visits by society members to the homes of potential 'pledgers'. For the year 1852–3 the society claims to have distributed 117,000 tracts, the breakdown of which is shown below:

Table 4.1: *Total Abstinence Society: Distributed tracts in Edinburgh, 1852–3*

Title of tract	No. distributed
Rev. W. Reid's Tract on Sabbath Statistics	50,000
Edward Baines' Testimony and Appeal	5,000
Scottish Temperance League's Narrative Series	20,000
Miscellaneous kinds	42,000
Total	117,000

Source: *The Seventeenth Annual Report of the Edinburgh Total Abstinence Society* (Edinburgh, 1853).

Despite what seems an enormous amount of distributed literature, the 1854 report called for 'a more complete series of tracts' to maintain the momentum of the campaign. The result of this plea was the publication of what was entitled the *Edinburgh Series of Temperance Tracts*. The twelve tracts are listed below; their titles provide a clear enough idea of their content.

[18] B. Harrison, *Drink and the Victorians: The Temperance Question in England, 1815–1872* (London, 1970), p. 19.
[19] O. and S. Checkland, *Industry and Ethos: Scotland, 1832–1914* (2nd edn, Edinburgh, 1989).
[20] See Checkland, *Philanthropy in Victorian Scotland*, pp. 90–101.

Figure 4.3: Edinburgh Series of Temperance Tracts

1. *Christian Witness – Bearing against the Sin of Intemperance.*
   Rev. H. Bonar, D. D., Kelso.
2. *Look before you Leap – An Appeal to Young Men.*
   John Stewart, Esq., ed. of *Edinburgh News.*
3. *Better Dwellings for the Working Classes, and how to get them.*
   A. Prentice, Esq., Manchester.
4. *A Word by the Way to the Wives of Working Men.*
   Rev. D. Ogilvie, A. M., Broughty Ferry.
5. *The Workshop and the Dramshop; or, a Bag with Holes.*
   Rev. Alexander Wallace, Edinburgh.
6. *The Working Man's Home.*
   J. H. Dawson, Esq., ed. of Kelso Chronicle.
7. *Christ or Bacchus: which ought the Church to Help?*
   Rev. William Reid, Edinburgh.
8. *Health, the Abstainer's Hope: Disease, the Spirit Drinker's Doom.*
   D. Brodie, Esq., M. D., Edinburgh.
9. *The Followers of the Young Mr Timothy.*
   Rev. James Morrison, Glasgow.
10. *The Household Blessing.*
    Miss Carla Lucas Balfour.
11. *Temperance as affecting the Interests of Employers and the Employed.*
    A. Prentice, Esq., Manchester.
12. *Juvenile Delinquency: the Fruit of Parental Intemperance.*
    Mary Carpenter, author of *Reforming Schools* and *Juvenile Delinquents,*
    their Condition and Treatment.

Source: *Edinburgh Series of Temperance Tracts.* Issued by the Edinburgh Total Abstinence Society (Edinburgh, 1859).

The published tract was certainly a heavily used tactic by a society such as the Total Abstinence Society, but so too was the public meeting. The eighteenth annual report of the society, for 1854, recorded over 100 meetings held in that year – including a series of meetings held weekly in the Free Canongate Church during the winter months.[21] The success of a series of lectures by John B. Gough on behalf of the society in January 1854 was such that 1,252 members joined, compared with only 384 for the corresponding month the previous year.

The use of the meeting and, also, the school, rather than the tract, was the campaigning tactic of another temperance society: the British League of Juvenile Abstainers. The great object of the British League was to:

save the young from the many evils by which they are surrounded, especially the evils connected with the use of alcohol, tobacco, snuff, and opium, by educating the mind in reference to the nature of these stimulants, and thus prevent them from forming those habits which many of riper years have felt to their cost.[22]

---

[21] *The Eighteenth Annual Report of the Edinburgh Total Abstinence Society* (Edinburgh, 1854).
[22] *Report of the British League of Juvenile Abstainers, for the Twelfth Year, 1857–58, and for the 9th Session of Apprentice School* (Edinburgh, 1859).

The British League in the session 1857–8 operated twenty children's meetings held weekly, thirty-six day schools and six apprentice schools, all held in Edinburgh. It laid great store by stating that each meeting opened and closed with a prayer and, especially, that all the schools were free.[23] The meeting, the lecture, and the school lesson were, therefore, powerful campaigning weapons for voluntary societies in this period.

The Edinburgh Association for the Suppression of Drunkenness was slightly different in its appealing techniques, in contrast to the Total Abstinence Society and the British League of Juvenile Abstainers. The association relied on the use of statistics to warn the population about drink. In its *Plea*, an introductory pamphlet to its work, the association carefully evaluated the value to trade, the spirit makers and sellers, and to the exchequer, of the sale of liquor.[24] The distillers, the wine merchants, and spirit dealers were all accused by the association of being 'content to rear splendid fortunes out of the ruins of other men's homes, and, like the poisonous fungi that live on decay, to grow rich on other men's corruption [and] we have no sympathy to waste on them'.[25] As an alternative to those profiting from misery, the association argued that the shopkeeper would and should benefit from the increased sales of tea, coffee and the like.

We are beginning to see how the association developed a rational argument against the sale of liquor. The debate moved away from rhetoric and eloquence and instead a rational, empirically based case was constructed. As to the charge that the association's proposals would be a restriction on trade, the association's retort was to the point: 'If anything could make Liberty stink in the nostrils of the people, it would be to hear her name profaned to such ignoble ends, and see her sacred shields hung up at the door of a dram shop.'[26] This is fine rhetoric, but the association then quotes the tabular returns of the Twelfth Report of the Inspector of Prisons in Scotland showing, 'THE CLOSE RELATIONSHIP BETWEEN DRINKING HOUSES, POVERTY AND CRIME'.[27] The association details the Inspector of Prisons' assertion that drunkenness was the cause, more than any other, of crime and misery in the population. The claim was that drunkenness cost an immense amount of human life and cost the country an enormous amount of money. In addition, the association presented the statistics of the Edinburgh Poor House, showing that:

Of 2,270 out-door pensioners, including adults and children, 1,816 have been reduced to the condition of paupers from habits of intemperance in themselves or relatives.

---

[23] Ibid., pp. 3–4.
[24] The Edinburgh Association for the Suppression of Drunkenness (n.d.) *A Plea, etc.*
[25] *Suppression of Drunkenness*, p. 6.
[26] Ibid., p. 8.
[27] Ibid., p. 2.

Of 631 in-door patients, including adults and children, 505 have been reduced to the condition of paupers from habits of intemperance in themselves or relatives.

This gives 80% of the pauperism in Edinburgh as the fruits of drunkenness.[28]

With the Edinburgh Charity Workhouse also claiming that two-thirds were brought to poverty by their own intemperance, the association believed it had built a sound case for the suppression of drunkenness.

Statistics were being employed more and more by mid-century Victorians. In 1851 there was 'An inquiry into destitution, prostitution and crime in Edinburgh', confident in its use of 'facts' to identify a problem and to find its solution:

> And now to portray crime in all its hideousness, – to show vice her own image in all its appalling loathsomeness, – to paint poverty in its squalid rags, and with its paralysing wretchedness, – and to do this strictly and truthfully, without borrowing a line from romance, a single colour from imagination, or the slightest shade from fancy, but letting the naked picture stand boldly forth in the harsh and stern reality of FACTS, such is our object.[29]

The statistics produced by the inquiry can be seen in Table 4.2, showing the comparative figures on consumption of spirits in England, Scotland and Ireland derived from the abstract of a paper presented to the British Association by G. R. Porter of the Board of Trade.[30]

It can clearly be seen that reasoned and logical argument, backed up by a few choice statistics, could become a powerful campaigning resource – it was one that the Edinburgh Association for the Suppression of Drunkenness exploited to its full advantage.

Table 4.2: *Comparative annual consumption of spirits: England, Scotland, Ireland*

	Men, women and children	Total expenditure
England	0.569 gallons	£8,205,242
Scotland	2.647 gallons	£6,285,114
Ireland	0.853 gallons	£6,319,852

Note: These figures are totally irrespective of an estimated outlay on beer (in which is understood porter and ale also) of £25,383,165, and for brandy of £3,281,250; while for tobacco £7,588,607.

[28] Ibid., pp. 28–9.
[29] *An Inquiry into Destitution, Prostitution and Crime in Edinburgh* (Edinburgh, 1851) [original emphasis].
[30] Ibid., p. 30.

In all the examples presented here recourse was made neither to the state nor to local government, but instead use was made of a number of activities which transmitted their message directly to, usually, the working classes. Four tactics were identified. The first was the use of the 'visit', the second the publication of the tract, the third the use of the lecture or the school room, and the fourth the use of statistics to back up reasoned argument. This was the way that intervention was carried out in mid-Victorian Edinburgh by the urban bourgeoisie. Its success and its ability to be effective stemmed as much from the range of activity as from its actions. Thus to extend this argument a little more, our attention is now turned to the multifarious charitable and benevolent institutions which filled many of the 'spaces' in Scotland's urban society.[31]

'Benevolent and charitable institutions'

Christianity underpinned much of the enthusiasm within the middle class for voluntary activity at this time, and its influence was therefore extensive within Edinburgh's network of voluntary societies. Those societies categorised as 'benevolent and charitable' by the compilers of the *Almanac* shared many of the motivations of those explicitly 'religious institutions', yet it is possible to identify six generic types which will enable us to elaborate upon the extent of self-organisation within Edinburgh's civil society:

(a)   'Industrial and improvement' Societies
(b)   'Area' Societies
(c)   'Clan' Societies
(d)   'Hospital' Charities
(e)   'Societies engaged with the Irish 'problem'
(f)   'Down at luck' Institutions

By taking each subsection in turn, the pervasiveness of voluntary activity in mid-nineteenth-century Edinburgh will be stressed. By so doing we will be able to complete our understanding of the practical content behind middle-class governing of urban society.

(a) 'Industrial and improvement' Societies

Unlike societies which campaigned using the tract, the lecture or case-study evidence from visits, and exerted moral persuasion, industrial and improvement societies centred their fund-raising activities on the exchange of goods and services. Hence their ethos was distinct from the straight charitable donation. Such societies also insisted that those who came to them for assistance be given either new skills or a semblance of education. This ideology of 'improvement' was not only aimed at benefiting

---

[31] The *Almanac* lists the benevolent and charitable institutions in Edinburgh in 1854 deemed worthy of inclusion – those societies are collated in Appendix 2.

its clients; it was also to discourage 'wasters', thereby reassuring patrons that their financial help would not go to the undeserving.

An example of this type of society is the Society for the Industrious Blind. The objectives of this charity were manifold, although in its report of 1858 three clear aims were laid out for the society:

(1)   It affords employment to the indigent and deserving blind; pays them certain wages or remuneration for work done; provides for them in sickness, and clothes them.

(2)   It instructs the youthful inmates in certain branches of manufacture, whereby eventually they may be enabled to turn their abilities to some account for their support, and so make them useful members of society, and less dependant upon others for that assistance which their want of sight would naturally imply.

(3)   The benefits of religious and secular education (and the Directors congratulate themselves in being enabled to dispense such great blessings), are afforded to those who might otherwise have remained in mental as well as visual darkness, or what, perhaps, is infinitely worse than total ignorance, might become vitiated and callous, not only to the things of time but of eternity.[32]

This was a charitable body that tried as much as was possible to be financially independent, free of complete reliance on donations. The ethos of the regime required that the residents were willing to work for their living. It was very much a case of offering a tangible return for a charitable 'donation'.

This notion of exchange was perceived as the central reason which maintained the existence of this society since its inception in 1793. However the society was all too aware of the impossibility of the manufactures of the 99 blind workers under its care trading successfully in the market place. In the annual report of 1857 it bemoaned that in fact the society could not compete 'with manufacturing establishments, where manufacturing is used, and artisans possessing the blessings of sight are employed'.[33] The money earned by the society for its goods and services was never sufficient to keep it in business. Thus an important qualification is that, while the society operated within an ideological framework where financial support was gained in receipt for work done, for its actual survival it was still heavily dependent on subscriptions and, especially, on one-off donations and legacies. That being said, such purely monetary donations were solicited and given on the assumption

32   *Report of the Directors of the Edinburgh Asylum for the Relief of the Indigent and Industrious Blind for 1858* (Edinburgh, 1858).
33   *Report by the Directors of the Edinburgh Asylum for the Relief of the Indigent and Industrious Blind for 1857* (Edinburgh, 1857).

that the patients would be morally and educationally 'improved' – a function the Society for the Industrious Blind was pleased to perform.

(b) 'Area' Societies

A second set of benevolent and charitable societies operating in the mid-nineteenth century were those which can be termed as 'area' societies, and were closely associated with the clan societies (see below). Based in Edinburgh, such societies existed to provide charitable assistance for specified geographical regions. Examples include: the Edinburgh Aberdeenshire Club, the Edinburgh Morayshire Club, the Edinburgh Morayshire Mechanics' Society, the Edinburgh Caithness Association, the Edinburgh Upper-Ward of Lanarkshire Association, the Edinburgh Galloway Association, the Edinburgh Angus Club, the Orkney and Shetland Charitable Society, the Social Peeblean Society, and the Edinburgh Kinross-shire Society. To take just one of these societies, the Edinburgh Angus Club, which was instituted in 1841, it formed a special bursary fund and planned to 'greatly ... promote the interests and cause of education in the county of Angus'.[34] The report quoted was from the Edinburgh society, but similar societies existed in Dundee, Arbroath, Montrose and in many other places on the east coast of Scotland as well as in Glasgow and the west.

The significance of these 'area' societies is that they formed a tangible link between Lowland, urban, Scotland and its rural and Highland 'periphery'. It is probable that such societies were not found in the rest of Britain, and they do indicate strongly the perception of certain local problems as Scottish national problems. As we shall see later, this point was no more apparent than over the issue of the relief of Highland destitution.

(c) Clan Societies

A related type of society is the 'clan' society. Leaving aside their relevance to the strength of Scottish national identity, clan societies performed important philanthropic functions. An example of this was the Clan Gregor Society, founded in 1822 following George IV's visit to Scotland in that year.[35] This story is now well known thanks, primarily, to the work of Prebble: his majesty arrived in Edinburgh on 13 August; he docked at Leith, then travelled in state to Holyrood Palace and from there to Edinburgh Castle to receive the Scottish regalia; he addressed all the clans, assembled in their plaids, and declared: 'Gentlemen, I shall give you another toast, in which you shall heartily join me. I shall simply

---

[34] *Reports by the Committee of Management and Minutes of Annual Meetings of the Edinburgh Angus Club ...* (Edinburgh, 1868).
[35] For an account of the visit, see J. Prebble, *The King's Jaunt: George IV in Scotland, 1822* (London, 1988).

give you: "the Chieftains and Clans of Scotland, and God bless the Land of Cakes".[36]

During George's visit to Scotland the Clan Gregor was entrusted along with the Celtic Society to guard the Scottish regalia – 'the sacred relics of our ancient and national independence'.[37] Appearing in the full garb and tartan of the clan this was the first time they had gathered together for almost a century.[38] From this gathering there developed a shared concern over the poverty of their fellow clansmen and women following the '45. The society was formed. Its chief objective was to:

> extend to the poor of the Clan the blessing of a sound and a Christian education ... To assist in the education of young men belonging to the Clan-Gregor, bearing the names of MacGregor, Gregor, Gregorson, or Gregory ... who give indications of talent and genius, and who intend qualifying themselves for any learned professions, for the army or navy, or for mercantile pursuits.[39]

This was not the first clan to resurrect itself as a society in this way. As early as 1725, and therefore between the two Jacobite uprisings, there was founded in Glasgow a Buchanan Society to assist the poor of that clan and to educate its children. While in 1806, also in Glasgow, a body of clansmen formed the Mackay Society. This was a group of city traders, grocers, vintners and the like who formed a society with the aim of helping their clansmen 'in time of affective dispensations'. This society was reconstituted as the Clan Mackay Society in 1888 when all the other clans began to follow the example of the Clan Gregor Society in both helping the disadvantaged bearing their name and also, by the 1880s, in an effort to preserve the history and literature of their clan.[40]

The Clan Gregor was certainly the most active of its type and it is the example about which most is known. Its office bearers for 1830 are shown below (Figure 4.4). They show clearly the importance of the clan name in its organisational structure.

The rules of the society demanded that the applicants for their bursaries had statements regarding their moral character certified by their minister and one of the heritors of their parish. The society was therefore a typical philanthropic charity offering a helping hand as aid to self-help, but was laced also with the usual trimmings of respectability and moral wholesomeness. In addition, and this is what makes this type of society distinct, the ideological justification for its role was one set heavily in the mythical memories and story-telling of Sir Walter Scott, and one rooted in beliefs about the clans' purpose of guarding both clan

---

36 *Full Account of King George the Fourth's Visit to Scotland in 1822.*
37 *Report Relative to the Objects and Progress of the Clan-Gregor Society* (1830).
38 For the history of this clan, see F. Macgregor, *Clan Gregor* (Edinburgh, 1977). W. R. Kermack, *The Clan Macgregor* (3rd edn, Edinburgh, 1979).
39 *Clan-Gregor Society.*
40 I. Grimble, *Clans and Chiefs* (London, 1980), pp. 256–7.

members and, importantly, Scotland's independence: the clan name acted as the point of continuity through history.

Figure 4.4: *Office Bearers elected to the Clan-Gregor Society, 21 May 1830*

Hereditary Patron: Sir Evan John Murray MacGregor of MacGregor, Bart.

President: Colonel Robert Murray MacGregor.

Vice-Presidents: Lieutenant-Colonel Robert B. MacGregor; Sir James MacGregor, Director-General of the Medical Department.

Extraordinary Directors: Alexander MacGregor, Esq., Merchant, Glasgow; Rev. William Gregor, Bowhill; Lieutenant-Colonel Duncan MacGregor, 93rd Highlanders; Malcolm McGregor, Esq., British Consul, Panama; Patrick MacGregor, Esq., Cashier, Commercial Bank of Scotland; John Gregorson, Esq., of Ardtornish; John Gregory, Esq., Advocate; William Gregory, Esq., Writer, Glasgow; Captain MacGregor Skinner, R.N.; Colonel J. P. MacGregor, India.

Ordinary Directors: Major Hugh McGregor, H.P., 63rd Regiment; James MacGregor, Esq.; Rev. James Gregory, Dublin; Rev. John Gibson MacGregor, Edinburgh; John MacGregor, Esq., Writer, Edinburgh; John MacGregor, Esq., Brunswick Place, Glasgow; Peter MacGregor, Esq., George Street, Edinburgh; Rev. Mr MacGregor Souter, Skye; Captain Malcolm MacGregor, 78th Highlanders; Rev. Wm. MacGregor Stirling, Edinburgh; Josiah MacGregor, Esq., Glasgow; James MacGregor, Esq., Fort William; Donald Gregory, Esq., Edinburgh; Alexander MacGregor, jun., Esq., Glasgow; Joseph MacGregor, Esq., Acct., Edinburgh; Alexander MacGregor, Esq., of Liverpool; William Gregory, Esq., Edinburgh; Rev. Simon MacGregor, Edinburgh; Captain John MacGregor, Rothesy.

Treasurer: John MacGregor, Commercial Bank, Edinburgh.

Secretary: James Murray MacGregor, Esq., Accountant, Edinburgh.

Convenor of Directors in Glasgow: Alexander MacGregor, jun., Esq., Glasgow.

Collector for Glasgow and West of Scotland: John MacGregor, Esq., Brunswick Place, Glasgow.

Source: *Clan-Gregor Society.*

Taken together, the 'area' and the 'clan' societies represent clear channels of philanthropic activity, narrow in direction, oriented to place of origin. They are important because they conjure up memories of an old Scottish society unchanged by industrialisation. Such societies were links between urban and rural Scotland, between Lowland and Highland. Equally, they again make the point that a dominant characteristic of philanthropic activity is its specificity of function. It is this specificity which makes it necessary that a vast number of societies be in operation. There was no one institution, or set of institutions, which was going to fill the gap – that had to wait for a new ideology of state intervention in the twentieth century.

(d) Hospital Charities

From the list of benevolent and charitable societies presented in Appendix 2 it can be seen that there were a number of charities directed specifically towards hospital care. The problem of urban poverty in Edinburgh was as great as in any large city in nineteenth-century Britain. As overcrowding worsened during urban expansion, it quickened the need for a response, from both existing and new societies, to the inevitable repercussions for the health of the poorest sections of society. One of the long-established bodies which had increasingly to systematise its response was the Royal Dispensary and Vaccine Institution, founded in 1776, incorporated by Royal Charter, and one of the first of its kind. It was proud of its reputation for the treatment of 'patients of all classes'.[41] For the year 1854 its Annual Report states that the Institution had dealt with over 10,000 such patients. The use of tabular information was a common tactic of societies relying on charitable donations to carry out their work. In this case statistics were provided in the Report to enable prospective subscribers to evaluate the relative success of the Institution in its work. In particular it wished to attract support away from its rival, the New Town Dispensary, which had been set up in 1815 – although eventually the two did begin to work together.[42]

Statistics were also used by the Committee set up to enact an appeal for the then proposed Hospital for Sick Children in Edinburgh in 1859.[43] By showing that half the infants died before they reached the age of six, and that the appalling level of infant mortality accounted for nearly half of all deaths in Scottish cities, the committee hoped to raise £6,000 for the cost of the building and £1,200 for its annual running costs. The argument presented to the people of Edinburgh was that 'poverty is so hard that intervention is necessary', but it was the people of Edinburgh who were to intervene. Equally, intervention was proposed to build better housing for the working population in an effort to improve their health. Unlike the Children's Hospital, this proposal was not enacted until the turn of the century,[44] but at no time during that wait was it proposed that the central state should be involved, although the scale of investment required to influence the housing supply meant that this concern was primarily one of municipal government. The ideology of intervention was, in the period from 1830 to 1860, a fragile construct which was able to survive only in civil society.

Thus fundamental to both appeals was the use of statistics and tabular returns to add weight and authority to any appeal for subscriptions, donations and legacies. Throughout our period of study, as the 'petitioning' middle classes become increasingly involved in their publishing activities, so too does their use of empirical evidence to support their case. Moreover, the appeal for the proposed hospital for sick children showed that 'intervention' was specifically called for to try to temper the perceived problem of dire infant mortality. But this intervention was not to involve the parliamentary state nor the

---

[41] *Annual Report for the Year 1854 of the Royal Dispensary and Vaccine Institution, for Affording Medical and Surgical Assistance to the Sick Poor of the City and County of Edinburgh* (Edinburgh, 1855).

[42] Checkland, *Philanthropy in Victorian Scotland*, pp. 202–3.

[43] *An Appeal on Behalf of the Proposed Hospital for Sick Children in Edinburgh, 1859* (Edinburgh, 1859).

[44] Smout, *Century of the Scottish People*, p. 50.

municipal state. The problem was to be tackled within the voluntary sector. A group of middle-class worthies had come together as a committee and sent out an appeal to the citizens of Edinburgh to provide the finance, both fixed and recurring, for setting up of a children's hospital. The path towards the solution to the problem of child mortality in the Scottish cities was to be reached within Scottish civil society.

It is now time to diverge slightly from the conventions of the *Almanac* and leave those societies encompassed within the title 'Benevolent and Charitable' and briefly to consider some of those societies who tackled the 'Irish problem' in a non-benevolent way. Rather than treat the 'Irish problem' as one of poverty – as the Edinburgh Irish Mission for one perceived it – a number of societies existed to turn the issue into a sectarian one.

(e) Societies engaged with the 'Irish problem'
At the same time as help for the Irish poor existed in Scotland, there was also a multitude of anti-Catholic societies, the main target for their ire being the Irish. The Mission for the Conversion of Irish Romanists was supported by 'all denominations', but was run (temporarily at least) by the Free Church Presbytery of Edinburgh.[45] The Edinburgh Irish Mission and Protestant Institute was founded in 1842 'by a Committee of zealous Christians, at a time when Protestantism was scarcely awake'.[46] This society was in the business of whipping up as much anti-Catholic/anti-Irish feeling as it could, and it used some very emotive language:

> By means of Ireland's terrorism, clothed in a British Constitution, it has assailed our Legislature, brow-beaten our Government, and extorted from our bewildered and embarrassed statesmen, concessions, revenues, and patronage, and repaid them with scorn, disaffection, and insolent defiance. Another and secret column of attack has undermined the walls of the English Established Church, and by means of Oxford, has poured down on an unguarded country a perfect blood of Jesuits.
>
> Churches, colleges and nunneries rise up in Protestant Scotland, we know not how; Jesuits and priests glide into our drawing rooms, we know not whence; and though we are occasionally startled by the perversion of Protestants in the better ranks of society, we go to rest again in a frame of spurious liberality, which will be compliant towards intolerance, provided it be sincere, and liberally regardless of the cause of Christ and truth, because we happen to call it our own.

---

[45] *Missions for the Conversion of Irish Romanists in the Large Towns of England and Scotland explained and recommended, being the Report of the Edinburgh Irish Mission for the Year 1851, with a list of subscriptions* (Edinburgh, 1852).
[46] *Edinburgh Irish Mission and Protestant Institute* (1852), p. 2.

Arise, Protestants, arise!
We know the evils of Popery, that oft threatens our liberties, drains
our resources, and sits like an incubus upon our national prosperity.
Let us rise, then, and do something worthy of the cause – something
for Protestantism – something for liberty – something for civilisation
– something for national independence and national prosperity, for
this is not one cause but many! It is emphatically the cause of the
age in which we live, and the country in which we dwell.[47]

It can be seen that the Edinburgh Irish Mission and Protestant Institute
had little doubt that there was a threat to the Protestant faith and that it
knew from whom that threat came. Both campaigned through the
published pamphlet in order to try to dominate the political agenda. A
more considered society, with a wider remit, but with similar fears was
the Scottish Association for Opposing Prevalent Errors. The object of
this particular association was not merely anti-popery; it was against
anything it perceived as anti-Christian. It was against superstition,
infidelity, pantheism, supernaturalism and socialism. It was also hoped
that its formation in 1845 would counter the Tractarian party in the
Church of England.[48] Its function was the 'circulation of works already
existing, and employing other kindred measures, to counteract the
efforts which may be made for the diffusion of error'.[49]

These societies can be seen to be sectarian, grown out of the perceived
social problems caused by the influx of Irish settlers into Scotland. The
important point to note for our purposes is that, once again, the
expression of this sectarian pressure was channelled through
associations within Edinburgh's civil society. Where politics became
involved, such as in the mid-century debates over Parliament's grant to
the seminary college at Maynooth (which cost Macaulay his Edinburgh
seat in 1847), this can be interpreted as the mobilisation of the middle
classes in civil society to bargain with the central state. By so doing, they
hoped to remove the influence of that state in their affairs. As with those
who perceived the 'Irish problem' to be one of poverty, the mechanisms
of dispute or of appeal were of similar form: the voluntary organisation
was the vehicle of dispute as well as of intervention. By returning once
more to the direct guidance of the *Almanac* and considering our sixth
identifiable subsection, 'down at luck' institutions, we can identify one
final characteristic – the voluntary society filling the perceived gaps of
inadequate parliamentary legislation.

(f) 'Down at luck' institutions
Closely linked to the 'hospital' societies, much work was being done in
Edinburgh to relieve the suffering of those who were temporarily down

---

[47] Ibid., p. 3.
[48] *Report of the Scottish Association for Opposing Prevalent Errors* (Edinburgh, 1848).
[49] Scottish Association for Opposing Prevalent Errors (Mar. 1847) '*Circular*'.

on their luck yet keen to avoid the trauma of poor relief. Examples include the Edinburgh Living-in Institution, the Society for the Relief of Poor Married Women, the House of Refuge and Night Refuge, the Edinburgh Society for the Relief of Indigent Old Men, and the Society for the Relief of Poor Married Women of Respectable Character when in Childbed. These societies provided a flexible response for the respectable poor in a time of crisis.

As part of this particular problem, certain charities and homes were set up to address a need left unattended, or even created, by state legislation. One such charity was the House of Refuge for the Destitute. Its origins stem from the attempts of the Board of Health to stop vagrants entering the city in a bid to halt the spread of cholera. This left a large population of the destitute homeless and, what is more, barred from the prospect of finding lodgings in Edinburgh – effectively stuck between a rock and a hard place. A home was founded to provide a temporary residence, with food and clothing, until employment could be secured elsewhere, or they could be sent back to their parishes. Those staying in the home would be taught certain trades, such as shoemaking, tin-making, bookbinding and tailoring, while their children were placed under a master and taught reading and writing, with the females being instructed in sewing and knitting.[50] All the education and the instruction acted upon the principles of religion and virtue. As always, charity was never free.

Homes and institutions were thus set up to deal with a section of the respectable poor who would otherwise have slipped through the net of poor relief and to help those whose misfortune was exacerbated by state legislation. This final sub-section demonstrates the great flexibility of voluntaryism and its ability to deal with specific issues. It is this specificity which explains the range of voluntaryism and in turn explains how this range is sufficient to deal with almost any social problem within its remit, without the need for parliamentary legislation. Through voluntaryism the middle classes had the mechanism to intervene in their urban world.

The *Almanac* has indeed revealed the range of concerns and issues dealt with at the level of civil society. Religious education, drunkenness, crime and missionary work were addressed by the 'religious' section; blindness, lunacy, poverty, single-motherhood, homelessness, destitution, illness, disease and educational disadvantage were all dealt with in 'benevolent and charitable institutions'. These are some examples of the range of social problems to which solutions were attempted by the voluntary sector. That is, to repeat, what is meant by 'governing' civil society. The very openness of the constitution of the voluntary organisation, yet with a rigidity of status divisions in its hierarchical

---

[50] *House of Refuge for the Destitute, and Asylum for their Children, Morrison's Close, 117 High Street, Edinburgh* (1832).

structure, made it an ideal medium through which the middle class, traditionally so reluctant to associate, could pursue their chosen collective action.

The power to legislate or tax was of course absent. Scotland and its middle classes did not have their own Scottish state of the democratically constituted and elected form as political scientists would, quite legitimately, define it. But if we are careful to use inverted commas, then this ability to deal with such a variety of social and economic problems within a civil society enshrined by a shared state at Westminster, encourages the realisation that the urban middle class effectively administered a *de facto* 'state'. It becomes increasingly apparent that the inter-network of voluntary activity allowed the Edinburgh bourgeoisie an autonomy to administer Scottish affairs – the nation – as if they had their own 'state'.

To develop our understanding of the importance of voluntary activity to middle-class formation, which in turn fostered the impetus to self-administration, the remainder of this chapter will consider the other side of the structure of Edinburgh's civil society: the channelling of status claims and cultural power through chosen activity careers in public life.

II: CULTURAL AND STATUS VOLUNTARY SOCIETIES

While the range, structure and tactics of middle-class voluntary societies as they administered civil society are vital to understanding how civil society was structured in mid-century, in this second section the analysis falls on the middle class itself – the societies, clubs and associations pivotal to its class formation. This analysis concentrates on the final major section of the *Almanac* not so far discussed, 'scientific and literary'.[51] The theme of the remainder of this chapter is to illustrate the nature of cultural and status reproduction which was so important to class formation.

'Scientific and Literary Societies'

Typical of the middle classes in other large towns and cities of mid-nineteenth-century Britain, the Edinburgh bourgeoisie formed a series of literary, philosophical and debating clubs. John Seed, in his examination of Manchester, identifies the local Literary and Philosophical Society – 'a platform for intellectual liberal debate with a strong scientific stress' – as a central focus of the Unitarian elite in the

---

[51] It will be remembered that the societies within subsection (7) of the *Almanac*'s account of Edinburgh 'Miscellaneous Lists' are discussed within their closest generic type, e.g. 'religious', of 'charitable and benevolent', etc. The much smaller 'commercial' section, which mainly listed the banking and insurance companies in existence, will be examined in chap. 5, when the Scottish Trade Protection Society will be the focus.

1820s and 1830s.[52] These were sources of status battles as much as cultural or recreational activities. One of the most prominent of such societies in Edinburgh was the Philosophical Institution, founded in 1846 following a meeting the previous year by the directors and members of the then defunct Edinburgh Philosophical Association (which had itself been formed in 1832).[53]

The institution was a prime focus for the more literary members of the upper reaches of Edinburgh's middle class. The institution was proud of its library which contained over 1,000 volumes, over half of which had been donated by T. B. Macaulay, Francis Jeffrey and other supporters. By the session 1853–4 the library contained nearly 7,000 volumes, immediately to rise to 9,000 by the next session following another gift from Macaulay. The rules and regulations of the Reading Room and the titles of available periodicals are reproduced in Figure 4.5, while the rules, regulations and the titles of available newspapers from around the world are reproduced in Figure 4.6.[54]

This was education as leisure, and the middle-class taste was an international one. The programme for the session 1857–8, for example, combined a lecture by Professor W. E. Aytoun on 'The Ballad Poetry of Scotland', with Simpson's 'Great Britain as a Roman Colony', while the undoubted highlight of that year was the visit of Charles Dickens. What treatment Scotland did receive was as part of European-wide learning. One was just as likely to have been lectured on Italian peasants as on the literature of Scotland. Music tended to be the strongest focus for all things Scottish, but again, usually within a British context. Thus, for example, in the series of lectures by Charles Mackay, lecture III was on 'The Popular and Historical Songs of England', while lecture IV gave the same treatment to Scotland.

An analysis of the membership of the Philosophical Institution is carried out in the next chapter; for the moment it is merely pertinent to understand that the institution was one of a number of societies, exclusive in membership, high in status, and all important to the networks of power in mid-century Edinburgh. Each society existed in a well-understood space within the finely graded status divisions of Edinburgh's public life. Similar routes to both obtaining and maintaining high status were the various debating clubs which, although each was small in size, abounded in Edinburgh. Membership of these societies was exclusive, and each targeted particular strata within the middle class.

52 J. Seed, 'Unitarianism, political economy and the antinomies of liberal culture in Manchester, 1830–1850', *Social History*, vii (1) (1982), p. 4.
53 W. A. Miller, *The 'Philosophical': A Short History of the Edinburgh Philosophical Institution and its Famous Members and Lectures, 1846–1948* (Edinburgh, 1949).
54 *The Philosophical Institution: General Syllabus of the Lectures, Session, 1858–59* (Edinburgh, 1859).

Figure 4.5: *Philosophical Institute Reading Room*

THE LIBRARY READING ROOM
THE READING ROOM is open every day, from half past 9 a.m. till half past 9 p.m. The newest works selected for the library, and the latest publications of the following periodicals are always on the tables. A collection of valuable Books of Reference, consisting of the Encyclopaedias, Dictionaries, Atlases, etc., is open to the Members. The Periodicals and the New Works are give out by ballot every evening at 9 o'clock.

Weekly

Athenaeum
Builder – Critic

Chambers's Journal
Illustrated London News
Illustrated Times
Lancet
Literary Gazette
Medical Times & Gazette
Punch

Revue des Deux Mondes
——

Monthly

Annales de Chimie et de Physique
Annals of Natural History
Army List

Art Journal
Banker's Magazine
Bentley's Miscellany

Blackwood's Magazine
Christian Witness
Civil Engineer & Architects Jnl.
Dublin University Magazine

Monthly – continued

Eclectic Review
Evangelical Magazine

Fraser's Magazine
Herald of Peace
Household Words
Journal of Jurisprudence
London Journal of Arts
Mechanic's Magazine
Notes & Queries

Philosophical Magazine
Photographic Journal
Railway Timetables
Repertory of Inventions

Scottish Jurist
Scottish Congregational Magazine
Scottish Educational Journal
Sharp's London Magazine
Tait's Magazine

Titan
United Presbyterian Magazine
United Services Journal
——

Quarterly

British Quarterly Review
British & Foreign Medico-Chirurgical Review
Calcutta Review
Christian Remembrancer
Dublin Review
Edinburgh Medical Journal
Edinburgh Philosophical Journal
Edinburgh Review
Journal of Classical & Sacred Philology
Journal of Homeopathy
National Review
Navy List
North American Review

North British Review
Quarterly Journal of the Geological Society
Quarterly Review
Scottish Review
Silliman's American Journal of Science & Arts

Yearly and otherwise: – The British Almanac, Dod's British Peerage, The Edinburgh Almanac, East India Register, Journal of the Royal Geographical Society, Year Book of Facts, Directories (Edinburgh, Glasgow, London, and Slator's), Astronomical Observations at the Edinburgh Royal Observatory, Reports of the British Association.

Figure 4.6: *Philosophical Institute News Room*

The Library
THE LIBRARY FOR CIRCULATION, to which important additions are made every month, consists of a valuable and extensive selection of Books (upwards of 11, 000 volumes) in every department of Literature and Science, and is open for lending and returning Books, every day from half-past 9 a.m. till half-past 9 p.m. except on Saturdays, when it is closed for lending at half past 8 p.m.; and on Tuesdays and Fridays *during the lecture season*, when it is closed for lending at 8 p.m.

The News Room
The News Room is open every lawful day from 8 a.m. till 10 p.m. and is supplied several times during the day, with the earliest TELEGRAPHIC INTELLIGENCE of every event of public importance, the state of the Funds, Prices of Shares, Market Reports, Arrivals of Overland Mails, etc. The London Papers of the Morning are received by EXPRESS on the *Evening of their publication*. The Room is supplied with the following Papers:

Edinburgh Papers

Advertiser
Caledonian Mercury
Courant
Evening Post
Daily Express
*Gazette
Ladies' Journal
Leith Commercial List
News
*North British Advertiser
North British Agriculturalist
North British Daily Mail
North Briton
*Scotsman (Daily)
Scotsman (Bi-weekly)
Scottish Press
Scottish Railway Gazette
Scotch Thistle
Witness
——

London Daily Papers
Daily News
Morning Advertiser
Morning Chronicle
Morning Herald
Globe
Shipping & Mercantile Gazette
Standard
Sun
*Times
——
London Weekly Papers Etc., Papers
Atlas
Oxford University Herald

London Papers – continued

Bell's Life in London
Civil Service Gazette
*Economist
Era
*Examiner
Field
Gardener's Chronicle
Guardian
Herapath's Railway Jour.
Homeward Mail
Illustrated London News
Illustrated Times
Leader
Mark-Lane Express
Mining Journal
Naval & Military Gazette
Nonconformist
Observer
Patriot Press
Punch
Record
*Spectator
Watchman
Weekly Dispatch

English Provincial Papers
Birmingham Journal
Cambridge Chronicle
Gateshead Observer
Leeds Mercury
Liverpool Albion
Liverpool (Gore's) Advertiser
Liverpool Mercury
Manchester Examiner

Glasgow and other Scottish Provincial Papers

Glasgow Citizen
Glasgow Herald
Glasgow Gazette
Scottish Guardian
Aberdeen Herald
Aberdeen Journal
Ayr Advertiser
Banffshire Journal
Dumfries Courier
Dundee Advertiser
Elgin Courant
Fifeshire Journal
Greenock Advertiser
Inverness Courier
John O'Groat Journal
Kelso Chronicle
Montrose Review
Perthshire Advertiser
Stirling Journal
——

Irish Papers
Belfast Northern Wig
Dublin Evening Mail
Dublin Evening Post
General Advertiser
Nation
Tablet
——

Foreign & Colonial
Allgemeine Zeitung
Journal des Débats
L'Illustration Français
Melbourne Argus
Aust. & Zetland Gazette
Montreal Gazette
China Mail
New York Herald

Of the more important of these Papers, several copies are received. In all, they form an average supply of *one hundred and twenty sheets* daily. *Those marked * are filed.
Institution Rooms, 4 Queen Street,   HENRY BOWIE, *Secretary*, October 1858

From the *Almanac* it is possible to choose a few short examples which neatly illustrate the subtle but specific class divisions played out through the Edinburgh debating societies. The Speculative Society, for example, owed much of its success to the help it received from Henry Cockburn, and the renowned librarian of the Signet Library, David Laing. Its admission of members was very limited; strangers were very definitely excluded; compulsory attendance and fulfilment of duty were very early conditions. Explicitly this society was not a political club – an essay was read and debate was confined to 'academical exercise and speculations'. Sir Walter Scott was secretary between 1791 and 1795, and Robert Louis Stevenson was later to be a member; and although its numbers were already small by 1841, it always claimed to produce many eminent men.[55]

The Juridical Society was composed exclusively of young men in training for, or already belonging to, one of the branches of the legal profession: 'Petitions for admission shall be received only from Advocates, or gentlemen studying for the bar, Writers to the Signet, or those who are or have been apprentices of Writers to the Signet.'[56] It was a debating society on legal issues, except for every third week when a non-legal matter was on the agenda. The society had sufficient funds to own its hall and library and its meetings were strictly private.[57]

The Scots Law Society, instituted in 1815, was another devoted to the discussion of 'legal and literary questions'. The Royal Physical Society debated the cultivation of physical sciences, and rose from the union in 1782 of the Medico-Chirurgical and the Physico-Chirurgico Societies. The Dialectic Society, instituted in 1787, 'meets every Saturday during winter for the prosecution of literary and philosophical composition, curriculum and debate'. The Hunterian Society was instituted in 1826, and had basically the same objects and constitution as the Royal Physical Society. In 1833 the five societies last named were united as the associated Societies of the University of Edinburgh.[58]

These societies were part of early and mid-Victorian elite culture. The high value of literary pursuits was fundamental to successful membership of the middle class.[59] These debating societies were places where knowledge could be gained, discussed, and a common understanding reached. The fact that such societies each had distinct memberships will be explored further in the analysis of Chapter 5, but it can be seen that the specificity of function which characterised the religious and charitable organisations outlined in the first part of this chapter, was repeated in occupational and status terms for cultural societies. In addition, and importantly, each occupational and status stratum remained

---

[55] *History of the Speculative Society of Edinburgh from its Inception in 1764* (Edinburgh, 1845).

[56] *The Laws of the Juridical Society of Edinburgh, Instituted Anno 1773* (Edinburgh, 1830).

[57] 'University debating societies', part of *History of the Speculative Society of Edinburgh*.

[58] Ibid.

[59] See Morris, *Class, Sect and Party*.

closed-in on itself – it was this mechanism which enabled the middle class to manage intra-class conflict internally.

This literary culture was also part of the 'bibliographical mania' which has been regarded by one influential author as a vital ingredient of Scottish society's self-image.[60] The search for literary knowledge can be identified equally in the growth of subscription libraries. Here, however, there is a much clearer inter-class divide between the middle class as a whole and the skilled artisans of Edinburgh. The Edinburgh Select Subscription Library held its first meeting on the evening of Friday, 21 March 1800 and it was a society for a closed section of the bourgeoisie. It did not appeal for public subscription, but instead opted to be self-financed by its members in order to remain exclusive. This exclusivity proved too expensive to maintain. To keep costs down, and to keep the library in operation, the members were forced, over the following decades, to offer regular share issues for new members to take up. Table 4.3, below, details the membership figures for the years 1837 to 1841.

Table 4.3: *Membership of Edinburgh Subscription Library*

Year	Membership	Year	Membership
1837	541	1840	595
1838	573	1841	593
1839	585		

Source: *Edinburgh Select Subscription Library. Sketch of the Origin and Progress of the Library* [reprinted from the third appendix to the former catalogue; with postscript in continuation to 1842].

In contrast, a quite different subscription library was formed under the title of the Edinburgh Mechanics' Subscription Library. Unlike the Select Subscription Library, which was run by members of the legal profession and accountants, with the occasional upholsterer and engraver thrown in, the Mechanics' version was run by a mixture of artisans and members of the petty bourgeoisie. This latter point can be seen by looking at the occupational titles of the office bearers of the society in a selected year: 1858–9 (Figure 4.7).

The society actually states that there is no law in the library's constitution which requires that the greater portion of its managers should be mechanics – 'yet it may be confidently affirmed, that during the whole of its history the greater portion of those who have directed its movements have either been mechanics, or very slightly raised above them in the social scale'.[61] This society charged 5s. for entry money and

[60] M. Ash, *The Strange Death of Scottish History* (Edinburgh, 1980).
[61] *Laws and Catalogue of the Edinburgh Mechanics' Subscription Library* (Edinburgh, 1859), p. v.

1s. 6d. as quarterly contribution, a rate fixed at the formation of the library in 1825 and still in force in 1859.

Figure 4.7: *Office bearers of the Edinburgh Mechanics Subscription Library, 1858–9*

President: Wm. Ross, Printer
Vice-President: James Keppie, Printer
Treasurer : James L. Maxwell, Clerk
Secretary: Henry Ranken, Upholsterer

Committee:

Alexander Aitken, Clerk	Peter Anderson, Tailor
Robert Allan, Clerk	Robert Beaton, Clerk
Alexander Brodie, Collector	Peter Campbell, Bookbinder
William Bryce, House Agent	David Cotlam, Printer
Dr Cochrane	John Johnston, Teacher
David Croall, Reporter	Alexander Kerr, Printer
David Fisher, Printer	James Morton, Teacher
James Glasgow, Umbrella Maker	John Stevenson, Bookseller

Auditors: John Maxwell, John Blair, John Morrison
Librarian: John Low.

Source:　*Laws and Catalogue of the Edinburgh Mechanics' Subscription Library* (Edinburgh, 1859).

Both societies aimed to be self-supporting and to be as limited in their membership, as 'exclusive' as they could afford. This charge for exclusiveness fits with ideas of status affirmation, with each social class having its own library. It also fits with the Victorian notions of 'industriousness' and self-help – that one makes 'learning' and 'knowledge' one's pastime. A well-documented part of the middle-class project was the concept of respectability through self improvement. Both these subscription libraries acted this part and, in creating a hegemonic agenda centred on intellectual self-improvement, these libraries were of great intra- and inter-class influence.

The search for knowledge and how it can help one advance in life and also impact on society in general was present amongst those who were members of the Phrenological Association. It was one of those fascinating Victorian societies which, in a pseudo-scientific manner, tried to graft the biological sciences on to the morality of the human race. In this it was very close in ideology to the Eugenics movement which was especially prominent at this time.[62] A whiff of the use of phrenology as a guiding principle for the conduct of one's life can be gauged from a letter written by George Combe to the society, which it then published:

In short, the applications of Phrenology are boundless; and if your association will first *learn* Phrenology in its full dimension, as the

---

[62] S. Shapin and B. Barnes, 'Science, nature and control: interpreting Mechanics' institutes', in R. Dale, G. Esland and M. McDonald (eds.), *Schooling and Capitalism: A Sociological Reader* (London, 1976).

philosophy of the brain and the philosophy of mind, and then apply it to expand their own intellect, improve their moral sentiments, and promote human welfare, every member in his own sphere and according to his own opportunities, your labours will provide high gratifications, and you will find the day far distant when your interest and progress will cease.[63]

The Phrenological Association's acceptance and display of skulls was a matter of great pride.[64] The belief that much information could be gleaned from an exploration of the cranium was common throughout most of the nineteenth century. When Sir Walter Scott died in 1832 his skull was opened up and inside they found a large brain, as expected of one so renowned. In addition, his brain was discovered 'to be in a soft state, and there were globules of water under the left lobe'.[65] This was also expected as it had been diagnosed that Scott had died of water on the brain. The search for the anticipated evidence of success, Scott's overly-large brain, was indicative of powerful strands of bourgeois thinking on the distribution of the classes in the mid-Victorian social structure.[66] A little bit of knowledge, perhaps gleaned from the Edinburgh Select Subscription Library, could go a long way to sustaining what are largely spurious empirical measurements of society. The use made of statistics by hospital charities for sustaining support has already been discussed in part one of this chapter. One society which is perhaps half way between such hospital societies and the Phrenological Society in using statistics as a tactic was the Medico-Statistical Society.

Like the Phrenological Society, but perhaps less controversially, the Medico-Statistical Association sprang up from the mid-Victorians' fascination with empiricism. It is likely that this association's lead came from Chadwick's use of statistics to argue the need for public health reform.[67] In its first report the Medico-Statistical Association stated that its aims were: 'to attribute more precise causes of death than supplied by the Registrar General'.[68] A group of twenty-three doctors, including Alison and Begbie, put their names to this report which included a detailed discussion on causes of death. It can be suggested that this society is another example of dissatisfaction with the function of central government, leading to the middle classes of Edinburgh setting up their own association to carry out the functional requirements deemed necessary for successful health care in Scotland.

---

[63] *Rules of the Edinburgh Phrenological Association, Instituted 1855* (Edinburgh, n.d.).
[64] *Agreement between The Phrenological Association and William Henderson's Trustees* (n.p., 1856).
[65] *The Scotsman*, 29 Sep. 1832.
[66] B. Barnes and S. Shapin (eds.), *Natural Order* (California, 1979).
[67] Flinn, *Report on the Sanitary Condition*.
[68] W. T. Gairdner, M.D., and W. J. Begbie, M.D., *First Report of the Medico-Statistical Association* (Edinburgh, 1852).

So far the societies discussed have concerned either the middle class coming together with their own kind to debate the political, philosophical or literary matters of the day, or to discuss in a more abstract way the social order and health problems of the age. In each case it has been suggested that the middle class administered its internal divisions through the appropriate society or organisation. A more explicit example of how the middle class was riddled with personal influence is the existence of the 'old-school tie' network. For example, a society less concerned with Scotland's poor than with the prospects of the children of the middle class was the High School Club. The club was instituted in 1849 with the object being, generally, 'to promote the interests of the High School, to maintain a good understanding, and form a bond of union among the former pupils of that institution'.[69] Like the Clan Gregor Society, it wanted to set up bursaries to allow talented children to attend the school and to reward scholarship with prizes. By this means it was an important route for former pupils to make contact with new pupils and with their own contemporaries.

The High School Club was not the only occasion for those who have prospered within the middle class of Edinburgh to look after their own. There was also the Signet Club, which consisted of about twenty 'friends' of whom all were members of the Society to His Majesty's Signet. It was formed in 1780 and was, in effect, an elite social club. In terms of its function, it was little more than a structured dinner club. An extract from the minutes of 23 November 1844 provides a flavour of the club's concerns: 'It was moved by Mr Wm. Mackenzie, and agreed to, that Cockieleekie with prunes should be a standing dish at the November meetings.'[70] Although merely an opportunity for making merry, the Signet Club existed to allow like-minded members of the Edinburgh bourgeoisie to come together to exchange information, ideas and trade, and it was an occasion to make contacts. For a member of the elite to be part of such a clique signalled one's arrival in a position of power.

Access to the 'inner-circles' of elite activity was central to the maintenance of status in the everyday life of the Edinburgh bourgeoisie, and this can also be seen in an analysis of one further example of this type – the Academy Bar List – which straddled the Signet and the High School Clubs in its role. It published the biographical details of 'the names of all old Academy boys who have come to the Bar, or who have practised at it, in England, Scotland, Ireland, India, and the Colonies'.[71] The Bar List and the Signet Club were cliques within the legal profession.

---

[69] *First Annual Report of the High School Club* (Edinburgh, 1850). For a list of members of the High School Club, Mar. 1851, see NLS: 5.1924.
[70] G. Dunlop (ed.), *An Account of the Signet Club with Extracts from the Minutes and a Complete List of Members, 1790–1902* (Edinburgh, 1902).
[71] *The Edinburgh Academy Bar List – 1824–1894* (n.d.).

These clubs are just three examples of elite membership within Edinburgh's middle-class activity in and around 1854. They are important alongside what are today better known societies such as the Royal Society of Edinburgh, the 'Bibliographical Clubs', and the New Club, which were made up of a very select band of Edinburgh's middle class. An analysis of the membership of such societies must wait until the next chapter, but by now the argument of this section should be clear: the Edinburgh middle class maintained its status differences through a range of cultural voluntary societies, and each organisation acted as a focal point for the exchange of information, contacts or influence. Yet in the wider sense, by these very acts the bourgeoisie homogenised its own class formation with such vitality that the inter-class intervention and hegemonic bargaining of the first section of this chapter could be possible.

From the foregoing analysis it should now be certain that the level of voluntary activity was all-pervasive, and that this philanthropy, along with the cultural and status actions of the elites, established a distinct social structure within Edinburgh's civil society. Voluntary activity was part of class formation as well as inter-class negotiation, but its impact on the nation/state axis was to create the mechanism whereby the middle class could engage and attempt to solve the social and economic problems of the town and city. As a day-to-day experience, mid-century 'governing' of urban society was carried out within civil society.

This chapter has concerned itself with the ways and means by which the middle class overcame its internal differences under a principle of piety to make the transition, in Marxist language, from a class-in-itself to a class-for-itself. This it did in the first instance by creating a consensus through the common ground of philanthropy in a way that nullified the potential divisions of class, sect and party. The structure of the voluntary organisation was such that it allowed all hierarchical divisions to be played out in the controlled arena of the rules and regulations of what has been termed a subscriber democracy. Secondly, inter-class relations between a hegemonic elite and the various sub-sections of the poor and the working class were also negotiated through the mediating structure of voluntaryism. One of the prime points of contact, and therefore of bargaining between the classes, was the voluntary organis-ation within civil society. Religion, education and charity were all dispensed by voluntary organisations. Self-advancement, literary and philosophical, commercial and social contacts were achieved through a structured, self-administered, public life. It was the very process of inter-class relations and intra-class formation which created the social structure which existed in the 'spaces' left between the household and the state.

In many ways the *Almanac* and the *Directory* have done the work for us by delineating this structure and so easing our ability to identify and to analyse its workings. What the split in this chapter has suggested is that

both the inter- and intra-class bargaining has involved the industry of
some sort of active elite. The status and cultural organisations were
clearly set up and run on what were perhaps fairly small and pedantic
social boundaries, but they were important ones to contemporaries.
Indeed, it is possible that the voluntary activity of the Edinburgh middle
class was run by a social elite who were part of both the high status
cultural societies and equally a part of the general philanthropic
subscriber activity. If, as is argued here, the extent to which civil society
was structured by voluntaryism was great, then it is important to test the
extent to which those who subscribed were in any way different from the
rest of the middle-class population. If the Scottish nation in the mid-
nineteenth century was 'governed' from within, which sections of the
urban middle class were pulling the strings?

CHAPTER FIVE

A Governing Elite: Edinburgh's Subscriber Population

Edinburgh is not only in point of beauty the first of British cities – but, considering its population, the general tone of its society is more intellectual than that of any other. In no other city will you find so general an appreciation of books, art, music and objects of antiquarian interest. It is peculiarly free from the taint of the ledger and the countinghouse. It is a Weimar without a Goethe – Boston without its nasal twang. But it wants variety; it is mainly a city of the professions.[1]

The Edinburgh middle classes were engaged in a whole range of issues, problems and causes of which all were conducted within civil society. Public life became structured by a series of philanthropic and voluntary societies by a class creating its own self-definition. This network of associational activity was the very machinery necessary to deal with almost any social, economic or political issue in the city and without recourse to the parliamentary state. To this end it has been suggested that there existed an 'inner elite' within Edinburgh's middle class which acted as a social, political and cultural vanguard. Their ability to 'govern' was a function of their class formation. The purpose of this chapter is to test the extent to which Edinburgh was an elite-led middle class, one that can be identified as a 'subscriber-class'.

A frequently accepted shorthand definition of the 'middle class' in British towns and cities at this time is: those who held the £10 property franchise entitling them to vote. The occupational distribution of the 7,735 individuals recorded in the Edinburgh pollbook for the 1852 general election, a list updated in 1854 with new enrolments, is employed here to represent Edinburgh's (male) bourgeoisie.[2] This frequency count, coded in terms of the organisation in which the paid employment was located, is reproduced in Figure 5.1, below.

---

[1] A. Smith, *A Summer in Skye* (London, 1865), p. 26.
[2] This pollbook's representativeness of the Edinburgh bourgeoisie was established in comparison with letter cluster samples of local post office and trade directories in Morton, 'Unionist-Nationalism', chap. 4.

Figure 5.1: *Edinburgh pollbook (1852/4): distribution of occupational titles*

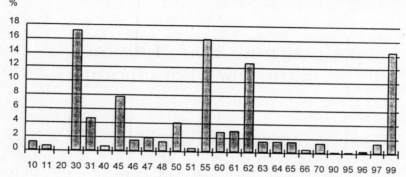

Occupation (coded by 'organisation')

10	Land	60	Professional (general)
11	Gardeners	61	Medical
20	Quarries	62	Legal
30	Distribution & processing	63	Religion
31	Dealers	64	Education
40	Transport	65	Miscellaneous services
45	Commerce	66	Printing & publishing
46	Bankers	70	Construction
47	Agents & travellers	90	Independent income
48	Clerks & bookkeepers	95	National government
50	Manufacturing	96	Local government
51	Managers & employers	97	Defence
55	Craft	99	No occupational title

The three largest groups discerned were 'distribution & processing' (mainly shopkeepers), 'craft' (small manufacturers and traders), and the 'legal profession' (Writers to the Signet, solicitors, etc.). These three occupational categories will structure our analysis of middle-class subscriber activity. To contextualise this, 'unique-name' record linkage was carried out between the 1852/4 pollbook and the seven sub-sections of Oliver and Boyd's 1854 *Edinburgh Almanac*. This produced 4,037 named individuals who were identified in the pollbook as being connected to at least one society or association.[3] By these means it is possible to gauge the level of subscriber activity and the societal power of

---

[3] *Oliver and Boyd's New Edinburgh Almanac and National Repository for the Year 1854* (Edinburgh, 1854); *List of the Electors of the City of Edinburgh, arranged according to their residence, Corrected after Appeal Court 1854, showing the voting at the general election, July 1852* (Edinburgh, 1854); for a detailed explanation of the technicalities of unique name linkage within the methodology of nominal record linkage, as employed in this study, see Morton, 'Unionist-Nationalism', chap. 4.

the Edinburgh middle class as it was channelled through the forms of associational action outlined in the previous chapter.

To develop our theme, this chapter is an attempt to identify the trends of middle-class network association. Obviously this cannot include all associations, and all networks, as such a task would necessitate a different and dedicated research topic. Linkage across the seven subsections of the almanac was precluded, and instead only linkage between the almanac's subsections and the pollbook was carried out. To compensate, and to try to reflect the range of subscriber action, a number of lists of memberships from societies not included in the almanac of 1854 have been included. Even with these additions, the figures presented throughout this chapter can only be underestimates of the level of potential interlinkage. Having said that, by looking at Table 5.1 it can still be seen that the degree of subscriber activity by those who were linked from the almanac to the pollbook was pervasive, and for a select few it was startling:

Table 5.1: *Frequency of appearance in 'public life':*
Edinburgh almanac-pollbook (c.1854)

Appearances	N	Appearances	N
34	1	9	11
24	1	8	20
17	2	7	39
16	1	6	28
15	1	5	63
14	1	4	93
13	3	3	248
12	7	2	689
11	7	1	2,816
10	6	Total	4,037

Over half of the subscribers were active only once, yet even with the imposed limitation to the potential interlinkage, it can be seen that the top end of subscriber activity was prolific, with one individual named thirty-four times.[4] What is clear from the Edinburgh activity count is that

---

[4] It is useful to compare this result with Morris's study of Leeds, where he uses similar techniques. Morris calculated that 86% of the middle-class population could be identified as appearing in three or fewer lists, whereas the corresponding Edinburgh figure was 93%. The top end of Morris's scale is 14, with 28 (4.96%) individuals identified as appearing in six or more lists. In Edinburgh the top of the scale reached 34, and appearance totals were recorded at 24, 17 (twice), 16 and 15. In addition, 128 individuals (3.14%) were identified as appearing in six or more lists. In percentage terms there is little difference between the two studies; the range of multiple associations in Edinburgh is due to the greater number of cases examined: R. J. Morris, 'Petitions, meetings and class formation amongst the urban middle classes in Britain in the 1830s', *Tijdschrift voor Geschiedenis*, cii (1990), pp. 299–301.

certain individuals habitually appeared in a number of lists and there-fore supported a wide range of causes and had a voice throughout Edinburgh's public life. Table 5.2 identifies those who appeared in ten or more lists:

Table 5.2: *The most active subscribers: number of memberships* (≥10)

No.	Name
34	Lord Provost of Edinburgh
24	Duke of Buccleuch and Queensberry, K.G.
17	Rev. D. J. K. Drummond (Episcopalian)
17	William Muir, D.D. (Established, St Stephens)
16	James Grant, D.D. (Established)
15	Lord Murray
14	Rev. Thomas McCrie, D.D.
13	Duke of Argyle
13	Rev. John Hunter, D.D. (Established)
13	Lord Advocate
12	Rev. R. S. Candlish, D.D. (Free Church)
12	Sir Wm Gibson-Craig, Bart.
12	Robert Kaye Greville, LL.D.
12	Lord Panmure
12	Rev. Wm Robertson (Established)
12	Dr George Smyttan, M.D.
12	John W. Tawse, Esq.
11	Marquis of Breadalbane
11	Lieutenant-Colonel George Cadell
11	Dr J. Mathews Duncan, M.D.
11	Sir Adam Hay, Bart.
11	John Scott Moncrieff
11	Alexander Pringle, Esq., VP., MP
10	Sir John Stuart Forbes, Bart
10	R. Grieve
10	Rev. George Johnston
10	Earl of Rosebery, K.T.
10	Right Hon. Lord A. Rutherford
10	Prof. A. Campbell Swinton

At the top end it is obvious that the Lord Provost, as patron, headed many societies because it was a duty of the office. Equally, the duke of Buccleuch's role was predominantly that of figurehead. For both indi-viduals subscription was not necessarily out of choice, but part of their social role, although nevertheless indicative of their potential for influence. The office of Lord Provost in particular was a tangible link between a number of different causes and issues in Edinburgh society. These, then, were positions of patronage, but if one examines the list, six out the next nine names are those of ministers of religion. This activity from the clergy of Edinburgh might be expected for a number of reasons. One is the historical role of the Established Church, and from 1843 the Free Church also, in the national affairs of Scotland. Patronage from the

Church was a necessary form of legitimacy for many campaigning societies. A second reason, as Chapter 4 has demonstrated, was the sheer profusion of religious and missionary societies which reached the far corners of Edinburgh's civil society. Callum Brown is the leading exponent of the argument in favour of the dominance of religiosity in nineteenth-century urban Scotland, and the indications here support this view.[5] Generally, then, the evidence of the almanac is that there existed a small active elite who were involved in most areas of Edinburgh's civil society, although the majority only subscribed once in any one of the subsections.

How are we to understand this activity? Was Edinburgh led by a small, bounded subscriber class, or was the act of subscription a universal one? Are those who used the voluntary society as a means of intervening in their urban world divorced from the rest of Edinburgh society, or were they representative? Our goal is to highlight the political activity and the subscriber activity of the people behind that level of social structure between household and state that is termed 'voluntaryism'. This chapter will analyse the distribution of votes at the 1852 election (broken down by occupation), and this will be compared with the occupational, the political and the financial profile of Edinburgh's active subscribers. In this exercise, we will explore the value of the very idea of a 'subscriber class' to understanding the link between political power and economic and social power. If it is legitimate to identify a self-governing bourgeoisie in Scotland, who were these 'elites' who ran Edinburgh's urban life?

Edinburgh's enfranchised elite: mid-century voting

The political history of reformed Scotland has been covered extensively by Iain Hutchison.[6] It is quite right that for this period his focus, and that of Fry, should be a religious one, because by mid-century Scotland's politics, and Edinburgh's in particular, had become dominated by the issues stemming from the Disruption and the decade of dispute which led up to it. Within this wider debate, the central focus of the post-1843 sectarian divide was education. Attempts by the Free Church of Scotland to constitute itself as an alternative established church were a serious threat to the hegemony which the Church of Scotland had enjoyed since it had been appointed the state's Church, although both were under threat from the Voluntaries' attempts to discredit the very idea.

[5] C. B. Brown, 'Religion, class and church growth', in Fraser and Morris, *People and Society in Scotland*: vol. II, p. 313; C. B. Brown, 'Secularisation: a theory in danger?', *Scottish Economic and Social History*, xi (1991), pp. 52–8.

[6] I. G. C. Hutchison, *A Political History of Scotland, 1832–1914: Parties, Elections and Issues* (Edinburgh, 1986); Fry, *Patronage and Principle*; for a case study of Edinburgh, see J. C. Williams, 'Edinburgh Politics: 1832–1852' (Edinburgh University Ph.D. thesis, 1972).

Religion had split the Liberal vote in Edinburgh mid-century. Macaulay had been defeated in 1847 over the issue of state funding for Maynooth, the Catholic seminary school, and this issue remained at the root of bitter campaigning between the candidates. When Macaulay regained Edinburgh City constituency at the 1852 general election, the announcement produced a noisy reaction:

> I hereby declare that the Right Hon. Thomas Babington Macaulay – (Vehement cheering from Mr Macaulay's friends) – and Charles Cowan, Esq. – (great cheering) – duly elected and returned as members of Parliament for the city of Edinburgh. (Long continued cheering and hissing).[7]

The full result was as follows:

Table 5.3: *Distribution of votes at 1852 general election: Edinburgh City*

Rt Hon. T. B. Macaulay (Liberal)	1872	(27%)
Charles Cowan (Liberal)	1754	(26%)
Lord Provost Duncan McLaren (Liberal)	1559	(23%)
Hon. Thos C. Bruce (Conservative)	1066	(16%)
Alexander Campbell (Liberal-Conservative)	626	(9%)

Source: C. R. Dod, *Electoral Facts from 1832 to 1853: Impartially stated, constituting a complete political gazetteer* (1853), ed. H. J. Hanham (Brighton, 1972), p. 105; *The Scotsman*, 17 Jul. 1852; the latter gives McLaren thirteen votes less at 1,546.

Analysis of this election result tells us a great deal about the Edinburgh bourgeoisie at this time, and it will allow us to contrast the subscriber population. Each voter had two votes, both could have been used – 'split' for separate candidates of different parties, 'straight' for separate candidates of the same party – or only one vote could have been cast (to 'plump' for a single candidate). As the *Caledonian Mercury* explained:

> As to the present contest it may afford an idea of its complication when we state that there are fifteen different courses an elector may pursue, or a sixteenth providing he does not vote at all ... and we should not be surprised if most of them are travelled.[8]

Because each member of the electorate had two votes, any analysis must start with the distribution of 'first' and 'second' votes between the candidates.

---

[7] *The Scotsman*, 14 Jul. 1852.
[8] *Caledonian Mercury*, 12 Jul. 1852.

Table 5.4: *1852/4 Pollbook: percentage distribution of first and second votes*

First Vote		Second Vote	
Cowan	33.1	Macaulay	36.2
McLaren	31.3	Campbell	13.8
Bruce	26.3	Cowan	10.4
Macaulay	9.1	McLaren	6.5
Campbell	0.2	Bruce	0.1
		No second vote	33.1

Note: Percentages derived from the pollbook. Because of minor inaccuracies in the work of the pollbook's transcribers, especially following the book's revision two years after the event, the actual votes totalled in this source is misleading. The most prudent course of action is therefore to speak only of the percentage distribution.

Table 5.5: *1852/4 Pollbook: cross tabulation: First vote by second vote*

	V O T E 2						Row
Row %							Row
Col. %							total %
	Macaulay	Cowan	McLaren	Bruce	Campbell	No Vote	
V *Macaulay*		0.9	0.3	0.6	7.6	90.5	
		0.8	0.4	50.0	5.1	5.6	9.1
O *Cowan*	38.7		16.9	0.1	34.2	10.0	
	35.4		86.3	25.0	82.4	10.0	33.1
T *McLaren*	61.3	0.2		0.1	3.9	34.6	
	53.1	0.5		25.0	8.9	32.7	31.3
E *Bruce*	15.9	38.7	3.3		1.9	40.3	
	11.5	98.4	13.2		3.6	31.8	26.3
1 *Campbell*						100.0	
						0.5	0.2
Col. total %	36.2	10.4	6.5	0.1	13.8	33.1	100.0

By concentrating on the distribution shown in Table 5.4, the obvious point to be made is how few first votes Macaulay received in contrast to his gain of second votes. If only first votes had counted Macaulay would have been well beaten into fourth place instead of securing election. This was despite 90.5% of his first voters plumping (Table 5.5). He won – it was argued – because he received the so called second votes of those who gave their first vote to the other main candidates: 15.9% of those who gave Bruce their first vote gave their second to Macaulay, 38.7% of

Cowan's first voters did the same, and, whereas a third of McLaren's voters plumped, nearly two-thirds supported Macaulay (with no other candidate entertained).

Figure 5.2: *Aggressive opposition to McLaren at the 1852 general election in Edinburgh*[9]

THE DRAPER'S DIRECTORY.

Who was most active in ousting Mr Macaulay in 1847 ?	SNAKE the DRAPER.
Who prostrates himself before the image of Macaulay in 1852, and implores the help of Macaulay's friends ?	SNAKE the DRAPER.
Who thought to win by advising the electors to disfranchise themselves by plumping for himself ?	SNAKE the DRAPER.
Who made the City of Edinburgh Bankrupt ?	SNAKE the DRAPER.
Who, after doing the City Creditors out of Five Shillings in the Pound, said he had two Imposts that he could remit, yielding £3000 a-year ?	SNAKE the DRAPER.
Who spoiled the Oyster beds ?	SNAKE the DRAPER.
Who can tell what has become of Dons Close ?	SNAKE the DRAPER.
Who lost the Annuity Tax Bill ?	SNAKE the DRAPER.
Who forgot that (his friend of 1847) Mr Cowan was an active promoter of that Bill ?	SNAKE the DRAPER.
Who has a "better memory for facts" than any three men in Scotland ?	SNAKE the DRAPER
Who must have a large majority of the 6000 electors of Edinburgh before he condescends to represent them ?	SNAKE the DRAPER.
Who cuts down the Salaries of all Public Officers whenever a vacancy takes place ?--then adds and ekes if one of his own toadies be appointed ?	SNAKE the DRAPER.
Who made Money by the Exchange Bank ?	SNAKE the DRAPER.

VOTE FOR SNAKE THE DRAPER!!!

McLaren badly misjudged his campaign. He had expected Macaulay's supporters to reciprocate in an exchange of second votes for an 'agreed' Macaulay–McLaren ticket: 'Mr Macaulay got a great many votes of my friends ... but I received very small support from them', McLaren claimed at the declaration of the poll.[10] The Lord Provost also blamed his defeat on the Conservatives giving their spilt vote to Cowan, despite Bruce having denied that such a coalition 'whether formal or tacit'

9 Edinburgh Public Library: Edinburgh election, 1852, press cuttings, etc. (fYJS 4248.852, D35245).
10 *The Scotsman*, 17 Jul. 1852. Table 5.5 shows that only 0.3% of those giving Macaulay their first vote gave their second to McLaren.

existed.[11] Of the Conservative splits from Bruce, 38.7% went to Cowan, 15.9% to Macaulay and only 3.3% and 1.9%, respectively, to McLaren and Campbell. For the Liberal Charles Cowan virtually all his second votes came this way. McLaren therefore argued that it was he, ignoring the splits of the Conservatives, who received the largest share of the Liberal vote, claiming that even the Free Church *Witness* said that he won the Liberal vote over Cowan by two to one.[12] Because 16.9% of Cowan's supporters split with McLaren, making 86.3% of McLaren's second vote, and that this was not reciprocated, to an extent the figures support McLaren's assertion that he did receive a significantly greater proportion of the Liberal vote than his rival.

Table 5.6: *1852 general election: Edinburgh poll at each hour*

Name	9 o'clock	10 o'clock	11 o'clock	12 o'clock	1 o'clock	2 o'clock	3 o'clock	4 o'clock
Macaulay	365	687	1,014	1,275	1,494	1,624	1,769	1,872
McLaren	315	613	894	1,110	1,274	1,377	1,482	1,546
Cowan	319	587	839	1,090	1,279	1,459	1,628	1,754
Bruce	352	513	672	793	876	954	1,015	1,066
Campbell	171	292	415	497	540	575	603	626
Total	1,522	2,692	3,834	4,765	5,463	5,989	6,497	6,864

Source: *The Scotsman*, 14 Jul. 1852.

It was McLaren's anger at being so well supported amongst the Liberal voters than his rivals yet still failing to be elected which prompted him, under his guise of the Lord Provost's Committee, to take what *The Scotsman* described as 'a course unusual in England and unprecedented in Scotland of publishing in full the Pollbooks from the late contest for the representation of the city'.[13] Through this action he hoped to discredit Cowan and to resurrect his own reputation. He had wanted to prove the 'conspiracy' which was apparent on the day of the count whereby Conservative support for Cowan, 'deliberately' to hinder his own election, 'appeared at a late hour' (see Table 5.6, above).[14]

The Scotsman's review of the pollbook stated that 'it told us what we already knew', that Cowan was successful above McLaren because of the help of the Tories. It also mentioned the ecclesiastical support from

[11] *Edinburgh Advertiser*, 6 Jul. 1852.
[12] *The Scotsman*, 17 Jul. 1852.
[13] Ibid., 4 Aug. 1852.
[14] Ibid., 14 Jul. 1852.

which Cowan benefited. Cowan was 'helped' by 491 splits with Campbell, a second Free Church adherent. The newspaper, however, is wrong to say Cowan received help in this way. Campbell received only a handful of his 626 votes from first voters. The votes he received were thus, by the definitions so far used, the second vote of supporters of other candidates. In fact it should of course be argued the other way round: that 34.2% of *Cowan's supporters* gave their second vote to Campbell (making up the vast majority of his total vote). The only way the ecclesiastical issue could have benefited Cowan was that his supporters did not use their second vote to help a serious rival candidate.[15]

This point reveals a certain tension which runs throughout the results. The convention of analysis by means of 'first' and 'second' votes suggests the first vote is the more important one; that the 'second' is what is termed today a 'floating vote'. Such an assumption was behind McLaren's belief in the Macaulay–McLaren ticket, yet, as we have seen, he completely misjudged the electorate.

> It is plain that of none but a very few of the electors voting for Mr Macaulay and the Lord Provost, can any man tell which of the two candidates they regard with the greatest favour – whether this or that elector derived as the chief object the return of the Lord Provost and gave his second vote to Mr Macaulay as the second best or vice versa; and it is probable that the Lord Provost's mistake arises from too rash an assumption on this point.[16]

Because the votes were cast together, and because voters might see their candidates as of equal preference, a perhaps more meaningful analysis is of candidate 'pairs', of first and second votes being regarded as a continuous act, examined in an identical manner to plumpers. Indeed the whole reason for casting a second vote, if not to challenge an opponent tactically, is to make at the very least an equal choice. By treating the candidate pairs as a single entity, as one would with a plumper, greater flexibility is achieved in the analysis of the election result.[17] In particular, it makes it methodologically possible to bring in occupation as a profound explanatory variable in the analysis.

---

[15] Although, one could just have easily have argued that Cowan's supporters could have plumped rather than give a second vote to an outside candidate – the influence on the final placings would have been the same.

[16] *The Scotsman*, 4 Aug. 1852.

[17] Hutchison, *Political History of Scotland*, p. 69, based on the figures of *The Approaching General Election, being the past and present state of the various political parties in Edinburgh and the possible result of the Election* (Edinburgh, 1866), p. 29, is the authoritative guide to this election, yet it is one based entirely on the split between first and second votes. Indeed, the contemporary analysis conflates from whom the second vote was split.

By shifting the focus in this way, the most popular pairs of candidates amongst all classes of voters, in terms of share of the vote, were as follows:

Macaulay/McLaren: 19%
Macaulay/Cowan: 13%
Cowan/Campbell: 11.3%
Cowan/Bruce: 10.2%.

The importance of this form of analysis is that these pairs were more popular, or at least as popular, as any single plumper. In their own right McLaren (10.8%) and Bruce (10.6%) received the biggest share of the vote (that is, their respective plumpers as a percentage of the votes cast), while Macaulay received 8.2%, Cowan 3.3% and Campbell 0.2%. By comparing pairs with plumped candidates we see that McLaren failed as a compromise candidate. The *Caledonian Mercury* had predicted on the eve of the poll that Macaulay's return was straightforward, and that the 'strain of the contest will lie between the Lord Provost and Mr Cowan'.[18] And so our concern is why McLaren failed to be picked up as a 'pair choice' by the electorate. The McLaren/Bruce pair gained less than 1% of the vote, while McLaren/Campbell faired little better. To explain this election we must discover why McLaren did so badly in comparison with his rival Cowan as a pair choice with either Bruce or Campbell, and also examine that pivotal pairing of Macaulay/McLaren. The method used was to focus on the numerically largest occupational groups and compare them against the norm for the total voting population, to discover who were especially prominent or not in their support for Lord Provost Duncan McLaren.

As we have seen, the three largest occupational groups classified in the pollbook were 'distribution & processing', 'craft' and the 'legal profession'. Table 5.7 below details the distribution of votes for paired and single candidates by these three groups. The first feature to note from Table 5.7 is that the legal vote contained the strongest Tory support (Bruce) amongst the three largest occupational groupings:

29.9% plumped for Bruce (compared to 10.6% for the population as a whole).[19]
14.5% (10.2%) chose the Cowan/Bruce pair.
0.8% (0.9%) chose McLaren/Bruce.

---

[18] *Caledonian Mercury*, 12 Jul. 1852.
[19] The figures given in parentheses refer to the voting population as a whole (as presented in Table 5.7).

Table 5.7: *Selected occupations by vote: candidate pairs and plumpers*

	Votes Cast for each Candidate or Pair (%)															
	M C	M Mcl	M B	M Ca	M	C Mcl	C B	C Ca	C	Mcl B	Mcl Ca	Mcl	B Ca	B	Ca	Total votes
Law	17.9	5.5	5.3	0.4	14	0.8	14.5	5.9	2.9	0.8	0.4	1.3	0.2	29.9	0	13.2% N=475
Distribution & processing	12.2	26.4	4.3	1.1	5.1	9.3	7	11.1	3.9	1.1	1.4	15.5	0.5	1.1	0.2	18% N=647
Craft	11.9	26	2.7	0.5	4.9	6.1	6.9	10.8	4.1	1.9	2	18.2	0.9	3.3	0	17.8% N=639
Pollbook voting population	13	19	4.2	0.7	8.2	5.6	10.2	11.3	3.3	0.9	1.2	10.8	0.5	10.6	0.2	100% N=3597

Note: M = Macaulay; C = Cowan; Mcl = McLaren; B = Bruce; Ca = Campbell. The exclusion of 'non-voters' (i.e. those newly enrolled and listed when the pollbook was updated in 1854), accounts for the difference in the occupational distribution of these three groups. The overall spread in the pollbook was Legal (12.8%); 'distribution & processing' (17.3%); 'craft' (16.2%).

At the same time, the legal vote was also strongly Liberal, with much support for Macaulay and for Cowan, although not for McLaren. While 17.9% (13%) chose the Liberal pairing of Macaulay/Cowan and 14% (8.2%) plumped for Macaulay, significantly only 5.5% voted for the pair Macaulay/McLaren (otherwise the most popular pairing for the population as a whole at 19%). Moreover, only 1.3% (10.8%) of the legal profession plumped for McLaren and only 0.8% (5.6%) chose McLaren/Cowan. It can thus be seen that within the legal profession both its Liberal and its Tory wings voted against McLaren. So the acceptance by Hutchison and Anon (1866) of McLaren's laying of the blame for his failure solely at the feet of the Tory splits, fails as an adequate explanation of the result.[20] Instead, occupation, as a controlled variable, has now been shown to influence the distribution of first and second votes. This is particularly relevant to explaining why the Liberal straights of Macaulay and McLaren failed as a pair choice.

This anti-McLaren preference within the legal profession was in contrast to the two largest voting blocs which each showed a consistent preference for Edinburgh's Lord Provost. 'Distribution & processing', with 18% of all occupational titles, voted:

McLaren: 15.5% (10.8%)
Macaulay/McLaren: 26.4% (19%)
McLaren/Cowan: 9.3% (5.6%).

[20] Hutchison, *Political History of Scotland*, p. 68; *Approaching General Election*, pp. 26–33.

The radical leanings of the Edinburgh shopkeepers was perhaps a factor here.[21] McLaren was quite clearly the most popular choice, both as a plumper and as a pair, for this occupational group. The 'craft' sector, with 17.8% of all titles, mirrored this support for McLaren, while avoiding involvement in Conservative splits with Cowan:

McLaren: 18.2% (10.8%)
Macaulay/McLaren: 26% (19%)
McLaren/Cowan: 6.1% (5.6%)
Bruce: 3.3% (10.6%)
Cowan/Bruce: 6.9% (10.2%).

The election result was strongly determined by the voting of these three occupational groups, for, combined, they represented nearly half of all votes cast. It can be seen that the 'legal' bloc was split between Tory and Liberal: either plumping for Bruce and the Cowan/Bruce pair, or supporting Macaulay and the Macaulay/Cowan pair. The 'craft' and the 'distribution & processing' sectors preferred McLaren as the Liberal, were happy with Macaulay/Cowan, but were anti-Bruce and anti-Cowan/Bruce. Both these latter voting blocs voted in a similar way, but their combined 36% of the poll was, to all intents and purposes, counteracted by the 13% polled by the 'legal' sector. The homogeneity of the respective wings of the 'legal' vote was enough to restrict McLaren's gains from the lower socio-economic groups, especially considering that he lost out to Charles Cowan by a mere 195 votes. It was the sheer unpopularity of McLaren within the legal profession, both as a candidate to plump for and as a pair candidate with Macaulay, which produced the decisive figures in McLaren's narrow defeat.

The middle class and the subscriber class: one and the same?

Did the subscriber class reflect this psephological profile in the middle of the century? Or were the voluntaryists a distinct breed whose vote and choice of subscription were symbiotically fused? By bringing occupation into the analysis of the vote distribution we can link directly into Edinburgh's voluntary activity to test the hypotheses that the subscriber class acted as a unique elite or that they were a mirror image of the bourgeoisie.

Our route will be an occupational analysis, a political analysis, and an analysis of the amount of money subscribed. Taking each in turn will reveal the characteristics of Edinburgh's 'subscriber class' and will highlight the everyday experience of an urban 'governing' class. The

---

[21] Gray, *Labour Aristocracy in Victorian Edinburgh*, would agree, although the opposite conclusion is reached for later in the century in D. McCrone and B. Elliott, *Property and Power in a City: The Sociological Significance of Landlordism* (Basingstoke, 1989).

first task, then, is to explore whether there was an occupational difference between the associations.

Unsurprisingly it is no great presumption to suggest that the subscriber activity of the Edinburgh middle class was divided on status and intra-class grounds. It has already been noted in the previous chapter that certain associations and certain subscriptions were more 'exclusive' than others. Some of the debating societies, for instance, were shown to be premised upon a strictly vetted membership, as indeed was the Select Subscription Library, with its battle to balance the books while maintaining a limited personnel. The aim of this section is to explain in more detail the occupational profile of these groupings and to establish the parameters of Edinburgh's bourgeois civil society. Two contrasting examples of these outer limits are the subscription to the Edinburgh Apprentice School and the members of the Edinburgh New Club.

The objective of the Apprentice School Association was 'to institute and superintend Evening Schools, in different locations in Edinburgh and Leith, for the purpose of affording to Shopmen, Workmen, Apprentices, etc., the means of acquiring a solid education'.[22] This was not an unusual association and similar ones with identical objectives existed throughout Britain. It is also not untypical in the sense that it was what can be termed a 'low subscription' association. It did not solicit, nor did it receive, relatively large amounts of money. A subscription of only 5s. was enough to gain 'entitlement to attend and engage in the business of the General Meetings'. Figure 5.3 below compares the average subscription of each occupational category with the overall average for the year 1848. To allow the computer to handle pounds, shillings and pence – with 20 shillings to the pound and 12 pence to the shilling – all monetary values are expressed in terms of 'decimalised' shillings. Thus an example of a subscription of 2 shillings and 6 pence was converted to 2.5 shillings and so forth. To smooth the discussion of the results presented in the tables it has been decided to refer to decimalised shillings at all times.[23]

[22] *Apprentice Schools: Third Annual Report of the Association for Promoting Education among Workmen, Apprentices, etc.* (Edinburgh, 1848); *Apprentice Schools: Plea for Education* (Edinburgh, 1849).

[23] A simple conversion rubric is offered in Appendix 3 for those still uneasy with 'decimalised currency'.

Figure 5.3: *Apprentice school, 1848. Average subscription by occupational category (expressed in decimalised shillings)*

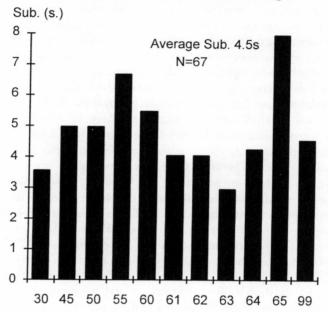

30	Distribution & processing	62	Legal
45	Commerce	63	Religion
50	Manufacturing	64	Education
55	Craft	65	Miscellaneous services
60	Professional	99	No occupational title
61	Medical		

Note: See Appendix 5 for explanation of achieved linkage.

Out of the 183 subscribers for 1848, only 67 were linked successfully to the pollbook. In part, the four-year time difference between the two sources explains some of the gap, but overwhelmingly the cause of so many failed linkages is the low status of the Apprentice School subscribers. Simply put, many of its subscribers were not franchised and would not then appear in the pollbook. The Apprentice School did have the Lord Provost as its honorary president, and, like many associations, it invited ministers from a range of religious denominations to be extraordinary directors so as to encourage 'much variation in religion of those enrolled'. However, with 473 pupils enrolled for 1848 and only 183 subscribers that year providing an average subscription of 4.46s., it is unsurprising that the society reported an increase in its debts. It was very reliant on appeals for help to the merchants and tradesmen of Edinburgh, and it can be seen that the legal profession paid in below the average (although the small numbers involved makes discussion of the occupational categories very tentative). This indeed was a low subscription society and therefore marginal to middle-class concerns.

A different type of society was the New Club, a very exclusive social club. It was instituted in 1787, and although there is no actual record of how the club originated, its fore-runner was the Poker Club of 1762.[24] From the analysis carried out its membership, only 90 out of the 774 who subscribed in 1847 were successfully linked. Of those linked just under half were classified as having no vote and just under one third had no occupational title, showing the gap between this club and the pollbook population.[25] The New Club was a society for the county elite of Lothian, its urban membership was always less important. Its members were admitted by a ballot held on the second Wednesday in the months of January through to June. The proposer and seconder of any new additions had already to be members of the club, must personally know the applicant, and to be successful over thirty voters must be in favour, with more than one black ball in ten leading to rejection.[26] The membership was increased only to alleviate debt – as in 1852, when an additional fifty members arrived following the failure the previous year to raise money by reducing the costs of the servants' board and selling the contents of the wine cellar.[27] The New Club tried to model itself (in particular its coffee room and its dinners), on the best London clubs. It had an appeal to those serving abroad, the East India Company or those in the forces. To attract specifically this type of member the 'Supernumerary List' was expanded in 1851 to which 'a very large number of members who were absent from the United Kingdom availed themselves'.[28] The focus of the New Club's membership was not Edinburgh's citizens, but was instead a club for those of eminent status when 'in town'. Most of its members, therefore, lacked the municipal franchise and were not part of the urban bourgeoisie.

---

24 *The New Club, Edinburgh, from its foundations in 1787* (Edinburgh, 1900), p. 17; H. A. Cockburn, *A History of the New Club, Edinburgh, 1787–1939* (Edinburgh, 1938), p. 15.

25 *Alphabetical List of the Members of the New Club corrected to 30th April 1923* (Edinburgh, 1923).

26 *Rules and Regulations of the New Club, Edinburgh* (Edinburgh, 1847).

27 Ibid., p. 41.

28 Cockburn, *History of the New Club*, p. 88; *Rules of the New Club, Princes Street, Edinburgh* (Edinburgh, 1923), p. 15.

In both cases, for different reasons, the New Club and the Apprentice School Association were not essential to middle-class subscription activity. On the one hand, the Apprentice Schools, although with no little eminent patronage, lacked the appeal to attract great financial support from the middle classes – it was indeed a low subscription society. On the other hand there was the New Club, which was a prime focus of networking – so vital to the construction of status – but was largely irrelevant to bourgeois concerns. For the Edinburgh middle class there was the Royal Institution and its off-shoots, the Royal Society Club, the Royal Society New Club and the Royal Society Supper Club, which acted as foci for contact making.[29] Both these societies, then, were in some ways tangential to middle-class civil society, but together they serve the purpose of setting the outer boundaries of this action. The Apprentice School was an example of the lower limits of respectable middle-class subscriber action, while the New Club represented the outer limits of middle-class associations.

The subscriber class: mainstream activity

The issue now is how in terms of occupation, the mainstream middle-class societies should be characterised. How should the societies in which the middle class were especially involved, and which were central to their administration of mid-century society, be defined? The first feature of this mainstream subscription activity was the society that replicated the occupational profile of the middle class: the society that transcended occupational interest. Such a society was the Total Abstinence Society, and it can be seen from Figure 5.4, below, that its occupational profile for the year 1853 was, in percentage terms, fairly close to that of the pollbook.[30]

The Total Abstinence Society was successful in its appeal to all sections of the middle class, and this was reflected in the occupational distribution of its membership. Its share of the big three occupational groups was consistent, if slightly over-represented, as Table 5.8, following and emphasising Figure 5.4 below, shows:

[29] D. Guthrie, *A Short History of the Royal Society Club of Edinburgh, 1820–1962, Published privately by the Royal Society Club* (Edinburgh, 1962); S. Devlin-Thorp (ed.), *Scotland's Cultural Heritage*, vol. I: *One hundred medical and scientific fellows of the Royal Society of Edinburgh, elected from 1783–1832* (Edinburgh, 1981); vol. II: *100 Literary Fellows, 1783–1812* (Edinburgh, 1981); vol. III: *100 Medical Fellows, 1783–1844* (Edinburgh, 1982); A. Boyle, *et al.* (ed.), *Scotland's Cultural Heritage*, vol. IV: *100 Medical Fellows, 1841–1882* (Edinburgh, 1983); A. Boyle (ed.) *Scotland's Cultural Heritage*, vol. V: *The Royal Society of Edinburgh: Scientific and Engineering Fellows, elected 1784–1876* (Edinburgh, 1983).

[30] *Seventeenth Annual Report of Edinburgh Total Abstinence Society.*

Figure 5.4: *Edinburgh pollbook and Total Abstinence Society: distribution of occupational titles*

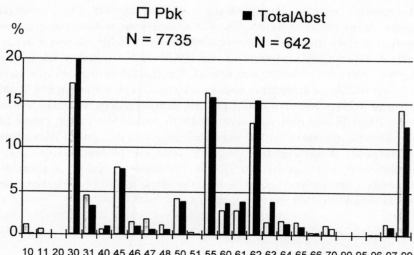

10	Land	60	Professional (general)
11	Gardeners	61	Medical
20	Quarries	62	Legal
30	Distribution & processing	63	Religion
31	Dealers	64	Education
40	Transport	65	Miscellaneous services
45	Commerce	66	Printing & publishing
46	Bankers	70	Construction
47	Agents & travellers	90	Independent income
48	Clerks & bookkeepers	95	National government
50	Manufacturing	96	Local government
51	Managers & employers	97	Defence
55	Craft	99	No occupational title

Note: See Appendix 5 for explanation of achieved linkage.

Table 5.8: *Total Abstinence Society: largest occupation groups*

Occupational title coded by 'organisation'	Code	Tot. Abst. %	Pollbook %
Distribution & processing	30	19.94	17.30
Craft	55	15.73	16.20
Legal	62	15.42	12.76

The second feature of mainstream activity is that certain occupational groups dominated specific voluntary organisations, sometimes for particular sectional concerns, sometimes not. The latter was especially the case when we note the general over-representation of the Edinburgh lawyers. If we examine three charitable causes (which are in no way unusual in this instance), Female Delinquency,[31] the Society for the Indigent and Industrious Blind,[32] and the Ragged or Industrial School Society,[33] then the over-representation of the legal profession amongst the ranks of the subscribers is apparent. In all three instances, the legal profession is counted at or above 26% of all subscribers, a figure double that of the pollbook population in general, and it reached a figure of over 35% in the case of the Relief of the Indigent and Industrious Blind.[34]

These three societies have no particular reason to be dominated by the Edinburgh lawyers. Unlike the debating societies described in Chapter 4 where, as it were, the legal profession was at play, the three societies here were occupationally 'neutral'. There was no professional incentive for the high representation of any occupational category, let alone the lawyers and their kind. The reason for this over-representation is the social role, self defined, that the Edinburgh law community had created for itself. As an occupational group, the legal profession used such subscriber activity to rise to the forefront of class consciousness. Time and time again, analysis of the subscriber activity of the Edinburgh middle class throws up a body of legal men (and their wives, mothers and daughters) who composed the bulk of the most active subscriber population. They may have been led by the ministers and aristocracy as presidents and patrons, but in most cases the rank-and-file was drawn from the legal profession.

Of course, the legal profession did not dominate every society. 'Distribution & processing' and 'craft' tended not to be over-represented within the occupationally 'neutral' societies, such as the three societies displayed in Figure 5.5, but they remain important foci of analysis. One particular society where occupational interest was uppermost was the Scottish Trade Protection Society, formed in 1853, and which had as its aim: 'to protect the honest trader from the fraudulent efforts of those who went about "seeking whom they might devour"'.[35] This society forged information links between Scotland and England so as to aid

---

[31] *Report of the Dean Bank and Boroughmuirhead Institution for the Reformation of Juvenile Female Delinquents* (Edinburgh, 1857).

[32] *Edinburgh Society for the Relief of the Indigent and Industrious Blind, 1856–57*, 'Town Subscriptions' (Edinburgh, 1858).

[33] *Eleventh Annual Report of the Edinburgh Original Ragged Industrial Schools, Ramsay Lane, Castle Hill, for the year ending 31st December 1857* (Edinburgh, 1858).

[34] Note that in all instances N refers to the number of subscribers successfully linked to the 1852/4 pollbook (the 'base').

[35] *General Meeting of the Scottish Trade Protection Society* (n.p., 1854).

security of traders in cross-border transactions of goods, and especially of credit. In its first year of operation the society had a membership of 180; by February 1854 its roll stood at 760. In that year, it distributed to its members a document which contained entries for 1,500 companies with a synopsis of credit worthiness in each case. Also distributed was a 'legal proceedings book', from which one trader could find out about another 'if a judgement had been got; if the debt had been paid promptly or in instalments, or paid at all; and whether the party had been prosecuted once, twice or thrice'.[36] It was claimed that, with this information, for the guinea a member invested in joining the society, he might expect to save £50.

Figure 5.5: *Occupational frequency of selected voluntary organisations*

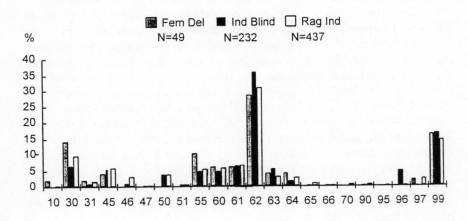

10	Land	62	Legal
30	Distribution & processing	63	Religion
31	Dealers	64	Education
45	Commerce	65	Miscellaneous services
46	Bankers	66	Printing & publishing
47	Agents & travellers	70	Construction
50	Manufacturing	90	Independent income
51	Managers & employers	95	National government
55	Craft	96	Local government
60	Professional (general)	97	Defence
61	Medical	99	No occupational title

Note: See Appendix 5 for explanation of achieved linkage.

[36] Ibid., p. 3.

Buchan's statue to Sir William Wallace at Dryburgh, completed in 1814.

Inscription on Buchan's Wallace statue at Dryburgh.

The statue to Bruce at Stirling Castle, with the National Wallace Monument in the distance.

Eglinton Castle, Kilwinning. The earl of Eglinton held his famous tournament here in 1839, and he was to become the first chairman of the National Association for the Vindication of Scottish Rights.

The Barnweil Tower in the Barony of Craigie, Ayrshire. The monument was initiated by Robert Park and completed in 1855 to a design by Robert Snodgrass.

Wallace's Tower in Ayr. The name most likely comes from the Wallaces of Craigie rather than from the patriot, but a statue (1833) by the sculptor James Thom was added to signify where Wallace may have been imprisoned.

The legs of this Wallace statue in Ayr (1819) were shortened to fit into the niche of the building.

Aberdeen's statue to Wallace was completed in 1888 with £3,000 left by Edinburgh's John Steill, a strong critic of the aristocracy's exploitation of the Wallace memory.

This society, in 1858, was very much a concern of 'distribution & processing' (32.5%), 'craft' (19.4%), 'commerce' (17.8%) and 'manufacturing' (9.3%).[37] This was occupational interest dominating, but it does demonstrate the willingness and the ability of different sections of the Victorian middle class to instigate the means of safeguarding their own class interest. The society acted as a control mechanism on the commercial life of Edinburgh. It was a regulator of trading activities. Thus a link can be postulated between credit worthiness and social acceptance within Edinburgh's 'inner-circles'. It was part of a process whereby social power within Edinburgh's civil society was 'managed' through the regulatory mechanisms of certain societies and associations. The hierarchies of influence which structured the public life of Edinburgh can be seen to have had their day-to-day influence in the membership content between associations as well as the membership arrangements within associations (Chapter 4).

The politics and economy of subscribing: between the societies

With the existence of such a range of societies, and the tendency for a hard core of individuals to be active within an important number of this range, the task of identifying the direction of 'cause and effect' in the actions of the subscriber population is made a difficult one. Taking on board the occupational analysis above, it is possible to discern certain themes which are important to understanding the functioning of Edinburgh's civil society mid-century. The first is that it is possible to determine the relative effect of the act of subscription on the voting choice of the Edinburgh middle class; the second is that the pattern of subscription was a distinct one, and that it indicates an identifiable 'membership culture'.

(a) The money givers and voting pair choice
Analysis was done by cross-tabulating occupation by monetary subscription or occupation by voting pair choice. In the graphs the results are often given in terms of 'residuals'. The 'residual' value is the difference between the 'expected' value and the 'observed' value for each cross-tabulation. The 'expected' value is that which would be produced from a proportionate distribution of values in line with the occupational distribution. The difference in the observed vote from that expected is the residual.

In Chapter 4 it was noted that the Philosophical Institute was a prime example of a middle-class 'status' association at this time. The distribution of its major occupational groups can be identified as 'legal'

---

[37] *List of Members of the Scottish Trade Protection Society* (Edinburgh, 1858).

at 15%, 'craft' at 7.8%, 'distribution & processing' at 8% with the addition of those coded 'commerce' amounting to around 6% of the subscribers.[38] To uncover its political proclivities, Figure 5.6 shows the relationship between the largest occupational groups and the largest difference in voting pair choices of its subscribers.

Figure 5.6: *Selected occupations by voting pair: major differences in residuals*

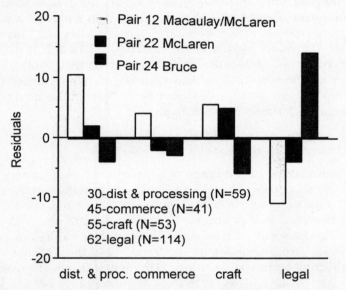

The Philosophical Institute had a solid legal support, and in its voting choice the institute produces residuals of up to ±10 and more; indeed, there is a definite opposition in the choice of Macaulay/McLaren as a candidate pair between the legal profession and the other occupational groups, particularly 'distribution & processing'. As previously shown, Macaulay/McLaren was the most popular pair choice with 19% of the vote. (In that election McLaren and Bruce both received just under 11% of the total vote from their respective plumpers.) The contrast within the Philosophical Institution subscribers between the legal profession and the rest is apparent in the other voting choices, especially that of the Conservative, Bruce, where a residual of +13 was recorded. This conforms with the pollbook population at the general election where between two and three times as many legal voters plumped for Bruce compared to the overall electorate (see Table 5.7).

---

[38] *Roll of Members of the Philosophical Institution, Edinburgh, 10th February 1857* (Edinburgh, 1857).

The Philosophical Institute's legal membership at 15% was only marginally more than the expected 13% – so no great difference there. 'Distribution & processing' and 'craft' were under-represented within the Institute, but it was a high-status organisation and most of these two occupational groups would be more likely to appear in, for example, the Mechanics' Institute. In this instance it can be said that membership of the Philosophical Institute did not overcome the definite opposition between legal and the other two main occupational groups, but it did homogenise the Conservative vote of the Edinburgh lawyers.

Figure 5.7: *Total Abstinence Society and pollbook: 'Distribution & processing' by voting pairs*

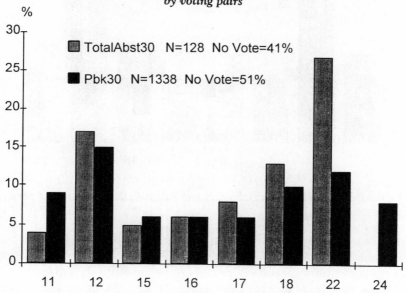

To take another example, the Total Abstinence Society, Figures 5.7 to 5.9 present the output from a cross tabulation between occupation and most popular voting pairs for the three dominant occupational groups, in comparison with the pollbook.[39] The identifying codes for the 'voting pairs' are presented below (and are reproduced in Appendix 4).

Table 5.9: *Coded voting pairs: 1852 general election*

11	Macaulay	Cowan	17	Cowan	Bruce
12	Macaulay	McLaren	18	Cowan	Campbell
15	Macaulay		22	McLaren	
16	Cowan	McLaren	24	Bruce	

[39] *Seventeenth Annual Report of Edinburgh Total Abstinence Society.*

Figure 5.8: *Total Abstinance Society and pollbook: 'Craft' by voting pairs*

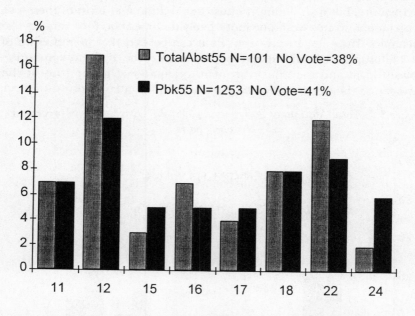

Figure 5.9: *Total Abstinance Society and pollbook: 'Legal' by voting pairs*

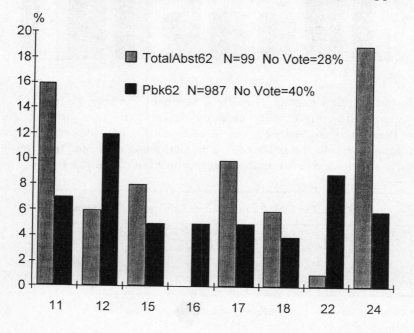

Two trends are most apparent from this comparison. The first is the large numbers of subscribers within, especially, 'distribution & processing', but also 'craft', who plumped for McLaren (code 22) in contrast to their colleagues in the pollbook population. This was to be expected. McLaren was in business as a draper, and he was therefore seen as the representative of small retailers – the very people coded 'distribution & processing'. McLaren was also a champion of the temperance move-ment. The point has been made in the previous chapter that it was McLaren, as Lord Provost, whose licensing controls introduced in Edinburgh were the forerunner of the Public House (Forbes Mackenzie) Act of 1853. Here sectional interest – total abstinence – was working in conjunction with occupational interest to reinforce the choice of McLaren as a plumper (a point re-iterated in Figure 5.11 which records a residual of +15 from this group in favour of McLaren and a slightly higher preference for the Macaulay/McLaren pairing also – Figure 5.10).

Figure 5.10: *Total Abstinance Society: residuals for Macaulay/McLaren (12)*

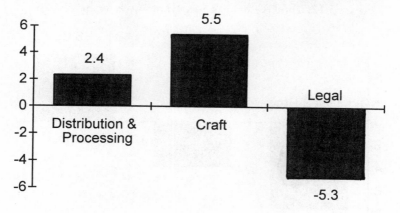

In contrast, the legal subscribers tended to be put off by McLaren's teetotalling crusade. Note that the legal subsection of subscribers were slightly more likely to have plumped for the Tory candidate Bruce (a residual of +5.9, Figure 5.12) than non-subscribers within the profession, and the Macaulay/Cowan pairing was also popular (Figure 5.9, coded 11). It appears their Total Abstinence subscribers have a greater preference for all the other main candidate pair choices. Legal's variance from 'distribution & processing' and 'craft' is clear when the residuals are highlighted, and it shows a general hostility to McLaren. For the legal subscribers it remained occupational identification – and class interest – which were stronger than sectional identification.

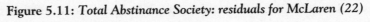

Figure 5.11: *Total Abstinance Society: residuals for McLaren (22)*

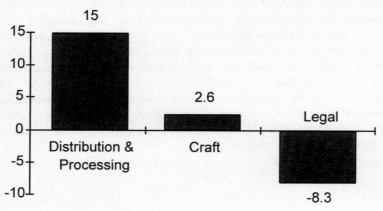

Figure 5.12: *Total Abstinance Society: residuals for Bruce (24)*

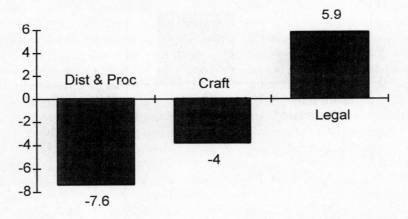

From these two case studies a contrasting picture is painted. For the Philosophical Institute subscription did not influence voting patterns, although it did solidify Conservative support. Arguably it was the under-representation amongst its membership of the lower socio-economic classes which give this society a legal-Tory tinge, but not enough to influence the election. In contrast, subscribers to the Total Abstinence Society were split between those voting in terms of its sectional interest, and those who favoured their class. The legal profession resisted, but for 'distribution & processing', membership of the Total Abstinence Society did tend to emphasise their preference for McLaren at the ballot box.

The subscriber population was therefore mixed in its variations from the general pollbook population. The best guess would be that 'campaigning' societies had a much greater influence on voting preference than social/status societies.[40] Our conclusion must be that the match between the subscriber class and the pollbook population is extremely close, and also that the subscriber class was, politically speaking, well in line with the aims and aspirations of the Edinburgh bourgeoisie as a whole.

To complete this line of investigation, the focus now is upon the amount subscribed; the question again is whether or not significant occupational differences were apparent amongst the subscriber population.

(b) The money givers: who subscribed what?

In between the boundaries of the Apprentice School and the New Club were a number of societies which were of relatively high status, of high subscription, and central to the philanthropic activities of the middle class in Edinburgh. Such societies, and such appeals, often involved the cause being built up into national importance. Appeals such as the Sick Children's Hospital in 1859,[41] or the Royal Lunatic Asylum and its success at achieving national patronage and £50 subscription bestowed by the Queen,[42] are cases in point. Three such causes which obtained national significance were the industrial schools for the most disadvantaged, the relief of destitution in the Scottish Highlands and Islands during the famine years between 1836 and 1850, and the temperance movement. It is easier to understand the process of subscription by looking at the response of the Edinburgh bourgeoisie to problems which became major concerns to Scottish urban society.

Thomas Guthrie's Original Ragged Schools were dominated by the Free Church but with a 'sprinkling' of members of the Established Church and the United Presbyterians. It was this clear Protestantism which prompted the United Industrial School to be set up in opposition, claiming to proceed on the principle of *'securing that religion be taught, but not of itself teaching religion'*.[43]

Both schools were established to deal with society's flotsam. Especially dominating the roll were the children of Irish immigrants, generally the most disadvantaged in Scottish society in this period. Guthrie's schools were specific in the role they were to play in the lives of the children

---

[40] The point is highlighted in Morris, *Class, Sect and Party.*

[41] *Appeal on Behalf of Proposed Hospital for Sick Children.*

[42] *Report by the Managers of the Royal Edinburgh Lunatic Asylum for the year 1842, presented to the Annual General Meeting, held on Monday 30th January, 1843* (Edinburgh, 1843).

[43] Original emphasis, *Public Education: The Original Ragged School and the United Industrial Schools of Edinburgh: Being a Comparative View of their Respective Results* (Edinburgh, 1855), pp. 5–6.

they educated, 'to give such children a position in the social scale'.[44]
Often the chosen place was not in Scotland, but this was a genuine
attempt at securing a better life for those less fortunate in society.[45] Thus
the Ragged Industrial Schools were part of middle class society's self-
defence mechanism.

The predominance of the legal population amongst the subscribers
was again notable (31.1%), but so too were the respectable totals
recorded by the medical professionals (6.4%) and the general professionals
(5.7%), in contrast to 'distribution & processing' (9.8%), 'commerce'
(5.7%) and, especially, 'craft' (5.5%) who were all under-represented.[46]
The structure of its subscription profile is presented below:

Figure 5.13: *Ragged Industrial School, 1858: most common subscriptions*

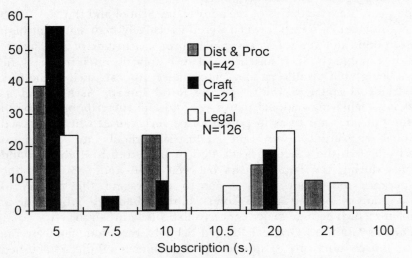

Over 60% of subscribers coded 'distribution & processing' gave either 5
or 10 shillings and nearly 60% of 'craft' subscribers gave only 5 shillings.
For both these groups there was little range in the amounts subscribed,
with few subscribing more than one guinea. The legal subscribers
showed more variation, with a noticeable number subscribing as much as
100 shillings. But there was significant bunching, with just under half
giving either 5 or 20 shillings.

---

[44] *Second Annual Report of the Edinburgh Original Ragged or Industrial Schools: With a List of
Subscribers and Donations* (Edinburgh, 1849), p. 5.

[45] 'This plan of emigration is one deserving of favourable consideration, as a matter of
police arrangement, whereby not only great good would be done to the community,
but by which there would probably be an actual saving to the public purse': ibid., p.
15.

[46] *Eleventh Annual Report of Edinburgh Original Ragged Industrial Schools.*

This quite distinct tendency to subscribe similar amounts was also apparent in an analysis of Edinburgh subscribers towards the relief of famine in Highland Scotland. The Edinburgh group which formed to organise this relief was soon followed by a Free Church initiative in Glasgow, which in turn prompted a separate Glasgow Committee to be formed. All three joined together under one Central Board of Management before being formally split into an Edinburgh Section and a Glasgow Section, each taking responsibility for a portion of the country.[47] The remit of the Edinburgh section covered Skye, Wester Ross and Shetland.[48] The occupational and subscription profile of those citizens who subscribed to the relief of Highland destitution *c*.1846, and who were successfully linked to the 1852/4 Pollbook, are presented in Figures 5.13 and 5.14:

Figure 5.14: *Highland destitution: occupational frequency count, percentage distribution (cases > 10)*

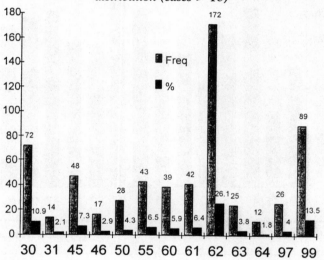

The Edinburgh lawyers, at 26.1%, are quite clearly the dominant occupational group active in the relief of Highland destitution. Additionally interesting is how generous the average subscription was at 65.8s, and there are a number of reasons for this. The first is the desperate need for money to deal with such an extensive calamity. A published letter from Thomas Chalmers in March 1846 argued that more funds must be raised: 'don't let either those in relief or the highland proprietors over-rate the extent of relief from without, and

[47] *First Report of the Edinburgh Section of the Central Board for the Relief of Destitution in the Highlands and Islands of Scotland, for 1848* (Edinburgh, 1848), p. 16 [SRO: HD 6/14].
[48] Ibid.

relaxing somewhat, their own efforts and their own responsibilities'. The favoured solution from Chalmers was to refuse applications from the able-bodied 'who may be living in voluntary idleness', and to send more seed-corn. Ultimately, he argued, the government needs to help: 'but the public needs to keep contributing *as if* the government won't'.[49] This demand for more and more money recurred throughout the crisis and the society frequently exclaimed the need to 're-double its efforts'. Even before Chalmers's warning, *The Witness* had made clear that citizens and their families in some districts of Edinburgh should be prepared for a visit and 'should have their contributions in readiness'.[50]

Figure 5.15: *Highland destitution: average subscription by occupation (> 10)*

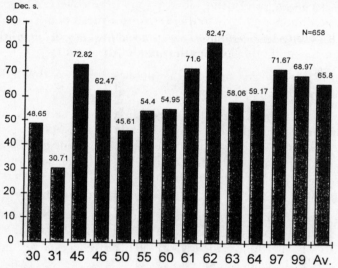

30	Distribution & processing	61	Medical
31	Dealers	62	Legal
45	Commerce	63	Religion
46	Bankers	64	Education
50	Manufacturing	97	Defence
55	Craft	99	No occupational title
60	Professional (general)		

Note: See Appendix 5 for explanation of achieved linkage.

Many methods were used to raise more money: the published sermon or tract, such as one advertised in *The Witness*, was a common tactic:

[49] Original emphasis, *The Witness*, 6 Mar. 1847.
[50] Ibid., 6 Jan. 1847.

In a few days will be published a Sermon, preached in aid of the Destitute Highlanders, by the Rev. D. J. K Drummond, incumbent of St Thomas' English Episcopal Chapel. Any profits arising from the sale will be given to the funds for the Destitution of the Highlands.[51]

It has already been seen that Rev. Drummond was one of the most active subscribers (Figure 5.3). In Edinburgh the organisation of collection was done by district, and this brings us to the second point concerning this appeal: its need for public accountability. The committee was firm in its resolution that a fullest possible list of the subscribers be published because of the scale and haphazard nature of the collection:

A very great portion of the subscriptions were collected by parties who accounted irregularly to the Treasurer; there were committees in each county or district – collectors of upwards of 30 wards in Edinburgh – and other parties throughout the country.[52]

In addition the society needed the public's trust so that additional subscriptions would be forthcoming:

The object of the Committee in sending these accounts to the Accountant, although they have already been audited by the Finance Committee, is that subscribers and the public may have the assurance of a professional Accountant, unconnected with the Board, that the sums entrusted to their charge have been duly accounted for.[53]

All such societies had to be publicly scrutinised, but for the relief of Highland destitution, the sheer size of the subscriptions and their irregularity of collection, made outside regulation necessary. Figure 5.15 showed a high level of subscription from all the professional groups, with commerce, medical and defence joining the lawyers as above-average subscribers. What the figures hide, however, are: the degree of multiple subscriptions from certain individuals; and, importantly, that the average was kept up by a few very large subscriptions from the likes of Sir James Colquhoun, who gave £100, and the earl of Zetland, whose third subscription was also £100.[54] Multiple subscriptions and a significant few large subscriptions combined to make the relief of Highland destitution a well-funded society.

Not all societies could rely on such large donations. To conclude this examination of the relationship between occupation and subscription the

[51] Ibid.
[52] *Reports of the Accounts of the Edinburgh Section of the Relief of the Destitution of the Highlands and Islands of Scotland* (Edinburgh, 1851), p. 7.
[53] Ibid., pp. 3–4.
[54] SRO: HD 16/70.

focus is again turned to the Total Abstinence Society, a society with an extensive subscription raised from relatively small amounts of money. Taken together, 'distribution & processing', 'craft', and 'legal' made up 51% of assigned occupational titles of those who subscribed to the society (and were successfully linked to the pollbook).[55] A distribution of amounts subscribed, controlled by occupation, is presented in Table 5.10:

Table 5.10: *Total Abstinence Society: occupation by subscription (decimalised shillings)*

	1.0	1.5	2.0	2.5	5.0	7.5	10.0	20.0
D & P (N=128)								
Count	24	8	10	54	20	1	4	1
Expected	18.1	5.0	7.4	63.0	22.9	0.8	3.0	2.0
Residual	5.9	3.0	2.6	−9.0	−2.9	0.2	1.0	−1.0
Craft (N=101)								
count	22	8	8	46	11	0	1	3
Expected	14.3	3.9	5.8	49.7	18.1	0.6	2.4	1.6
Residual	7.7	4.1	2.2	−3.7	−7.1	−0.6	−1.4	1.4
Legal (N=99)								
Count	5	1	2	52	30	0	4	3
Expected	14.0	3.9	5.7	48.7	17.7	0.6	2.3	1.5
Residual	−9.0	−2.9	−3.7	3.3	12.3	−0.6	1.7	1.5

Note: The discrepancies in the totals are due to the rarely chosen subscription amounts being excluded from this table for sake of brevity.
Source: *The Seventeenth Annual Report of the Edinburgh Total Abstinence Society* (Edinburgh, 1853).

For the three lowest subscription amounts (1s., 1.5s. and 2s.) 'distribution & processing' was over-represented, with the residual, respectively, +5.9, +3 and +2.6. The 'craft' occupations were also over-represented at the lowest level: residuals of +7.7, +4.1 and +2.2 respectively. Both 'distribution & processing' and 'craft' were, moreover, under-represented at the most common subscription level of 2.5s. (−9 and −3.7 respectively). These two occupational codes are of the lower socio-economic status of the voting population measured in the pollbook. It is therefore interesting, and intuitively correct, that they should be over-represented at the lower end of subscription amounts, under-represented at the average amount and, in addition, under-represented at virtually the remainder of the scale of subscriptions (although with a respectable presence at the higher amounts – but N is really too small to provide confidence). It is also intuitively correct that the legal profession, which is at the higher end of the socio-economic spectrum, is found for the three lowest amounts to be under-represented to the extent of, respectively, −9. −2.9 and −3.7. For the

[55] See note below Table 5.10.

average of 2.5s., legal was over-represented by +3.3, and it is noteworthy that the second most common amount subscribed was 5s., an amount at which it was strongly over-represented (+12.3).

This analysis must remain tentative because the number of cases is sometimes rather small – note that for 1.5s. and 2s. N is 10 or less in all three examples. Yet the main purpose of presenting this table is to demonstrate that a distinct 'bunching' of amounts subscribed tended to occur. In the case of the Total Abstinence Society this bunching occurred at 1 shilling, 2.5 decimalised shillings (two and sixpence) and 5 shillings. In all three instances, each occupational group assigned over half of their subscriptions to the latter two amounts, and, in the case of the lawyers, 83% subscribed either 2.5 or 5 shillings.

The subscriber class

The phenomenon of bunching, that is of pockets of subscriptions, is a clear one from this analysis. The class difference in the subscriptions, whereby those of higher socio-economic status who could afford to, and did, contribute higher amounts, is tempered by the universal tendency to subscribe certain specific amounts whether joining a society or putting money into a collecting tin. The study of the subscription lists for Highland Destitution, Total Abstinence and the Ragged or Industrial Schools saw all groups tending to subscribe very near to the average, and although the wealthier occupations had a scattering of subscriptions at the higher end, they still tended to fall back to an 'appropriate amount'. Whether it be a high subscription society or a low one, bunching occurred. It is this action which enables the subscriber class to operate. It created an identifiable vanguard within Edinburgh's general voluntary activity which involved itself in many different causes and issues throughout the length and breadth of civil society. It was by bunching the subscription at an acceptable minimum – a figure socially determined in each instance depending on the aims and function of the society – which (importantly) allowed such a spread of activity to be a practical reality.

The subscriber class gave the same amount as their neighbours, colleagues, and friends would have subscribed, and it was the amount the collector would have expected from someone of their status and in their neighbourhood to have subscribed. This was structured by the publication of subscription lists in newspapers or separately as 'Accounts of ...' or 'Proceedings of ...' Vital to the legitimacy of all such associations was the public dissemination of their financial statement and lists of the names, addresses, occupations and subscriptions of their membership. The middle classes had to maintain and manage fine gradations of rank and protocol, and one could not under-subscribe one's social standing.

Yet there is evidence of 'subscription fatigue', and those who organised the many re-openings of the subscription to the Scott monument (see Chapter 7) were well aware of the reluctance of Edinburgh's citizens continually to dip into their pockets for more money for a cause they were already likely to have subscribed to before. So to create the conditions for multifarious activity, and for the reasons of status maintenance and subscription weariness, the majority of the middle class tended to give the minimum their circumstances and conscience would allow.

The explanation for the range of amounts subscribed, which follows from this argument, is both that many people would subscribe once or twice each year, often to wildly different associations, but also that a limited number of individuals were always around to give relatively large amounts to the many different causes they believed in. These people continually changed between societies, depending on particular interests or concerns, but such a group, however fluid, always existed. Equally, there was always the large one-off subscription from, occasionally, the Queen or Prince Albert, although more usually from the duke of Buccleuch or Roxburgh, or in the case of Highland Destitution, the earl of Zetland. But the majority gave their subscription within a limited range and in fact they were concentrated in pockets of subscriptions.

One final point is that the most active subscribers may not have been the most financially generous, but their role was the contribution of their time, and more importantly, their name. The most active, usually the Edinburgh clergy but also many aspiring parvenus as well as titled patrons, headed the subscriber class. This group of activists managed the subscriber population; it organised, prioritised, and made respectable the many causes in which the members involved themselves. The most active ran the agenda of Edinburgh's civil society – together with the subscriber class, they governed urban Scotland.

The governing of civil society: subscriber activity and national identity

Taken together, Chapters 4 and 5 have dissected Edinburgh's civil society in the middle decades of the nineteenth century. By means of this empirical overview, the everyday reality of 'civil society' and 'governing' the 'nation-state axis' – the conceptual underpinning of nationalism proposed here – has been brought into historical focus. The purpose has been to show that the local bourgeoisie had all the resources necessary to structure and administer the towns and cities in Scotland, and that they were willing to do so. If the role of the 'state' in the state/civil society relationship is that of the exercise of infrastructural power, then for the mid-nineteenth century that power was in the hands of the middle class. The mantle of 'state' was embodied within the urban middle class, and this is critical to an understanding of Scottish national identity in this period. The descriptive aim of Chapters 4 and 5 has been to outline Scottish civil society in all its varied and penetrative forms. At the same time the analytical purpose of these two chapters has been to indicate how that society was 'governed'.

Chapter 4 was divided between those societies which were set up to deal with problems and to dispense philanthropic financial, educational and moral help, and those societies which acted as power and status foci for the urban middle class. This subscriber action allowed the middle class to define itself both in relation to itself and in contrast to others. This action also allowed the middle class to deal with the challenges of urban society without recourse to the parliamentary state. Education, destitution, orphanages, the blind, the unemployed, unmarried mothers, and temperance were just some of the social issues dealt with by a range of societies formed under a principle of piety by a bourgeoisie which negotiated its own class consciousness through those societies as well as through a range of scientific, literary and cultural associations.

The present chapter has extended the analysis of middle class control over civil society. It has addressed the question as to whether those who subscribed were in any way different from the Edinburgh middle class as a whole. An active elite has been identified which was spread between a number of societies and supported a number of causes. They gave their time and their name, and some gave very high subscriptions, too. There was a certain group of high-status individuals who exerted a great deal of influence over Edinburgh's civil society, an influence that at best could only be underestimated.

A second set of analyses concerned the occupational, voting and the subscription profile of the subscriber class. The lawyers were shown to be over-represented within a number of different societies, and this was indicative of their social power. 'Distribution & processing' and 'craft' were numerically important subscribers in most of the societies. In terms of voting, the subscriber population followed the general pollbook distribution in many instances, although the subscriber population often threw up some strong extremes in their candidate pair choice. In one instance it was found that for the Total Abstinence Society, the cause of temperance outweighed class for many subscribers. Yet civil society – as it was structured through this associational activity – was flexible enough to sustain the conflicting electoral choices of its three main occupational groups. Each shade of political opinion could co-exist within the same voluntary organisation, and this was of immense benefit to concerted class action and to underpinning class coherence. Indeed, the analysis of the amount subscribed to different causes produced the expected split between 'low' and 'high' status societies, but showed that irrespective of occupation or society, the majority of subscriptions tended to favour set amounts. In this sense the subscriber population acted as one – the culture of subscription across all societies was coherent; it cut across occupational and party lines. This was the middle-class formation which in turn administered Edinburgh's civil society. Material, social, religious and class concerns were all negotiated under the mechanism of voluntaryism. The Edinburgh bourgeoisie became a coherent class upon the playing fields of urban Scotland.

It was the self-sustaining independence of this class action which dominated the nation-state axis and was the means whereby Scottishness was encapsulated. Through voluntaryism Westminster centralisation was resisted, and a Scottish parliament equally so. This, then, sets out new parameters for an interpretation of Scotland's *ethnie*, focusing on nation and state as mediated through the practicalities of civil society. If a Scottish Westminster-style state was not a goal for Scotland's enfranchised elites, then it cannot be valid to judge the expression of Scottish national identity in those terms. The time has come to place Scotland within a typology of nationalism whereby the nation was internally governed by those externally enfranchised. Decentralisation is the key to the empowerment of the middle classes and the infrastructural enshrinement of urban Scotland (the axis of 'reciprocity' in the language of Hall).[56] It is from this basis that Chapters 6 and 7 complete this study by an examination of the symbols, icons and rhetoric of Scottish national identity in the mid-nineteenth century.

[56] Hall, 'In search of civil society', p. 16.

CHAPTER SIX

Symbols and Rhetoric: The National Association for the Vindication of Scottish Rights

Scottish nationalism: why symbols?

The lack of parliamentary nationalism in the middle decades of the nineteenth century, either in the form of a nationalist party or as part of the Home Rule programme of a British party (as with the Liberals in the 1880s), makes it difficult to measure the importance of national identity to the Scottish people. Simply put, there were no votes to count. Nevertheless, scholars have tried to make sense of Scottishness in this period, as Chapters 1 and 3 have explained, but their answer is a Scotland characterised by either romance or kailyard – because of the lack of imagined nation-statehood. Yet even in the late twentieth century there is no direct correlation between Scottish national identity and votes for the Scottish National Party, especially as Labour and the Liberal Democrats play the 'Scottish card'.[1] The fluidity in which the Union is placed in the lexicon of Scottish national identity is a function of four civil societies and one shared state, one that creates a 'duality' in the party political process.[2]

Politics is clearly one characterisation of nationalism, but it should not dominate. In contrast, national identity can be linked to an ethnic past which is manifest in many different ways over time and which can exist outwith the parliamentary system; that is the aim of this chapter. National identity is related to contemporary concerns, and ultimately that means the nature of governing *a* people in *a* defined territory. Chapters 4 and 5 explained the essence of that 'government' in Scotland's civil society in the middle decades of the nineteenth century: they and the preceding chapters have set the parameters of the 'nation-state' axis, and the framework of national identity.

---

[1] The lack of correspondence between 'Scottishness' and votes for the SNP is explained in McCrone, *Understanding Scotland*, pp. 164–73.

[2] E.g., the three main British political parties all have Scottish versions which hold their own conferences and have made their own party structure and who compete with the Scottish National Party; likewise there is a Scottish Trades Union Congress and a Scottish Confederation of British Industry, distinct yet joined to their 'British' counterparts.

The present task is to examine how the construction of identity is linked to the symbols, icons and rhetoric of Scotland's ethnic past. The idea from Goffman of the total immersion of the individual in others, of living in 'a hall of mirrors', is a useful way for starting to think about how we gain our identity. How we understand others and how we understand the reflection of ourselves is fundamental to the construction of self. The next step is to determine how individuals come to seek commonality with a nation. W. J. M. Mackenzie, with regard to political identities, has attempted to explain the slide from 'personal identity' to 'identification with' to 'common sense of identity' to 'larger national identity'.[3] To chart this change, Mackenzie uses the work of Erik Erikson to show, as in Goffman, the determining influence of an individual's surroundings on their 'identity'.[4] Although Erikson accepts that the self can only be understood in interaction with others, there are important differences and sentiments which are possible. There is no one-to-one relationship between a particular set of surroundings and the construction of self. Thus while using the Gramscian idea that the 'individual makes their own history', Erikson qualifies this by saying that 'they do not make it as they please, they do not make it under circumstances chosen by themselves, but under circumstances directly found, given and transmitted from the past'.[5]

Individuals are dependent on their surroundings and their past histories to determine their identity. But the creation of the self-conscious identity involves a certain degree of structuring of the situation. What is required is the emergence of leaders to 'tell one who one is', through the use of the rhetoric of identity, the use of 'we'.[6] The implication of this for the creation of identity is that those who share an interest, share an identity; that the interest of each requires the collaboration of all. This is activated through the idea that all those who share a network of communication share an identity.[7] The important group is that which manages or controls the use of 'we'.

By accepting Mackenzie's argument, we can appreciate the power of the common meaning given to common symbols for the construction of common identity. This is the reason for an emphasis on the rhetoric of understanding applied to symbols in the construction of the Scottish national identity. A shared sense of identity is based on the perception of

---

[3] W. J. M. Mackenzie, *Political Identity* (Middlesex, 1978), p. 31.

[4] Recent anthropological thought goes further and roots the self in modern society in a 'reflexive project': A. P. Cohen and N. Rapport, 'Introduction: consciousness in anthropology', in A. P. Cohen and N. Rapport (eds.), *Questions of Consciousness* (London, 1995), p. 6.

[5] Mackenzie, *Political Identity*, p. 37.

[6] Ibid., p. 117.

[7] Cf. Deutsch, *Nationalism and Social Communication*; and Anderson, *Imagined Communities*, for the use of common communication for common 'imagination'; but also note how we need to be told 'who we are', that is, the importance of hegemonic dominance.

mutuality. It is important, then, that the discourse of mutuality be examined. Certain symbols have been, and continue to be, common to Scottish national identity, although interpretations have changed over time. In particular, William Wallace, Robert Bruce, Robert Burns, and Walter Scott have dominated as icons within the Scottish *ethnie*. It was argued in Chapter 3 that the *ethnie* is dependent upon the lucky-dip of the historical past, fundamentally shaped by contemporary interpretation, being therefore inherently malleable.

The question which must now be addressed is: if the view of the state/civil-society relationship so far argued is accepted, then how should we now understand the common meaning given to the common symbols of Scottish national identity? Given the nature of government in the mid-nineteenth century, whereby the effective state was a local one, what shape was subsequently given to the Scottish *ethnie*? If it were not rational to think in terms of Scottish independence, then how should Scottish nationalism in the mid-nineteenth century be interpreted? This chapter, and Chapter 7, will examine contemporaries' interpretation of the symbols of Scottish nationalism. The National Association for the Vindication of Scottish Rights [NAVSR] was, in Mackenzie's, terms the group that structured the nationalist 'we' in Scotland. As a movement the NAVSR's reign was brief (1852–6), but in our period it provided the most consistent critique of Scotland's relationship with England under the Union of 1707. Indeed, it was a critique which was part of a wider discourse on Scotland's national identity from 1830 to 1860, and in Chapter 7 the understanding hereby established will be used to analyse the commemoration of Scott, Burns, Wallace and Bruce, and the building of the National Monument on Calton Hill.

The National Association for the Vindication of Scottish Rights

In order to understand the vaporous concept of national identity, an important first step is to demonstrate how nationalist leaders, self-appointed or chosen, interpret people's past and identity. Within their aims and objectives these leaders may conflict with themselves, but their purpose is to set the terms of the debate, to set the agenda for others. In the mid-nineteenth century, the leaders who most coherently expressed how the nation should understand its common past were members of the National Association for the Vindication of Scottish Rights.

The NAVSR was dominated by three personalities: James Grant; the earl of Eglinton and Winton; and Charles Cowan. James Grant was a second cousin of Sir Walter Scott, and his early fame rested on the writing of romantic historical adventures. He and his brother, John, were joint-secretaries of the Scottish Rights Society (as the NAVSR was known), and wrote most of its petitions and campaigning literature. The

earl of Eglinton and Winton, the association's chairman, was claimed
(somewhat erroneously) to be 'second in influence only to Lord Derby
within the Conservative party'. This falsity sustained the rhetoric of
national self-sacrifice for their leader. '[He] threw away all political
aspiration in contending for the national cause of his country' (since he
had become minister for Ireland in 1852).[8] Politically, the Association
was a real mixture: 'Whigs, Conservatives, Radicals, Free Traders and
Protectionists, the adherents of every political section and religious sect,
have ignored their petty squabbles to demand justice for their country.'[9]
Charles Cowan, the Free Church Liberal, and Scottish Rights supporter,
offered 'to shower Scotland in gold', as *The Scotsman* put it, before his
election to Westminster in 1852. Cowan made his promise in response to
a challenge from John Grant, on the eve of the 1852 election, in a letter
dated 13 April, to resist 'centralisation' in London.[10] It was in a letter the
following week that Grant proclaimed that after the election an
association for the protection of the Scottish people would be formed.[11]
Grant kept the issue of Scottish rights in the forefront of the letters
pages of the Scottish newspapers until November 1853, when the
association finally held its first public meeting.

Representations of support and subscription to join the Scottish
Rights Society were made by the Lord Provosts of Edinburgh, Glasgow,
Perth and Stirling, as well as by many other notable early supporters.
The politicians Charles Cowan and Duncan McLaren were at the top of
the first subscription list, adding their weight to the public profile of the
association.[12] Yet despite its 'large and influential meetings in
Edinburgh, Glasgow, Perth and Inverness', rank-and-file membership
was more in the 100s than the 1,000s.[13] In a petition to the English and
Irish members of the House of Commons, the association claimed to
consist of

> many thousands of the Gentlemen of Scotland, and numbers
> amongst its members 14 Scottish Peers, the Chief Magistrates and
> Town Councils of 50 of the cities and Burghs of Scotland, upwards
> of 1,000 Magistrates, and the Presidents of Colleges and chairmen
> of the leading commercial bodies in Edinburgh, Glasgow and
> elsewhere.[14]

[8] Major Scott of Gala, reported in his speech to a meeting of the Associates of the National
   Association for the Vindication of Scottish Rights (n.p., n.d.).
[9] James Grant, 'Nemo Me Imusse Lacesset!' (n.p., n.d.), p. 170.
[10] Ian [John Grant] 'Centralisation', *Edinburgh Advertiser*, 13 Apr. 1852.
[11] John Grant, 'Justice to Scotland', 20 Apr. 1852.
[12] Scottish Rights Association (1853), *Address to the People*.
[13] 'Address to the People'.
[14] *Address to the English and Irish Members of the Honourable the Commons House of Parliament
   for the United Kingdom of Great Britain and Ireland* (1855), p.1.

Yet the association rarely got the mass of the people, let alone the more literary-minded middle class, on its side. In part this is because of its failure to identify any one particular sectional or political interest which could underpin 'Scottish rights', and this diffuseness was reflected in the voting profile of its subscribers as they had voted at the 1852 general election. Figure 6.1, showing those linked between the NAVSR in 1853/4 and the pollbook population for 1852/4, indicates that the two politicians who went on to support the Association – Cowan and McLaren – were in no way appealing to their own supporters. Most notable from this comparison was the doubling of support from NAVSR subscribers to the Macaulay/Cowan voting pair, the popularity of Macaulay as a plumper, and the unpopularity of McLaren both as a plumper and a candidate pair. Indeed Macaulay won most support from Scottish rights supporters, while Charles Cowan's vote remained steady and Duncan McLaren's plummeted in comparison with the pollbook population. It was Macaulay, who was not even identified with the NAVSR, who did best!

Figure 6.1: *NAVSR and 1852/4 pollbook: largest voting pair and plumper choices (%) (all figures exclude non-voters)*

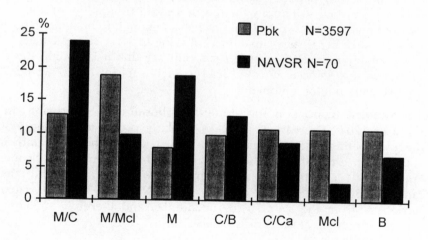

Note: M = Macaulay; C = Cowan; Mcl = McLaren; Ca = Campbell; B = Bruce
See Appendix 5 for explanation of achieved linkages

The lack of any clearly identifiably enhanced electoral support for Charles Cowan is all the more surprising, considering he was the Free Church candidate, for there is often assumed to be a link between the Free Church and opposition to Westminster. To test this assumption, the 110 subscribers to the NAVSR who could be linked to the 1852/4 pollbook were examined, and it was found that twenty-five of them could be related back to the list of supporters of Charles Cowan in the 1847 general election, a list detailing religious adherence. Of this small sub-set, 48% turned out to be Free Churchmen, in comparison with 28% of Charles Cowan's voters in 1847.[15] Perhaps this does suggest (but no more strongly than suggest) that there was a link between the Free Church's challenge to the British state and the cause of Scottish rights. Yet as Figure 6.1 indicates, despite this implied 'dominance' of the NAVSR by adherents of the Free Church, the Scottish Rights Society did no more than reflect the general pollbook percentage of support for Cowan.

While the links between Scottish rights and theological independence remain inconclusive, the campaigning language of the association was crystal clear. The whole tone of the rhetoric of nationalism from the association, which remained consistent throughout its existence, was set by the chairman, the earl of Eglinton and Winton, at its very first public meeting, held in Edinburgh in 1853:

> I am not wrong-headed enough to wish that the Union, which has been established so happily for the peace and tranquillity of both, should be interfered with. I am not foolish enough to imagine that, if such were my wishes, any efforts of mine to sever those, I trust, indissolubly united (cheering). I can only say that if I thought the result of this Association could lead to such a misfortune, I would not remain in it for a moment.[16]

The National Association was not in the business of destroying the Union of 1707. The earl of Eglinton similarly proclaimed at the first Glasgow meeting of the association that 'The Union of the two countries is as firmly established as the House of Hanover on the throne. (Applause.)'[17] To maintain this support for the Union and the Hanoverian (not Stuart) dynasty, the NAVSR reappropriated 'patriotism' from the state so to romanticise, and therefore mobilise, their interpretation of the Scottish *ethnie*:

[15] As Appendix 5 makes clear, 110 out of 383 subscribers were able to be linked to the 1852/4 pollbook, however only 25 of this subgroup could then be linked back to the 1847 list of voters for Charles Cowan. The explanation for the largest extent of failed linkages (of NAVSR and pollbook) is because of the large number of institutions (not individuals) who made up many of the earlier subscribers.

[16] *Justice to Scotland. Report of the First Public Meeting of the National Association for the Vindication of Scottish Rights, held in the Music Hall, Edinburgh, on the evening of November 2, 1853* (1853), p. 4.

[17] *Justice to Scotland. Report of the Great Public Meeting of the National Association for the Vindication of Scottish Rights, held in the City Hall, Glasgow, December 15, 1853* (1853), p. 5.

We are not a province, as is proved by our having a separate Established Church, separate laws, and a Court of Session. (Cheers). But, it is asked, 'What is the Nationality of which they complain?' 'What is nationality?' It is patriotism! (Cheers). And what is patriotism? The most noble sentiment by which the human heart is animated. (Loud cheers.) The theme of the poet – the dream of the youth – the admiration of mature years – the foundation of all national greatness. (Much cheering.) It is the love of the husband for his wife – the parent for his child; it is something more ennobling still. It may slumber, but it never dies, and why are we alone to be decried for loving this old country of ours? (Loud cheers.) We love our English brethren, and we are proud to be associated with them in an empire on which the sun never sets – (Cheers.) – but we are Scotchmen still. (Cheers.) We glory in the triumphs of a Marlborough, a Nelson and a Wellington, but may we not look with pride to the achievements of a Wallace and a Bruce? (Great applause.) We read with delight the works of a Byron and a Wordsworth, and a Dickens, but may we not claim more specially our own, a Scott and a Burns? (Cheers.) We admire the pages of Gibbon, but may we not admire, with even more delight, the works of a Hume, a Robertson, an Alison, and a Macaulay? (Cheers.) We admire the works of a Lawrence and a Reynolds; but we claim as our own a Wilkie, a Grant, and a Swinton. (Cheers.) The feeling of patriotism which has aroused itself in Scotland may have been at first scouted as absurd and ephemeral. It may have been first given utterance to by men of no political eminence or hereditary rank; it may have been looked coldly on by those who were regarded as the hereditary and selected guardians of the liberties of Scotland, but it is a reality which will not die away, and which must be attended to. (Cheers.)[18]

The Scotsman's report of the original meeting noted that the hall was crowded to excess and that many hundreds had failed to gain admission; but in its analysis of the event the newspaper was very critical of the objectives of the association and its political mix-and-match who took to the platform. Of the public meeting in November, it proclaimed that 'the "Scottish People" were not there!' It criticised the 'multitude and confusion of objects' which the association stated were its aims, and argued that the Scottish MPs 'all know, that never since the Reform Bill has any Scottish measure been passed which a majority of them opposed, nor any Scottish measure refused when a majority of them asked'.[19]

Yet *The Scotsman* was mistaken in its hostility, because it was one based on the false premise that the association was demanding an independent

---

[18] *Justice to Scotland ... Glasgow*, p. 8.
[19] *Scotsman*, 5 Nov. 1853.

Scottish parliament. The NAVSR made various demands, but a Scottish parliament was not one of them. In contrast, Figure 6.2 lists twenty-four reasons why, in the opinion of 'A citizen of Edinburgh', Scottish rights needed attention:[20]

Figure 6.2: A *Vindication of Scottish Rights: Grievances*

(1) The Abolition of the Scottish Board of Excise and Custom in 1843
(2) The superiority of the English and Irish Poor Laws in comparison with the Scotch.
(3) Neglect of public charities in Scotland by the government
(4) Inadequacy of public defence in Scotland
(5) The inadequacy of money spent on harbours of refuge in Scotland in comparison with England
(6) The Great Famine of 1846: £8,000,000 donated to Ireland, nothing to Scotland.
(7) Scotland being, at present, without a special Secretary of State; the Lord Advocate is unfit to do all the duties expected of him.
(8) Demands the return of the Privy Council of Scotland – the ancient independence of the country.
(9) Holyrood and Linlithgow Palaces are crumbling
(10) Scotland contributes more to the Exchequer than Ireland
(11) Scotland lacks a fair number of MPs
(12) The General Post Office in Edinburgh is badly paid in comparison with Dublin
(13) The General Post Office in Glasgow is a crumbling building
(14) Postal mismanagement
(15) Inland Revenue Office
(16) The Scottish heraldic emblems have been down-graded.
(17) Scotland's revenue returns are no longer counted by the Exchequer
(18) Sale of Crown lands
(19) Scottish police not supported by the government
(20) The United Kingdom of England and Scotland should be always designated Great Britain
(21) Military spending on building barracks more so in England than in Scotland
(22) Ordnance survey work of Scotland lagging behind
(23) The Bank Act of 1845 restricts the Scottish Banking System
(24) Union Riots in 1706 – evidence of original unpopularity of the Union.

Clearly the Scottish Rights Society's demands were initially for a fairer treatment of Scotland from the Exchequer. There was also the demand for better administration, and better government; this was focused on the re-establishment of the post of Secretary of State for Scotland (lost in 1746). Since that particular Westminster response to the Jacobite uprisings, the administering of Scottish affairs had been included in the remit of the Lord Advocate, whom, it was argued, was overloaded with his own advocacy business, his judicial role, and the governing of Scotland. Lord Cockburn, who claimed in 1854 to have known all but one of the fourteen Lord Advocates since 1800, suggested that only about four had been suited to public life. This encouraged him to suggest that the possibility of a Lord Advocate being a good Scotch manager was so rare that for practical purposes it should not occur.

[20] A Citizen of Edinburgh, *A Vindication of Scottish Rights, Addressed to Both Houses of Parliament* (Edinburgh, 1854), pp. 6–30.

Therefore, he proclaimed:

> For myself, I am quite clear that, whatever he may be called, a recognised and responsible manager of Scotch affairs, distinct from the Lord Advocate, would be expedient. He may be the Home Secretary, or an under Secretary, or a Lord of the Treasury, or anything else; but he ought not *as a matter of course* to be also Lord Advocate.[21]

It is an understatement to say that Cockburn was generally hostile to the Scottish Rights Society, but he acknowledged that grievances existed and did ask: 'Why is it never proposed to make each successive Attorney-General the general minister for England?' As a Whig intellectual, his biggest fear was that the association would be antagonistic to Westminster and so block, in his view, more reasonable claims for constitutional equality. Indeed this view persisted throughout our period: in 1858 the Commons defeated (by 174 votes to 47) a motion by the member for Dundee (Baxter), 'That in the opinion of this house an Under-Secretary for Scotland should be appointed to perform the political duties at present attached to the office of Lord Advocate', despite the plea that he was actuated by no personal or party motives.[22] A similar motion by Sir James Fergusson, asking for a Select Committee to enquire into the administration of Scotland (because 'the duties which come under the province of the Lord Advocate of Scotland are so diverse, incompatible, and comprehensive, that no parallel can be found in the Administration of England or Ireland'), was equally dismissed.[23]

Wider support for the movement was mixed. On the whole the newspapers were split in their support. The historian R. M. W. Cowan surveyed the editorials and discovered that sixteen supported the movement, five were neutral and five were hostile.[24] A major boost for the Society, after the attacks it endured from *The Scotsman* and *The Times*, was the endorsement of the demand for a Secretary of State for Scotland by W. E. Aytoun in *Blackwood's Edinburgh Magazine*, where 'we have been careful to avoid rash strictures or unworthy reflections upon our neighbours'.[25] The NAVSR itself expressed its demand for a minister of Scotland with a warning over the experience of Europe, drawing parallels with the revolutionary movements so recent in their memories:

---

21 *Journal of Henry Cockburn, being a continuation of his Memorials of His Time, 1831–1854*, vol. II (Edinburgh, 1854), pp. 309–10 [original emphasis].

22 *Hansard's Parliamentary Debates*, 3rd ser., CL (1858), cols. 2118, 2150.

23 Ibid., 3rd ser., CLXXV (1864), p. 1169.

24 R. M. W. Cowan, *The Newspaper in Scotland: A Study of its First Expansion* (Glasgow, 1946); also quoted in Hanham, 'Mid-century Scottish nationalism, p. 167.

25 W. E. Aytoun, 'Scotland since the Union', *Blackwood's Edinburgh Magazine*, lxxiv (1853), p. 283.

There are several states on the Continent which owe fealty to sovereigns not resident within their boundaries, but I never heard of one which was left at least without a reasonable governor – and, recollect this, Scotland is no petty province. We have a population of three million living under our own laws and institutions; and the revenue that we contribute to the United Kingdom is larger than that of many independent states of Europe. It is larger than that of Holland, Belgium, Naples, Sardinia, or Sweden and Norway. It is larger than the combined revenues of Bavaria, Denmark, Greece and Switzerland. (Cheers.) Now, there is not one of these countries to which we do not send envoys extraordinary, with a diplomatic staff.[26]

In addition, it threatened the possible consequences of insufficient representation of Scottish interests. The immediate experience of Europe had been a revolutionary one and an inevitable worry for the British state. The Glasgow solicitor and historical author, William Burns, invoked events on the Continent to warn of the dangers of ignoring how Scotland was governed. In response to another English newspaper attack, he wrote to Lord Palmerston arguing that:

The Times, indeed, will have it that this 'jargon of nationalities' has been the source of all the evils Europe has endured since 1848, and therefore anything of the kind should be ignored. Is this your Lordships' theory as to the condition of Europe, and her sources of danger, since the Congress of Vienna – or will you not rather agree with me, in saying that these dangers have arisen, and continue to threaten, owing to the *violation of existing nationalities*, by the system of dealing with nations as if they were cattle, that could be allotted off and appropriated according to the arrangements of politicians? I do not expect your Lordship's answer; but perhaps the *Times* may deign to tell us what Poland, Hungary, or Italy, would say to the question, or what answer would be given by many portions of Germany. Happily, my Lord, our circumstances are different, and any contest we may have will be a peaceful one. *But the principle at the bottom of the contest is the same.*[27]

Such administrative neglect, to an extent that the NAVSR believed Scotland could soon follow the revolutionary path of continental Europe, was made accessible to the Scottish people through the romanticisation of Scotland's 'past'. Ever since Walter Scott made his highly dramatic re-discovery of the lost Crown jewels of Scotland in

[26] *Justice to Scotland … Glasgow*, p. 11.
[27] A North Britain [William Burns], *A Tract for the Times. Scottish Rights and Honour Vindicated, in letters to Viscount Palmerston, 'The Times', and 'Caledonian Mercury'* (Glasgow, 1854), p. 45 [original emphasis].

1818, locked in a forgotten chest in a bricked-up room in Edinburgh Castle, Scottish romanticists were highly sensitive to the protocol and honour of Scotland's heraldic past. Typical of their complaints was the petition sent to Victoria by John Grant:

> That your Majesty's Petitioners have humbly to represent that it has been the custom for some time to display upon the Forts, Garrisons and Military Positions of this part of the United Kingdom, and particularly upon the Castle of Edinburgh, on the occasion of anniversaries, certain flags and royal standards, quartered with the Arms of Great Britain, as borne in England, in so far as the Lion Rampant of Scotland is placed in the Second Quarter of the said standards, and not in the First and Fourth Quarters, and the arms of England are placed in the First and Fourth Quarters and not in the Second.[28]

The same problem of heraldic honour was also apparent, it was complained, with respect to the new two-shilling piece, the florin. Grant even applied, ultimately unsuccessfully, for the post of the Lyon King of Arms, so to follow his obsession and preside over the heraldry in Scotland. One correspondent for the *London Morning Post* was convinced of Grant's suitability,

> as his brilliant romances are found in every clime where the English language is read ... and the frequent references made to heraldry in his works show that he is well versed in the obtuse science, and the chivalrous sentiments which he has embodied in his writings bear evidence that it is an office which he is well suited to fill.
> ... An application has been made to the government on his behalf by his Royal Highness the Prince of Wales.[29]

Although concern with heraldry was common in national movements throughout Europe at the time, this theme was not the most successful campaigning weapon. Its most pointed critique came from *Punch*: 'SCOTLAND, having complained of the shameful treatment of her lion in the English standard, the complaint will, it is understood, be followed up by Wales, – the English heralds have completely ignored the Welsh rabbit.'[30]

---

[28] John Grant, 'May it Please Your Majesty. The Petition of the undersigned, your Majesty's loyal subjects, inhabiting that part of your Majesty's United Kingdom called Scotland' (n.p., n.d).

[29] 'The Lyon-King-at-Arms', *London Morning Post*, 11 Jul. 1856.

[30] *Punch*, xxv (1853), p. 179.

Figure 6.3: '*A Growl from the Scottish Lion*'[31]

A GROWL FROM THE SCOTTISH LION.

A more effective campaigning tactic was the use of the petition.
Petitions to both Houses of Parliament, to the Lords Commissioners of
the Treasury, and to Her Majesty were most common. They were
usually produced by the various town councils, as, for example, in the
case of the twenty petitions forwarded to the Home Secretary by Lord
Eglinton on 14 June 1853.[32] Another campaigning weapon was the use
of statistics to provide 'facts' demonstrating Scotland's ill-treatment. This
was explicitly the object of Robert Christie who, on behalf of the
association, wished to add some rigour to the 'universal complaints'
within Scotland concerning the grants of public money. Thus, with data
culled from various parliamentary documents, Christie produced a set of
tables which ranged from the expenditure on royal palaces – Table 6.1,
below – to comparative public money spent on safe harbours for the east
coast fishing fleet, improvements in London, the cost of the police of
London and Ireland, and other instances where Scotland supposedly
did less well out of the Exchequer in proportion to its input of six
millions.[33]

---

[31] *Punch*, xxv (1853), p. 179.
[32] *Petition of the National Association for the Vindication of Scottish Rights presented to the House
of Lords by its President, the Earl of Eglinton on Thursday last* (1854); *Memorial of the Council of the National Association To the right Honourable the Lords Commissioners of Her
Majesty's Treasury* (1854); *Address to the English and Irish Members of the Honourable the
Commons House of Parliament*.
[33] R. Christie, *Injustice to Scotland Exposed* ... (Edinburgh, n.d.).

Table 6.1: *Injustices to Scotland exposed, c.1853*

	England	£
St James's Palace		66,336
Royal Mews, Pimlico		17,570
Kensington Palace & Gardens		48,546
Carleton Stables		1,215
Buckingham Palace & Gardens, excl. £88,837 in 1828		184,270
Marlborough House, external repairs		399
Hampton Court Palace, Gardens, Shed, House and Bushby Park		152,916
Kew Palace Buildings, Royal Botanic, Pleasure Gardens/Palm-House		162,708
Windsor Castle, Parks, and Forest		435,853
Frogmore		38,737
Bagshot Park		325
Ascot Royal Stand, Stables, and Kennel		6,920
Victoria Park		133,266
Royal Pavilion, Brighton		16,384
Hyde, St James' and Green Parks		178,652
Regent's Park and Primrose Hill		70,540
Greenwich Park		12,137
Richmond Park		80,365
Sum for England		**£1,607,139**
	Scotland	
Holyrood Park		19,831
Holyrood Palace		3,597
Linlithgow Palace		558
Sum for Scotland		**£23,986**
	Ireland	
Phoenix Park		107,351
Sum for Ireland		**£107,351**
	Total	**£1,738,476**

This apparent neglect of public expenditure in Scotland was a frequent
irritation in the eyes of the Scottish Rights Society. Charles Cowan sent a
letter to the first public meeting in which he recalled the apathy he had
experienced in his dealings with government with regard to Scottish
interests, in particular with regard to his campaign to fund the endowments
of Professorial chairs at Edinburgh University.[34] He received similar
resistance over the issue of religious tests in the Scottish universities:[35]

[34] *Justice to Scotland ... Edinburgh*, p. 3.
[35] *Hansard's Parliamentary Debates*, 3rd ser., CXX (1852), cols. 1236–63.

Large sums are spent in England and Ireland for purposes not of
an imperial character at all, while scarcely a penny finds its way
north. England and Ireland received £185,754 for their charitable
institutions. The only amount of the kind made to Scotland was one
to the Dispensary of Kirkwall of £2.[36]

These, then, were some of the problems identified by the NAVSR of
which remedy was demanded. The initial public speech by Eglinton
made clear that the association supported the Union, and their petitions
always stressed loyalty to Her Majesty. But there was a consistent and a
clear recognition of Scottish nationality existing separately and indepen-
dently. In one of the association's tracts it was argued that England and
Scotland

> are distinguishable *historically* and *institutionally* and until Scottish
> history shall be forgotten (which is the same thing as saying until
> letters shall perish), and Scottish legal, ecclesiastical, and other
> institutions are revolutionised, the two countries must remain
> distinguishable in certain important features, suggesting separate
> local interests, and demanding a peculiar administration.[37]

In response to *The Times*, John Grant, writing as 'Ian', argued against
Scotland the province, and for Scotland the nation:

> You state, that there is hardly a county in England that does not
> think itself overlooked, and 'that they do not appeal to their
> separate *nationalities*.' Scotland is a *nation*, and possessed of all that
> constitutes a nation – a regalia, a peerage, a church, a code of laws,
> and the institutions dependent upon their possession. She therefore
> has a *nationality* to appeal to. But what county of England or Scotland is
> in present possession, or has even the memory of a nationality?
> None. Permit me to say your argument does not apply.[38]

As Aytoun tersely expressed the same sentiment: 'The Union neither did
nor could de-nationalise us.'[39]

Religion was, of course, another important distinguishing characteristic of Scottish nationality, and the potential influence of the recent
history of the Free Church has already been hinted at. Henry Inglis
argued in one of the association's tracts that it was Presbyterianism
which was the essential difference between England and Scotland: 'The
maintenance of Presbyterianism is so interwoven with the noblest
passages of Scottish history, that the extinction of the former is a certain

36 *Tracts of the National Association for the Vindication of Scottish Right, No. 2* (1854), pp. 3–5.
37 *Tracts of the National Association for the Vindication of Scottish Rights, No. 3* (1854), p. 4
   [original emphasis].
38 *Justice to Scotland; To the Editor of the Times* (Edinburgh, n.d.) [original emphasis].
39 Aytoun, 'Scotland since the Union', p. 273.

consequence of the extinction of the latter.'[40] John Grant also argued for the maintenance of the distinctive governing of Scottish religion:

> Patronage, forced upon the people by a foreign majority has caused schism after schism, until the Disruption rent the Church of the nation in two, and forced us to subscribe three millions for the maintenance of that form of church government solemnly agreed to be preserved by the people when the Union farce was enacted.[41]

If Presbyterianism was interfered with, then the likelihood was that it would make Scotland more at risk from Popery (it was argued).

Such statements were made to distinguish the Scottish nation from the English nation. However, the movement explicitly made the point that it was not racist. Patrick Edward Dove argued that there were two definitions of nationality – the first concerned race, the second concerned reason, the NAVSR was for the latter:

> Whoever – whatever man – whether he be black, white, red, or yellow, the moment he identifies with the institutions of Scotland, that moment he became a member of the Scottish nation, and Caledonia must throw around him the mantle of protection. (Applause.)
> We do not want Members of Parliament to represent our race, the race can represent itself; we want members to represent our laws, our institutions and our administration.[42]

Dove was the assistant to the Free Churchman Hugh Miller on *The Witness*,[43] and thus a perceptible link between Scottish grievances and the Disruption could here be suggested. In an address to the House of Commons, written in 1855, the demand for the recreation of this office of Secretary of State for Scotland was reiterated, but it was made clear that this was not an expression of anti-Englishness:

> The Council of this Association, while strenuously asserting the rights and honour of their native country, most explicitly disclaim any but the most friendly feeling towards England. It is their sincere prayer that no such feeling may ever rise between the two countries, and if from misrepresentation or misconception, any Member of your Honourable House should believe otherwise, it is hoped that such an impression will be at once discarded as unworthy of the intelligence and good feeling of the Scottish people.[44]

---

[40] *Tracts of the National Association for the Vindication of Scottish Rights*, No. 6 (1854), pp. 4–5 [NLS].
[41] Ian [John Grant] 'English Aggression on Scotland', *Edinburgh News*, 16 Jun. 1854.
[42] *Justice to Scotland ... Glasgow*, p. 20.
[43] Hanham, 'Mid-century Scottish nationalism', p. 151.
[44] *Address to the English and Irish Members of the Honourable the Commons House of Parliament*, p. 3.

The Scottish Rights Society was careful not to proclaim anything that could be construed as xenophobic nationalism, but it was adamant in its principle of the better government of Scotland. The society stood to maintain not the letter but the spirit of the Treaty of Union.[45] It did not wish to damage the Westminster Parliament, but in fact wanted to increase the number of Scottish members. Yet a tension existed in its vision of government and the association was strongly against the 'centralising principle' which, it argued, had occurred with 'the merging of the Institutions of Scotland into those of England'.[46] This opposition to centralisation was at the heart of the Scottish Rights Society's critique of the governing of Scotland. The association joined the anti-centralisation bandwagon, active in the towns and cities of England, to defend local government. William Burns, once again addressing Lord Palmerston, argued that he was a 'fan of local government' and that he 'had long been convinced that such a system [centralisation] is peculiarly opposed to the true interests of my native country'.[47] In a later tract the association condemned centralised government as 'Undoubtedly the greatest problem of the present age', and stated that its core concern was 'how far the central government of a nation should directly interfere with matters affecting the social or material interests of the people':

> The Association for the redress of Scottish Grievances wish nothing more than a just observance of the Treaty of Union, and to prevent the crushing policy of centralisation, which has placed Scotland in a position little better than Yorkshire or any other English county.[48]

Building on this theme, James Grant sent out warnings of the effects of centralisation on the states of Europe:

> Centralisation hurled Louis Phillipe from the throne of France, Centralisation plunged Hungary in woe and Austria in war, Centralisation blotted Poland from the map of Europe, and Venice and Lombardy from the States of Italy. Centralisation is the curse of modern Europe; let us be aware that it does not become the curse of Britain.
>
> It has disgraced and demoralised Scotland, it has depopulated her highlands; it has violated her laws and subverted her institutions; it has levelled the kingdom of the Bruces and Stuarts to the rank of an English county.[49]

45 North Britain [Burns], *Tract for the Times*, p. 25.
46 *Address to the English and Irish Members of the Honourable the Commons House of Parliament.*
47 North Britain [Burns], *Tract for the Times*, p. 29.
48 Red Lion [John Grant sen.], *Scotland and 'The Times': To the Editor of the 'Edinburgh Evening Post' and 'Scottish Record'*, 26 Jul. 1853.
49 James Grant, 'Scotland for ever!' (*c*.1853), p. 222.

The Boards of Customs and Excise, the Scottish Mint, and the Scottish Household had been abolished and not replaced. The separate revenue returns for Scotland had been abolished in 1851; the Stamp Office had been centralised in London, and there were many other instances where some of the more obvious layers of government had been stripped.[50] These were all indicators of the creeping grip of Westminster. There was a strong distrust of centralisation – of concentrating all in the capital – and of 'functionary government', where paid officials, either in the civil service or on boards of control, administered Westminster government. The association proclaimed that:

> The question is one, then, between self-government, local administration and action, generally, on the one hand, and centralisation, with its necessary accompaniment of *functionaryism*, on the other. England, Scotland and America exemplify the former; France and the Continental states exemplify the latter.[51]

Its worry was, for how long could Scotland resist even greater centralisation at the Imperial Parliament.

This, then, was the governmental structure the association wished Great Britain to adopt: a Scottish Secretary of State in a harmonious House of Commons, with re-emphasis upon a powerful local state. Dominating its thinking was the perceived real fear that the British state would succumb to the temptation of centralisation. In fact, even critics of the Scottish Rights Society, those who argued that the Union of 1707 did incorporate separate identities within a full union of equals, still feared centralisation and the perpetuation of *'functionaryism'*. One NAVSR critic feared that a Scottish Parliament would increase centralisation. As an alternative, the answer of this 'Scotsman' was the need for a different form of centralisation – one that dispensed with Boards and *functionaryism*. Instead, it was centralisation which went hand-in-hand with strengthened local government:

> The existence of a strong central executive power, designed to *protect* the subject in the exercise of his freedom, combined to an almost unlimited encouragement to *local* legislation, are essential features of an enlightened, liberal system of Government ... Centralisation, then, in its true sense, is essential to good *government*; but local action, and local appointments are equally essential to good *legislation*.[52]

---

50 Hanham, 'Mid-century Scottish nationalism', p. 165.
51 *Tracts of the National Association for the Vindication of Scottish Rights, No. VII* (1854), pp. 3–4 [NLS] [original emphasis].
52 A Scotchman, *Scottish Rights and Grievances: A Letter to the Right Honourable Duncan McLaren, Lord Provost of the City of Edinburgh* (Edinburgh, c.1854), pp. 12–13 [original emphasis].

The 'Scotchman' wished to diminish the number of state-appointed functionaries in all three kingdoms, and with reference to Scotland, 'the superintendence of a popularly elected local council is much more efficacious than that of a distant Home-Secretaryship'.[53]

> It is to this worship of state functionaries that France is indebted for its political slavery. The all but complete destruction of Municipal Government in that lively, happy, and [now] unhappy country, is an example of the justly dreaded system of imperial centralisation – the appointment by the *state*, in the different localities, of Government officials to manage *local* affairs.[54]

So, although it argued against centralisation, the NAVSR, according to this commentator, would increase centralisation by taking power away from the municipalities and giving it to a Secretary of State for Scotland, a functionary of the central state. Both this individual critic and the Scottish Rights Society were concerned that any tendency away from local power (and arguably the Boards of Control were the thin edge of this wedge) was going to result in standardisation through Westminster to the detriment of Scotland's distinctiveness and fair return from the Union. Centralisation, which made slow gains from the mid-century before its ultimate success over universal elementary education in the 1870s and a Scottish Office in the 1880s, was the evil the Scottish Rights Society set its stall against. Equally, John Steill, one of the few of the association's pamphleteers to demand an independent Scottish parliament, was ultimately concerned with the dangers of anonymous centralisation at Westminster and the benefits of traditional local government. He argued for 'the re-establishment in Scotland of a native Legislature, based on Scottish principles, and devoted to Scottish interests'. But his premise was not so much on Scotland's ancient sovereignty, but on the chance to improve the governing of Scotland: 'I would cling to no thing, merely because it was Scottish, but because it was good and true; and on this I would be my own judge'.[55]

The resistance to centralisation is the key to understanding the kind of state the Scottish Rights Society demanded for the Scottish nation. Its effective aim was to ensure power remained with the local state, but that a Secretary of State would allow such matters that required consideration at Westminster to receive more effective attention. At this level, then, we can begin to understand why the Scottish Rights Society should be so explicit in its support for the Union. If everyday government remained effectively local, Westminster would rarely enter the equation – likewise, neither would the Union.

53 *Scottish Rights and Grievances*, p. 13.
54 Ibid., p. 14 [original emphasis].
55 J. Steill, *Scotland and her Union with England* (Edinburgh, 1854), pp. 8, 17.

The impact of this conceptualisation of the nation/state relationship on the symbols of Scotland's *ethnie* can be seen in one of the most lavish and stage-managed publicity stunts executed during the lifetime of the NAVSR. It took place on the evening of 18 September 1854 and was the earl of Eglinton's banquet. The published account gives a wonderful description of the mixture of symbols which comprised mid-nineteenth-century national identity:

> The great national banquet in the honour of the Earl of Eglinton, President of the Association for the Vindication of Scottish Rights, took place on Wednesday evening, when upwards of 600 Associates from various parts of the kingdom sat down to sumptuous enter-tainment in the City Hall, which was splendidly decorated for the occasion. At the east end, and behind the chairman's table, were suspended two royal standards of Scotland, one on each side of the organ, attached to blue covered staves, with ornamented yellow coloured tops and rich tassels. The end of the hall was also taste-fully adorned with wreaths of flowers and evergreens. At the back of the croupier's chair, at the west end of the hall, and behind the gallery, a Union Ensign of the United Kingdom was suspended on the wall, with wreaths of evergreens and flowers on either side. The north and south large windows were draped with curtains of the tartan of the Association, and between the windows, pending from the curtains, were festoons of evergreens, interspersed with flowers. On the north side the St Andrews standard was suspended from a dark blue flag-staff, with carved top, tinted yellow. In front of the platform, at which sat the Chairman, were the Royal Arms of Scotland, admirably painted on canvas; and to the right and left were the well-known armorial bearings of the Earl of Eglinton and the Duke of Montrose. Underneath were festoons of heather and evergreens. On the side railings of each side of the Chair, and fronting the assemblage below, were four Lochaber axes and four claymores of admirable workmanship, with targets to match; and besides these grim emblems of the rough play of olden times, were some tokens of the more peaceful game of modern days, in the shape of curling stones, of finished workmanship, with brooms to match, not forgetting the fine old national amusement of golf.[56]

The standard of St Andrews, the Royal Arms of Scotland, four claymores, and the Union Ensign of the United Kingdom: the glorification of the nationality of Scotland, but under the umbrella of the Union. At the banquet the duke of Montrose proposed the first toast,

[56] *Banquet in Honour of the Right Honourable the Earl of Eglinton and Winton, K. T., President of the National Association for the Vindication of Scottish Rights to be held at the City Hall, Glasgow, on Wednesday, the 4th October, 1854* (n.p., 1854) [Scottish Rights Association, vol. II).

which was a traditional one to the Queen, but nevertheless interesting for the European context he outlined:

> notwithstanding all those changes which we have seen on the Continent, and those great disturbances which have shaken both countries and monarchies, her Majesty remains strong in the attachment of her people, and in England, still more in Scotland – (Applause.) – universal loyalty prevails. (Cheers.) Gentleman, Scotland has always been famous for her loyalty ... Her Majesty the Queen.[57]

The toast was drunk with all the honours, 'followed by the National Anthem on the organ, and *Hail to Victoria*'. Montrose took the chair, and in his speech the desire for government by the local municipalities was again stressed:

> The principle of centralisation is a principle entirely foreign to the constitution of this country. It belongs to foreign lands, it belongs to a system of government where the head of the government is autocratic, but does not belong to a free constitution which has been nursed by independent and by local government, which has found in its municipal corporations in the early instances of history to have been some of the great leading obstacles to power, that have been the first pioneers in the way of liberty and commercial freedom, and which at this day is still the great principle of our free and liberal institutions. (Cheers.)[58]

Centralisation was regarded as a breach of the articles of the Union, a 'breach of contract'. It is again clear that the NAVSR was responding to challenges to Scotland's ability to govern its own territory, and a strong local government was regarded as a vital component of this structure. It was believed that anti-centralisation would make the Union work more fairly. It was not the Union which was the problem for Scottish nationalists, instead it was a British state that was drifting towards centralisation and functionaryism. Unionist-nationalism was a rational response in an effort to resist this process.

Eglinton's banquet was one of the last big set-piece occasions orchestrated by the association. Because the NAVSR was never widely backed by influential people, nor ever gained enough grass-roots support, it was soon to dissolve itself. The council of the association met in Falkirk on 20 January 1855 to discuss future action. At that meeting a resolution was unanimously adopted whereby 'in the present state of the affairs of the country [the Crimean War], and particularly the position of Great Britain, in regard to foreign powers' the Council decided to abstain from petitioning the House of Commons,

[57] Ibid.
[58] Ibid.

until a more suitable period shall arrive for the discussion of domestic questions ... We do not forgo our claims as Scotsmen; but we forbear from urging them prominently in an exigency, common to the whole United Kingdom.[59]

Despite this resolution, the 'Address to English and Irish Members of Parliament', previously agreed to and already printed, was circulated. It stated that petitions to Parliament upon the issue of Scottish Rights had already been made by the Convention of Royal Burghs, the Magistrates and town councils of Edinburgh and Glasgow and many other town councils throughout Scotland. But the association was in no way committed to distracting the House of Commons when the concerns of foreign affairs were pressing. Loyalty to Her Majesty and British patriotism were stronger than the demand for Scottish grievances when, because of the Crimean war, a choice had to be made.

Figure 6.4: *English satire:*
'The sad Scottish lion
lists its grievances'[60]

By 1856 the association had collapsed: its arguments dissipated by a mixture of the war, the growing willingness of the government to listen to Scottish complaints, and the instability which the wide and heterogeneous membership brought.[61] Disloyalty to John Bull as the Crimean war progressed was a familiar charge 'radicals' faced, and one

---

[59] W. Burns, 'Association for the Vindication of Scottish Rights' (1855).
[60] *Punch*, xxv (1853), p. 39.
[61] Hanham, 'Mid-century Scottish nationalism', p. 170.

the NAVSR did not wish to encourage.[62] A gap then existed in the organisation of nationalist expression. The field was left to particular, *ad hoc*, celebrations of nationalism. William Burns, for example, had already formed a St Andrews Society in 1854 in Glasgow, while in 1858, under his editorship, an appeal was made for all parties to join together to demand an increase in the number of Scottish MPs. The next major occasion of nationalist expression was the movement to built a monument to William Wallace (Chapter 7).

The NAVSR was the body which led Scottish society into a general understanding of its national identity during the middle years of the century. It mobilised many facets of the Scottish *ethnie* in its pursuit of better administration of Scotland under the terms of the Union. The whole spectrum of Scotland's historical lucky-dip was dredged up in three years of intense activity, to proclaim the independence of Scottish civil society and thus attempt to hold back the tide of centralisation. This chapter has explained the intellectual framework which underpinned the way in which Scots saw themselves and perceived their identity. By linking their fears around the issue of centralisation, the NAVSR was explicit in its concerns about the government of Scotland. In effect, its members were reactive rather than progressive. They did not want a Scottish Parliament, they demanded instead the maintenance of a locally governed civil society, where the state kept its distance and removed its functionaries. To preserve this governance, the NAVSR mobilised Scottish ethnic identity as a vehicle for protest. The rationale of their argument was that the Union of 1707 was being violated by the spread of centralisation. Their use of national identity was thus to preserve the Union, as they perceived it – this is what has been termed Unionist-Nationalism.

But what else can be said of the period from 1830 to 1860? How did others interpret the Scottish *ethnie* and so define Scottish nationality? The purpose of Chapter 7 is to analyse in more detail the rhetoric used to celebrate particular elements of the Scottish *ethnie*. This will be different from the above analysis of the Scottish Rights Society, because the focus will be on particular icons, outwith the context of a political project, and because it will, to a greater extent, include involvement from all classes in society.

---

62 *The Economist* had recently criticised Cobden, Bright, Disraeli and Lord Derby for disloyalty to the British state at various times when battle was being waged: 'John Bull must be assured that everything is going wrong and that everyone is doing wrong; that his statesmen are betraying him; and his allies deserting him; that his admirals don't like fighting, and his generals don't understand commanding; that his army is ill found, ill fed, ill officered, and in a position of most helpless peril; and if he can only prove that he is going rapidly, inveterately, and altogether to the dogs, his delight and their triumph are alike complete. Accordingly the dish which he desires is served up to him, with equal disregard of his indigestion, and of evil consequences which may ensue in the meantime': *The Economist*, xii (592), Sat. 30 Dec. 1854, pp. 1442–3.

CHAPTER SEVEN

Icons and Rhetoric: The Monuments of National Identity

The only uncontentious aspect about defining national identity is the very complexity of the problem itself. Many words have been written, and indeed much blood has flowed, to defend or to demand a selfhood. The National Association for the Vindication of Scottish Rights was strong on words – blood letting rather than blood spilling – but it tapped a nerve still tender in Scottish society. It was able to mobilise the Scottish *ethnie* in a campaign to resist centralisation of government and state. It was able to do this because of what seems a perverse use of the symbols of Scotland's past, by arguing that the independence of Scotland's civil society could only be guaranteed by greater Union with England. How was this claim justified throughout our period, and what is the timing of this rhetoric? The task before us is now, having expanded our range of examples a little, to explore some of the most important instances of the celebration of Scottishness.

In the mid-nineteenth century there were four explicit iconographic events which concentrated the collective mind of the Scottish nation and forced it to pinpoint its identity. These icons were 'Scottish national' components in any chosen model of dual or multiple identities. The first occasion was the death of Sir Walter Scott in 1832 and the ensuing debate over a suitable memorial; as we shall see, this culminated in the completion of the Scott Monument in 1846. A similar occasion was the centenary of the birth of Robert Burns in 1859, which led to a wide-scale outpouring of national sentiment and gave mid-century society the opportunity to re-interpret the life of the eighteenth-century poet. The third important focus of national sentiment was the commemoration of William Wallace; the construction of the national monument to Wallace, begun in 1856 and finally inaugurated in 1869, and the 1859 attempt to build a monument to Wallace and King Robert Bruce in Edinburgh, importantly defined Scotland's relationship with England mid-century. Our final example is the National Monument on Calton Hill, famously unfinished: the various attempts to complete this 'disgrace' unearths much about the changing rhetoric of Scottish nationalism throughout our period and beyond.

In our analysis we should keep in mind Marinell Ash's obvious but neglected truism that the building of monuments tells us more about the current state of attitudes than any notion of honouring past 'heroes'.[1] By analysing in turn the rhetoric of each of these icons it is possible to understand more fully the arguments of the Scottish Rights Society as well as wider expressions. More importantly perhaps, the rhetoric identified can only be explained within the analytical framework of self-governing civil society delineated in Chapters 2, 4 and 5. The depth of the example I will present is to illustrate the profundity of Scottishness at this time of 'missing' nationalism.

The commemoration of Sir Walter Scott: obituaries and monuments

After Sir Walter Scott – historical novelist, Scottish patriot – died in 1832, how was he remembered by his contemporaries? By examining his obituaries, a consensual interpretation of his life becomes apparent. Obituaries can be honest, but rarely are they uncomplimentary. They are 'original' only when they are idiosyncratic, and although they document lives, they are required to be succinct; they will always focus on what are perceived to be either the most important events and achievements in public persons' lives, or on the wider impacts of these lives on others. Therefore obituaries rarely differ; they reflect a common agreement on the role in society or the impact on society of the public figure – albeit a positive, glorified reflection. But if, as it is fair to suggest, the glossing of a life is usually the interpretation widely believed, then the justification of the value of this source is straight-forward.

Literary criticism, as an intellectual approach, has dominated interpretations of the life of Scott.[2] It has done so to such a degree that temporal changes in the views of contemporaries have been truncated and Scott has been kaleidoscoped through the fictional characters he created. By examining the obituaries instead, the focus moves to Scott's colleagues, friends and admirers, rather than the extrapolation of Scott's personality from his characterisation. Scott's commemoration by his contemporaries enables the closest possible fit to be made with the wider societal understanding of national identity.

Because of the success of his writings and his widespread fame, the biographical details of Scott's life generally went unrelated in the obituaries. Instead the line taken was the wider influence of Scott on Scotland. The obituary writers employed four recurring themes: (i) Scott the 'genius author', as Scotland's contribution to some sort of nineteenth-century Enlightenment and the 'civilised world'; (ii) Scott as a great British literary figure; (iii) Scott as the Universal Man who wrote for the 'common man'; and (iv) Scott as both the great chronicler of Scotland's

---

[1] Ash, *Strange Death of Scottish History*, p. 144.
[2] For a particularly good example of this approach, as carried out by a nationalist, see P. H. Scott, *Scott and Scotland* (Edinburgh, 1981). Many other examples could be given.

past and the writer who instigated pride in and recognition of the Scottish nation.

(i) Scott the 'genius author' and the 'civilised world'
In general the obituary writers elevated Scott to a position of centrality within world civilisation because of the believed genius of his intellect. In the estimation of the *Weekly Journal,* Scott's 'magnificent, and perhaps unrivalled, genius'[3] was the source of his fame. Or again, as the *Evening Post* remarked on noting the death of both Goethe and Sir Walter in 1832, 'and how much mightier the latter'.[4] This estimation of Scott's place at the pinnacle of modern civilisation was also taken up by *The Scotsman*:

> Scotland may well mourn the loss of the man who had spread the glory of her literature far and wide; but the events will awaken a feeling of grief in every part of the globe to which civilisation extends. It is the extinction of a mind of unrivalled gifts – the eclipse of a light whose splendour has filled the world. In an age fruitful of great writers, Sir Walter towered by the force of his genius, to a height which no other person reached.[5]

It was the sheer genius of the man, irrespective of his country of birth, which in the estimation of his contemporaries meant his place as an author was amongst the great intellectuals of the world. It was his genius, neutrally evaluated, that led them to place Scott as part of the world's 'high culture', although there was little attempt, if any, to regard Scott as a descendant of the Enlightenment. Therefore the view of David Daiches, amongst others, that Scott was a true descendant of the Scottish Enlightenment because of his belief in progress, rationality, moderation and reconciliation, does not square with these particular sources.[6] Scott is quoted as being a friend of Ferguson, whom he had looked up to for upwards of thirty years (Ferguson died in 1816),[7] and the young Scott attended the lectures of David Hume's nephew at Edinburgh University. However, the obituaries never compared Scott to Ferguson, Hume, Robertson, or any of the prominent Scottish intellectuals of the eighteenth century.

Nevertheless, Scott was regarded as truly a world figure. The *Edinburgh Evening Post* estimated that his death would be mourned everywhere: 'the tidings that the Author of *Waverley* has paid the debt of nature, will be felt, not as a British – not as a European – but as a

[3] *Weekly Journal,* 25 Sep. 1832.
[4] Reproduced in the *Glasgow Herald,* 24 Sep. 1832.
[5] *Scotsman,* 22 Sep. 1832.
[6] D. Daiches, 'Scott and Scotland', in A. Bell (ed.), *Scott: Bicentenary Essays* (Edinburgh, 1972), p. 40.
[7] Scott, *Scott and Scotland,* p. 59.

calamity which has befallen the human race'.[8] The *Dumfries Courier* also expected widespread grief at the news of Scott's death because of the popularity of his works in the 'civilised world'. Again, this is testament to Scott's (perceived) pre-eminent intellect, and to the belief that his fame would never die:

> Wherever civilisation has penetrated, his works are patent to the whole human race; and will continue to spread a charm over the surface of society, delight a smile, or invoke a sigh, immortalise and endear the land of the 'mountain and flood', sublimate, subdue, and electrify by turn millions on millions, to the latest posterity.[9]

That Scott was the property of the world, and not just of Scotland, was also argued by the *Edinburgh Observer and New North Britain*. This newspaper did regard the death of Scott as a national loss 'and, as such, ought it not to call forth the public demonstration of a nation's sorrow'; but still the loss belonged to more that just the Scots:

> Such men are few and far between. They are the great lights of the world, and when they depart, and their songs cease to be heard, we feel as if the earth grew dark and silent.[10]

(ii) Scott as British literary figure

As well as being an author of the civilised world, Scott was equally regarded as the leading British literary figure of his time. Rather than his place of birth being irrelevant (as the 'genius in the civilised world'), this time Scott's nationality was partially subsumed within his British identity. In his speech to the health of Sir Walter (at a dinner held by Mr Knowles on 21 September 1832, cruelly and ironically, with Scott, unbeknownst to the guests, having died that afternoon), Sir Daniel Sandford described him as a 'British Poet', who belonged to the exalted world status of Homer and Shakespeare (which thus combines our two themes). But, although Scott was British, he was also regarded as identifiably Scotland's contribution to British literature. This point was made explicitly by Thomas Atkinson, a correspondent to the *Glasgow Herald*:

> Yet, while his fame is the property of the world, as his writings are the heir-looms which we divide with the kingdom that has given us part in the heritage of Shakespeare – his ashes are the right of his own 'mountainland' – of Scotland – and there they must rest – more sacredly guarded by our own veneration than even those of 'Him of Avon' by his own solemn adjuration.[11]

---

8 *Edinburgh Evening Post*, 29 Sep. 1832.
9 *Dumfries Courier*, reproduced in *The Scotsman*, 26 Sep. 1832.
10 *Edinburgh Observer and New North Britain*, 25 Sep. 1832.
11 *Glasgow Herald*, 24 Sep. 1832.

Thus, whereas Shakespeare was England's contribution to British literature, Scott was Scotland's offering: both men were treated as expressions
of nationhood within a wider, 'British' national identity. Indeed, as we
shall see below, Scott's commemoration, in particular the preservation of
Abbotsford as the family home, became a deep-seated English concern.

(iii) Scott as the universal man

Scott was presented in a number of the obituaries as a champion of
egalitarianism and humanitarianism – as the proprietor of some sort of
(superior) Scottish 'spirit' or 'ethos'. Rather than being a descendant of
the writers of the Enlightenment, his 'enlightened views' appealed at a
lower, more popular level. According to *The Schoolmaster and Edinburgh
Weekly Magazine*, the writings of Scott 'embody the Philosophy of
Humanity, and the spirit of our own national history, with that finer
spirit, expansive as life, and enduring as time, which pervades all that he
has written'.[12] Scott was perceived as writing about Scotland's core, about
the ordinary Scot, about the DNA, as it were, which made 'the Scot'.

This 'Scottish spirit' helps explain this third strand in contemporaries'
interpretation of Scott, that of the author of *Waverley* as the Universal
Man – the man for all men [*sic*]. It is perhaps rather surprising to
conceive of this famous nineteenth-century Tory, a willing recipient of
the patronage of the duke of Buccleuch (making him sheriff-depute for
the county of Selkirkshire),[13] as an inheritor of the republican traditions
of Burns; but it was really the immense popularity of Scott which
persuaded his contemporaries to deny his politics as best they could and
to ennoble him as 'universal'. He was represented as being both a writer
for the people and a writer of the people. His reputation had reached all
men because, it is assumed, of the sheer quality of his work. He was a
literary great because he was populist. His romantic tales of chivalry
ensured mass sales. His novels quickly went to reprints and even his
narrative poems, such as *Lay of the Last Minstrel* and *Marmion*, sold over
50,000 copies.[14] Because his writings seemed to appeal to all men (and
obviously women as well) he was represented as being a writer for all
'men'.

The substance of his writings were characterised not merely as
sympathetic, but as mirror images of 'THE PEOPLE'. Briefly (because this
theme will be picked up in the next section), Scott was acclaimed as the
depository and the projector of the true, rustic, 'ordinary' Scottish
character.[15] Sir Walter Scott's choice of 'ordinary' Scots as his heroes was
emphasised in an enlightening argument in *The Schoolmaster*, as it tried
to cope with the problem of Scotland's literary hero being a Tory among
Whig-dominated literati, and of his being a Tory fount of Jacobitism to

---

12 *The Schoolmaster and Edinburgh Weekly Magazine*, 29 Sep. 1832.
13 Morris, 'Patrimony and Power', p. 77.
14 Scott, *Scott and Scotland*, p. 1.
15 *Glasgow Herald*, 24 Sep. 1832.

boot! *The Schoolmaster* denied Scott's politics, but in order to do so it had to link Scott's writings to the politically neutral, but emotionally valued, concepts of 'humanity' and the 'ordinary' man:

> Convinced that in heart and mind, in principle and affection, and (with a few incidental and casual aberrations into which he was hurried or betrayed) in conduct also, this illustrious person belonged to no state party, we would redeem his venerable and beloved name from the political party which claims it – and sound to a Crusade which should 'conquer his tomb from the infidels'. If SHAKESPEARE deserves the epithet of the myriad minded, to SIR WALTER SCOTT belongs that of the myriad-hearted; and with this large natural character, it will not be difficult to shew that he essentially belonged to the People – to Mankind, and that the tendency of all his writings has been to enlighten and expand the minds of men, by making them neither Whig or Tory, but something infinitely better than both.[16]

This defence of Scott's politics is a great deal more strident than the only other newspaper obituary to deal with Scott's Toryism, the *Dumfries Courier*, which confined itself to a quote in passing from James Hogg: 'he was no man's enemy, however much [we] may dislike his principles'.[17]

Moreover, when *The Schoolmaster* was obliged to attribute any political proclivities to Scott, it labelled him a Radical. This was especially for his treatment of kings and 'the law, as a profession, is the butt of the constant sly hints and direct thrusts of this UNIVERSAL LEVELLER', it claimed. He was apparently also good at insulting churchmen, statesmen and

> to the modern country gentry, the lower ranks of the rural aristocracy, and the worshipful members of the county quorum, he shows little more mercy. It is among the poor or the unregarded that we are taught to look for shrewdness, intelligence, disinterested attachment, and patriotism, which is not ambition or flimsy disguise ... If all this be evidence as Toryism, it is the Toryism after our own hearts.[18]

By representing Scott's politics as 'Radical', meaning a supporter of the 'common man', *The Schoolmaster* was thus able to deny the Toryism of Scott and set up this image of Scott as a hero to all.

(iv) Scott and the Scottish nation

The link between Scott and the ordinary man, and Scott as the embodiment of the Scottish spirit, was made even more explicitly in

---

[16] *Schoolmaster and Edinburgh Weekly Magazine*, 29 Sep. 1832.
[17] *Dumfries Courier*, reproduced in *The Scotsman*, 26 Sep. 1832.
[18] *Schoolmaster and Edinburgh Weekly Magazine*, 29 Sep. 1832.

relation to 'Scott and Scotland'. To varying degrees the newspapers concentrated on Scott as both the creator and the guardian of Scottish national identity. This is the main line taken by the *Edinburgh Evening Courant*. After first describing his importance to the civilised world in general, and then giving a brief potted biography, the *Courant* launched into its main theme – the important role played by Scott in maintaining Scotland's heritage:

> the Waverley novels will be prized by Scotsmen as permanent depositories of their language and manners, and of the genuine Scots character, which is fading before the fast encroaching tide of southern refinement. The classical language of Scotland, though it be discarded by the polite and the wealthy, has still its own simple graces ... How forcibly did he stretch the ludicrous points, as well as the loftier features of the Scots character, with all the vigour and truth of nature, without the slightest approach to caricature, even in his broadest and most rustic characters, while his dramatic scenes comprise the whole treasures of the language – the pure ore of expression without the alloy. He has given permanence in his immortal works to the fading images of the olden times, and has completed a gallery of portraits essentially Scottish, on which we daily gaze with still increasing adoration and pleasure.[19]

Likewise the *Caledonian Mercury* concentrated wholly in its obituary on the theme that Scott was the true and faithful guardian of Scotland's heritage:

> [Scott] boldly struck into a new path, and awakening the dying cadence of those strains which had gladdened 'Scotland's elder time', as well as evoking all that is most grand, gorgeous and romantic in the past history or traditions of a long history singularly rich in recollections of heroic daring or chivalric adventure, he at once introduced to us a new and unexplained region in the realm of fiction, and imported to the creations or rather reproductions of his genius the inexpressible charm of a glorious and indestructible nationality ... No man, perhaps, ever wrote so much, as a poet and a novelist, and yet absolutely speaking, invented so little.[20]

The *Edinburgh Evening Post* took such ideas one stage further by proclaiming the link between Scott's so-called reproductions and true representations of the Scottish character and what it terms 'Scottish patriotism':

> Scotland is glorious in the annals of patriotism, as the birth place of Wallace and Robert Bruce. She is now equally glorious in the

---

[19] *Edinburgh Evening Courant*, 24 Sep. 1832.
[20] *Caledonian Mercury*, 24 Sep. 1832.

annals of literature, as the country of Sir Walter Scott. 'To make a third he joins the freer two'; and although we had nothing more to boast of, the triumvirate are in themselves a host; – nor has the last been the least of the three in benefiting and adorning our native land. Our hills, our valleys, our history, and our manners, are consecrated in his immortal pages ... In fact, the benefits which Sir Walter Scott has conferred, and will continue to confer, although in ashes, on Scotland, are incalculable. Never more, while the world lasts, can we be a land unrenowned. In the political scale of nations we may rise, or we may fall. In his pages, we are a glorious people, and a favoured spot forever! Cervantes has done much for Spain, and Shakespeare for England, but not a tithe of what Sir Walter Scott has accomplished for us. In each of these great writers we find many localities sanctified by their genius, in their respective countries; but that of Scott pervades every corner of his native land.[21]

This last passage in particular shows us that what the obituary writers never did was use Scott as a symbol for Scottish independence. 'Nations' refers to 'native land', not self-governing nation-states, at least not for Scotland. The four themes identified from Scott's obituaries are, in one sense, too contradictory to refer to a self-governing nation-state (however defined). Scott was Scotland's contribution to Britain's literary heritage and to the literary achievements of Europe and the wider civilised world; Scott was perceived as preserving and presenting the essence of Scotland's past, and as such produced pride amongst ordinary Scots and wider acclaim of the beauties of Scotland (land of 'mountain and flood'). His immediate legacy was pride in the Scottish nation, but at a number of complementary levels. Scotland as a younger brother in the United Kingdom was one identity; Scotland as a contributor to some notion of a European intellect, and as a 'fully qualified member state' of the civilised world, was another; but there was also Scotland as the great country of equality where Scott followed in the tradition of Burns that a 'man's a man for a' that', which developed into a fully blown 'egalitarian myth'. These four Scottish identities were explicitly nationalist ones, but – we should note – a separate nation-state was never on the agenda. As the *Dumfries Courier* wrote in its obituary of Scott:

Patriotism and valour are undoubtedly virtues of the highest order – virtues which are no more conspicuous than among themselves – yet, when we divest ourselves of the prejudices engendered by the geographical distinctions of rivers, seas and mountains, and regard the different nations of the globe as members of the same great family, we are often forced to doubt whether the world has been

21 *Edinburgh Evening Post*, reproduced in the *Glasgow Herald*, 24 Sep. 1832.

more benefited or injured by those statesmen and warriors who in all ages have engrossed so large a share of its honours and applause.[22]

These four themes were complementary because the concept of nation-state was not an issue for Scotland – but the acceptance and equality of the Scottish nation within Britain and the wider world was all important. Our attention turns now to examine how perceptions of Scott, and the four complementary themes identified, were maintained or were changed over the next fourteen years – the time it took to complete and inaugurate the Scott Monument in Edinburgh.

The Scott monument and the memory of Sir Walter

Immediately after the death of Scott, a select band of gentlemen and noblemen met in the rooms of the Royal Institution to set up a committee to raise a subscription for the erection of a monument to his memory in the metropolis of Edinburgh. This preliminary gathering was quickly followed by a meeting held on 5 October which, according to *The Scotsman*, was one of the largest bodies of gentlemen ever in the Grand Assembly Room, and 'the most conspicuous in terms of rank and talent which ever assembled in Edinburgh'.[23] James Skene, appointed as a member and later secretary, of the committee, estimated in his reminiscences that around 1,200 turned out for the 'Great Meeting'.[24] An interesting feature of this gathering, as *The Scotsman* pointed out, was that those assembled were estimated to be of every political party. Scott's Toryism was no hindrance to the respect shown from all shades of the political spectrum. This really was a complete gathering of all the 'respectable' power in Edinburgh, where rivals rallied to a common cause and celebrated a national hero.

This meeting is an important occasion for analysing the rhetoric of national identity in the period. The purpose of the gathering was to satisfy the feeling that a monument should be built to perpetuate Scott's memory. Therefore those who attended had to signal to the population at large the reasons why they should subscribe. It was necessary in the first instance to display political unanimity, then the job was to delineate the importance of Scott to Scotland and to Scottish national identity. The Lord Provost, authorised by the magistrates and council to subscribe in their name such a sum 'as he may think proper', presided over the meeting.[25] The young duke of Buccleuch, on his first public appearance, spoke of the fame of Scott. In concurring with this view, the Lord Provost related that he had been asked, by many members of the

---

[22] *Dumfries Courier*, reproduced in *The Scotsman*, 26 Sep. 1832.
[23] *Scotsman*, 6 Oct. 1832.
[24] James Skene of Rubislaw 'Contents of Mr. Skene's Reminiscences of Sir Walter Scott, etc.' [NLS: MS. 965], pp. 286–7.
[25] *Council Record*, vol. 212, 3 Oct. 1832.

peerage and gentry of the country who could not attend, to ensure that resolutions were passed which would enable Scott's admirers to create a lasting testimony to him. When the duke of Buccleuch carried on to propose the first resolution he did so in terms of the work this warm-hearted, kindly man had done – 'who had always laboured for the welfare of Scotland'. Sir Walter Scott's patriotism 'was not out of declamation; his love to his own country was exhibited both in public and in private, and would be seen in every word or act of his life.'

In seconding the motion to build a monument in Edinburgh, Professor Wilson remarked that the loss would be felt throughout the whole of Britain, despite Scott's fame as a Scottish patriot:

> That great and generous country, too, with which they [Scotland] had long been running a race of generous rivalry, England, felt the same depth of sorrow of heart at the loss which human nature was about to sustain – the mighty heart of London beat with sorrow at the anticipated doom.

This is unusual for any symbol of national identity in that it was so well renowned by, as it were, the opposition. An important feature of the Scottish interpretation of Scott, as a focal point of reference in its nationality, was that Scott, especially from an English point of view, belonged to British national identity. Scott's chivalric writing and his romanticisation of the Highlands endeared him to polite English society and the English aristocratic leisure industry, which was approaching its mid- to late-century prime. For the Scottish frame of reference, this meant that Scott could not be appropriated solely for Scottish use – the love of Scott was polygamous, a claim to be shared with the world.

At the meeting, the Lord Provost then moved that a committee be formed, with power to sub-commit. Smaller committees were raised for London and for Glasgow,[26] and plans were laid to collect subscriptions from abroad. The sum subscribed at the close of the meeting amounted to about £1,100, the majority from twenty-four subscribers of the very highest rank.[27] A glance at the subscription list shows the dominance of the sub-committee and committee and of the contributions by the titled aristocracy, with relatively little input from the professional or merchant middle class of Edinburgh. However – as we shall see later – this balance of control shifted over the time it took to complete the monument.

The resolutions were then published in various forms, especially in the newspapers, but also as part of appeals made by the committee to

---

[26] A meeting of this General Committee was then held that week (9th) to appoint the Sub-Committee (*Scotsman*, 13 Oct. 1832).

[27] *Scotsman*, 6 Oct. 1832. A front page advertisement presenting the resolutions passed at this meeting, the composition of the sub-committee, and a list of the first subscribers, was published in *The Scotsman*, 13 Oct. 1832, which in addition stated that subscriptions will be received by the secretary, and by certain banks and bankers in Edinburgh, and also at booksellers' shops.

countries around the world.[28] This fits with the belief held by the obituary writers and the Monument Committee, as we have seen, that the death of Scott was a sorrow felt in every corner of the civilised world. But what the proposers of the monument wished to emphasise was not only that Scott's writings made the man famous in the civilised world, but also that his writings achieved the same for Scotland. As Sir Daniel Sandford argued in Glasgow:

> [His works] raised our country to a proud equality of fame with the most renowned nations of ancient or modern times – and they had done more than history itself to throw light and splendour round her annals.[29]

Soon after the formation of a Committee for the Erection of the Scott Monument in Edinburgh, there was also formed – on 9 November 1833 – a London committee with the aim of raising the finance to solve Scott's debts in order to keep Abbotsford in the possession of Scott's family and descendants for ever. With the collapse of his publishers, Bannatyne & Co. in 1826, Scott had taken it upon himself to pay off the debts amounting to approximately £120,000. By the time of his death, his prodigious literary output and commercial success had allowed him to pay off £70,000. The outstanding £59,000 owed to his creditors was met by various life insurances the author had set up.[30] Obviously this left little, if any, inheritance for Scott's descendants, although his sister was added to the civil list and received £200 per annum.[31] The London committee hoped that by raising a subscription they could secure Abbotsford for Scott's family, as an inheritance, and that would in their estimation be the most apposite action:

> It is thought no memorial can be appropriate to his name, as the permanent maintenance of the house which his residence has rendered classical, and the preservation of a library and collection of national antiquities, which his admirable taste selected, and which his genius made available to works that are in every hand, and have carried the glory of English literature through every civilised region of the earth.[32]

---

[28] 'Contributions at St Petersburg in the aid of the Fund now raising in Great Britain and on the Continent of Europe for Erecting a Monument at Edinburgh to the Memory of the late Sir Walter Scott, Bart.', appeal dated 15 Oct. 1832 from James Skene, Secretary. The sum raised, after costs, was £1,525; see also letter to Skene detailing a Public Meeting in New York to raise subscriptions, with a minimum contribution of $10 [NLS: MS. 965].

[29] *Scotsman*, 20 Oct. 1832, abridged from report in the *Glasgow Herald*.

[30] The successful agreement between Sir Walter Scott's family and his creditors was reported in *The Scotsman*, 3 Nov. 1832.

[31] 'Letter from King intimating pension conferred by him upon the sister of Sir Walter Scott', 24 Nov.(?), 1832 [NLS: MS. 1631].

[32] *Scotsman*, 1 Dec. 1832.

Therefore this London Committee did not think it inappropriate for the English nation to subscribe to a Scottish cause. It was organised by R. A. Dundas as secretary, and based in the Royal Society of Literature. The Abbotsford Subscription later advertised the formation of its (London) sub-committee, with Lord Melville as chairman. In the same advert in *The Scotsman* they also announced the formation of an Edinburgh sub-committee to raise funds for the preservation of Abbotsford – the majority of members of this sub-committee were already involved with the subscription for the monument in Edinburgh. The minutes show the strong sense of identification between England and the author of *Waverley*.

> the preservation of Abbotsford is of English suggestion. Englishmen have subscribed, and are subscribing, to accomplish this enlarged and liberal act of commemoration, – to entail property in Scotland on a race of Scotsmen; and that it is now requested of Scotsmen to give a favourable consideration to a measure for connecting Abbotsford for ever in the name of WALTER SCOTT. He whose inexhaustible and captivating power of description, has made the lochs, the rivers, the glens, and mountains of Scotland, objects of universal curiosity and admiration, while by a rare and intuitive faculty of penetrating into the recesses of the human mind, and, by possessing the most comprehensive knowledge, and masterly views of the history and antiquity of his country, he has unfolded the Scottish character, and exhibited it in all its genuine variety and dispelled prejudices, and has, with enchanting interest, made it to be familiarly known in every corner of the earth.[33]

That there existed a strong belief that Scott belonged to more than just Scotland, and was in fact part of England's heritage, was further made explicit by the earl of Haddington:

> Neither will I allow myself to be led away by those, I think not unbecoming, feelings of nationality, that make me proud to think this immortal genius owed his birth to my own native land. Whatever pleasure I may derive from this reflection, it would be most unjust to his fellow-countrymen on this side of the Tweed, not to acknowledge the great exertions they have made; and it must not be forgotten, that the idea of perpetuating Abbotsford in his family originated with them – it was of English, not of Scottish growth.[34]

This clearly conveys the impression that the English appeal was not just an Anglo-Scottish movement, but an English one. For the mid-nineteenth-

---

33 Ibid., 30 Jan. 1833; repeated in the note accompanying the third publication of the Abbotsford subscription: ibid., 20 Feb. 1833. See the membership of the Edinburgh Sub-Committee of the London Abbotsford Subscription in NLS: MS. 965.

34 'The Abbotsford Subscription' (1833), p. 31.

century Scottish nationalist it was, therefore, impossible to use Scott as an unambiguous symbol of nationhood, when England was highly committed to commemorating the memory of Scott itself – Scott as the tug-of-war nationalist symbol, indeed!

By May 1833, the amount of funds collected by the Edinburgh Committee for the Erection of a Monument to Sir Walter Scott stood at £5,752 14s., a sum which, apart from £300 from King William IV and £250 from other sources, was wholly raised in Edinburgh.[35] This total included £500 from the Bank of Scotland and other banks and banking companies in Scotland 'as a token of their admiration of the honourable feelings which induced him, after his embarrassments of 1826, to dedicate his talents, during the remainder of his life, to ensuring the full payment of his debts'[36] – conscience money if ever there was any. The contributors tended to refer simply to 'our distinguished son', or our 'illustrious countryman', rather than make any attempts to describe in their view the importance of Scott for Scotland.[37]

With over £5,500 in the committee's bank account, a sub-committee was appointed on 28 November of that year to look into a possible site for the monument.[38] They took two years to report, and ended up proposing nine alternative sites. At the same meeting a vote was taken on the design genre of the monument: an obelisk as opposed to a Gothic design. The latter eventually won out, chosen for being:

> peculiarly appropriate to this country – beautiful in its outline – capable of the greatest enrichment – of being raised to the most commanding altitude – exclusively and intimately associated with the events, areas, and characters, which occupied the genius of the man whose memory it is desired to honour.[39]

The style of architecture was to reflect the man – and also to reflect the man's influence on Scotland. This is the important point justifying our analysis of the meetings and appeals behind the construction of the monument to Scott. Any appeal for money, debate, or choice was successful if it was the truest reflection of the life and influence of Scott – it was on such terms that decisions were made.

After this meeting it was decided also that the architectural structure must include room for a statue 'of colossal dimensions' – something, again, not possible with an obelisk. Under these provisos, advertisements

---

[35] *Historical and Descriptive Sketch of the Scott Monument, Edinburgh* (Edinburgh, 1852), p. 4. Although a glance at the subscription papers shows this was not strictly true, with a small number of subscriptions from London, and occasionally from Liverpool and elsewhere. The likelihood is, however, that such contributors were Scots.

[36] *Subscription Paper for Memorial to Sir Walter Scott, to be erected in the Metropolis of Scotland*, broad sheet (n.d., *c*.1833).

[37] [NLS: MS. 825].

[38] *Second Annual Report of the Sub-Committee for Erecting a Monument to Sir Walter Scott* (Edinburgh, 1835).

[39] Ibid., p. 11.

were placed for the submission of designs, with prizes of 50 guineas for
the best three. In reply, forty-six different artists and architects sent for
inspection fifty-four plans, consisting of twenty-two Gothic structures,
eleven statues more or less accompanied with architecture, fourteen
Grecian temples, five pillars, one obelisk, and one fountain.[40] Again, like
the previous report, the sub-committee believed that since the
monument to Sir Walter Scott was to be built in his native city, it should
be erected in the

> ancient style of the country, not less desirable for its own intrinsic
> and most appropriate merits, than for the associations which it
> inspires, intimately associated as they are with the characters, the
> eras, and the events, on which he most delighted to dwell.[41]

Even John Steele, the sculptor chosen to create the statue to Scott, and
who had recently completed a highly commended likeness of Queen
Victoria, was given advice to ensure his work reflected Scotland's pride:

> That [the] monument must be seen from afar, to arouse the heart-
> felt feelings of Scotland's sons when they look upon the ancient
> seat. It must attach the citizen yet more to a home, honoured as the
> birth-place and adorned by the monument, as one of the greatest
> and best of men.[42]

In the event, despite the knowledge that more funds would be
required, the support of the residents and shop owners, and the
centrality and openness of the site, ensured the choice of the east end of
Princes Street. All that remained was for the committee to seek
empowerment through the requisite Act of Parliament, and to make the
arrangements with the tenant and others for construction to begin.[43] As
a consequence, on 30 April 1840, at the very meeting at which the choice
of site was finalised, the subscription was again re-opened. In an attempt
to overcome the Edinburgh public's subscription weariness, previous
subscribers were asked to contribute a sum equalling one half of their
original offering, although few did. In their publication of the list of
subscribers to the new appeal, the committee stated that an independent
meeting had been held in the Royal Hotel to form an auxiliary
committee to help fund-raising. This new committee had resolved to
divide Edinburgh up into one hundred districts, in which 'a certain

---

40 *Third Report of the Sub-Committee for Erecting a Monument to Sir Walter Scott* (Edinburgh,
    1838).
41 Ibid., pp. 7–8.
42 J. S. Memes, LL. D. Hons., S.A., *Letter to John Steele, Esq., S.A., Regarding the Scott
    Monument* (Edinburgh, 3 Apr. 1838).
43 *Council Record*, vol. 233, 7 Jul. 1840. The Bill ordered by the House of Commons 'for
    the erection at Edinburgh of a monument to the late Sir Walter Scott' was laid before
    the Council on 30 Mar. 1841, and remitted to the Lord Provost's Committee where
    assent was given and the City Seal granted in April: *Council Record*, vol. 234, 30 Mar.
    1841; vol. 235, 20 Apr. 1841.

number of influential Gentlemen have undertaken to wait upon the inhabitants of the District, to solicit subscriptions of any amount, however small'.[44] The auxiliary committee was formed separately from the sub-committee, and their organiser, Mr Dick of the Albion Company, was conscious of the view taken of his group by the 'higher ranks' in the sub-committee, which, as we have noted, was run by a landed and middle-class elite.[45] In fact, by 1844, Lord Cockburn, on behalf of the sub-committee, was delighted with this 'good practical committee ... of ... respectable tradesmen ... who ... entered on the business in a most business-like way'.[46] The plan adopted by the auxiliary committee was to give a schedule to three gentlemen or merchants residing in each district, for them to procure subscriptions in their vicinity, with the offer to present a 'splendid' engraving of the monument, from a drawing by the architect Mr Kemp, to those who subscribed one guinea or more. In tandem with concerts, theatrical and other amusements, and the offering of engravings and medals, the result was that in a few weeks £1,482 16s. 10d. had been added to the funds.[47] The auxiliary committee continued its activities until the completion of the monument in 1844. In total it collected £2,400, including £100 from Her Majesty Queen Victoria, £50 from the Queen Dowager, and £25 from Prince Albert.[48]

On 15 August 1840, the anniversary of the birth of Walter Scott, the foundation stone to the monument was laid with all due Masonic honour. The Masonic invitation to the ceremony (see Figure 7.1) shows the combination of Scottish and Masonic symbols with representations of Scott: the symbols of chivalric writings, the armour, harp, bible and flags proclaiming 'Marmion' and 'Veritas Vincit', are there beside a lion rampant standard, wild thistles and a crest of unicorns.[49]

Within the foundation stone was deposited a glass jar containing a range of contemporary newspapers and coinage, plus two plates inscribed with the words of Lord Jeffrey. In these, Jeffrey praised Scott's

---

[44] *Scotsman*, 3 Jun. 1840.
[45] The auxiliary committee consisted of: John Martin, banker; Robert Bryson, watchmaker; Robert Chambers, publisher; Ralf Richardson, tobacconist; William Marshall, jeweller; James Ballantyne, painter; William Donaldson, clothier; Wm Lindores, grocer; Frederick Shultz, Leith; John Dick, Albion Cloth Company, convenor of committee; John Castle, accountant, secretary of committee, *Historical and Descriptive Sketch of the Scott Monument*. Dick's reference to the sub-committee as being of the 'higher ranks' was reported in *Proceedings at the Public Meeting Regarding the Monument to Sir Walter Scott, 5th February 1844* (Edinburgh, 1844), p. 14.
[46] *Proceedings at the Public Meeting*, p. 13; *The Witness*, 19 Aug. 1846.
[47] See, e.g., *Theatre Royal, Edinburgh. In Aid of the Subscription to Erect a Monument to Sir Walter Scott* (Edinburgh, 1841), where on 29 Mar. the Officers of the Garrison will perform Planche's Historical Play 'Charles XII'.
[48] *Historical and Descriptive Sketch of the Scott Monument*, p. 9.
[49] This invitation can be found under the heading 'Scott Monument: Foundation Stone of Monument ... to be laid on 15 August 1840'; See also an ornate invitation, stating the officials at the ceremony: NLS: RY.1.1.23 (16).

writings as providing the greatest pleasure to the greatest number of any
except Shakespeare.[50] Thus unproblematic Scottishness was not
forthcoming, even at the time of Scott's greatest commemoration. Scott
and Shakespeare, like Scotland and England, were indelibly linked.

Many speeches were made that day, mostly stressing the image of
Scott as the man for all men, in the hope of striking a chord with all the
small subscribers who responded to the re-opening of the appeal. Once
the speeches were over, the band commenced playing 'Rule Britannia', a
salute of seven guns from the battery was fired, and the ceremony was
concluded. 'Rule Britannia' had not taken on its twentieth-century
connotations of English chauvinism, and, unproblematically, it rounded
off this day of Scottish national introspection in the metropolis of
Edinburgh.

Figure 7.1: *Ornate invitation to the Masonic procession and laying of the*
foundation stone of the Scott Monument, 1840[51]

The construction of the monument took place between 1840 and
1844. There was little debate concerning the monument during these
years, until it was realised that once again there were insufficient funds.
Appeals went out, stressing Scott as the Scottish contribution to British
literature, on a par with Shakespeare's contribution to the English

---

[50] *Historical and Descriptive Sketch of the Scott Monument*, pp. 7–8.
[51] NLS: RY.1.1.23 (16).

nation and Scott as the author venerated by all, but especially by the lowest classes, for his humanity – Scott as the universal man. In addition, over £3,000 was raised through 'several splendid assemblies, under the designation of Waverley Balls'. It was noted that on these occasions the 'elite of the rank, beauty, and fashion of the two cities assembled in vast numbers, and the scenes presented were of the most splendid and striking description'. The Waverley Ball in London claimed Prince Albert as patron, and included many eminent noblemen and famous public figures (such as Charles Dickens) as stewards. The London Waverley Ball raised £1,000, while a number of smaller Edinburgh Waverley Balls raised roughly a further £1,000 between them.[52] Thus the titled elite of society gave up the day-to-day running of the monument committee, yet their willingness to help raise money was still present, albeit in a more social, less committed, way. The construction of the monument was finally completed on 26 October 1844. It was inaugurated on 15 August 1846 and, as at the laying of the foundation stone six years earlier, a great public and Masonic procession took place.[53]

The commemoration of Scott: complementary national identities

By examining closely the discourse used to bind together the appeals to commemorate Scott, we have seen the constant recurrence of the four themes originally identified in the obituaries: (i) Scott the 'genius author'; Scott and the 'civilised world'; (ii) Scott as a great British literary figure; (iii) Scott as the Universal Man; and (iv) Scott as both the great chronicler of Scotland's past and the writer who instigated pride in, and recognition of, the Scottish nation. But because he was so greatly venerated in England, and in the world, he was not solely a Scottish icon. How could he be used as a product of Scotland's independent nationhood, and therefore a stepping stone to political independence, if he was part of England's literary heritage and part of a European enlightenment? The interpretation of Scott, by Scots, in the first half of the nineteenth century was firmly encapsulated in 150 years of Union. Sir Walter Scott was a Scottish icon forged in a society locked in a Union with England.

In much of the commonly cited discourse on Scott, the author has been taken a priori as a symbol of Scotland. Yet the rhetoric of commemoration presented here has exposed this view as too simplistic, hence the battle between Unionists and Nationalists for the 'true' memory of Scott's tradition.[54] If Scott continues to be used as a mirror whereby the Scottish nation sees itself, then we must accept that national identity is

---

52 Ibid., pp. 10–11.
53 *The Witness*, 19 Aug. 1846.
54 This has been explored superbly in J. Robertson, 'Walter Scott and the Crises of Unionist Patriotism', *Radical Scotland*, xlvi (1990), pp. 26–9.

not a unitary concept. To be 'Scottish' in the first half of the nineteenth century meant maintaining a number of different identities, four of which have been delineated through our examination of Scott. When we talk of Scottish nationalism in this period, including the formation of the National Association for the Vindication of Scottish Rights in the 1850s, we would be mistaken to use our twentieth-century eyes and look only for expressions of anti-Unionism and demands for a Scottish nation-state. As the analysis of the discourse employed for the commemoration of Walter Scott has demonstrated, at its fundamentals, Scottish nationalism in the first half of the nineteenth century was all about an independent Scottish nation locked into both the Union with England and the wider 'civilised' world.

The Burns centenary, 1859

Many of the themes in the discourse of celebration employed for Scott had been culled from an earlier view of Robert Burns – none more so, of course, than the cult of the common man. In their own ways, each author was the 'universal leveller'. The romantic and the ordinary, the noble and the pauper: contrasts which shaped Scotland's celebration of its most renowned literary sons. In 1859, one hundred years after the birth of Burns, a series of celebrations took place throughout Scotland, England and the world. It has been estimated that, in total, 872 formal events took place, and their breakdown was as follows:[55]

Table 7.1: *Burns Suppers, 1859*

Scotland	676
England	76
Ireland	10
Colonies	48
United States	61
Copenhagen	1
Total	**872**

Burns had been dead for over 60 years. In Edinburgh the monument and statue to the poet had been first mooted in 1812, the foundation stone was laid in 1831, and the completed statue handed over to Edinburgh City Council five years later.[56] Thus, by 1859, those celebrating the Burns centenary, unlike the obituary writers of Scott who were locked into recent memories of the man, could engage in a little more

[55] J. Ballantyne (ed.), *Chronicle of the Hundredth Birthday of Robert Burns* (Edinburgh, 1859) contains a comprehensive selection of the contemporary and newspaper reports of these celebrations.
[56] *History of the Burns Monument* (Edinburgh, 1961).

objectivity, and were much more concerned with their own contemporary national identity, than with that of Burns's own lifetime.

The biggest, and highest status, celebration was held at the Music Hall in Edinburgh. Tables were laid for 700 guests. The occupational profile of the top table was predominantly legal, but included a fair mixture of all sections of the middle class.[57] After the usual toasts to the Queen, the Prince Consort and the Prince of Wales, the chairman Lord Ardmillan then proposed a toast:

> I rise to propose to you 'The Arms of the Country' – not the heraldic arms, blazoned though they may be with the historic glories of disputed ages; but the two brave and powerful armies with which Britain now guards her shore, maintains her rights, and achieves her triumphs – the Navy and the Army.[58]

In particular the toast was made to the Scottish veterans within the British army, who were inspired by Burns, when 'in the desperate onset which sweeps the enemy from the field, how has there run along the Scottish line the sound ... that noblest of martial odes, – "Scots wha hae wi' Wallace bled"'. This was greeted by enthusiastic applause. The Scottish regiments were a proud symbol of Scotland who maintained their own identity, through their own clothing, within the British army. The heroic fighting of Wallace against the English now inspired the Scots to fight alongside the English against a common enemy. At this celebration to Burns, Professor Blackie then rose to propose 'The Meaning of Sir Walter Scott':

> There are six great names in Scottish History round which all true Scotsmen must gather as the proudest symbols of their nationality – two in the political world, Robert Bruce and William Wallace; two in the world of Christian heroism and devotedness, Patrick Hamilton, the first Protestant martyr, and John Knox, the founder of the National Church; two in its literary world, Robert Burns and Walter Scott. To which of these truly representative men we are most indebted for the inheritance of our great birthright of national feeling it is foolish to inquire; enough that they have all contributed to make us what, by the Grace of God, we are – a free, an independent, a thoughtful, a sober minded, and a conscientious – an earnest, determined, and preserving – and, so long as we cherish these virtues, a prosperous and invisible people.[59]

Scotland may not then have had political independence, but there was a strong sense of a nation independent in spirit, and that this independence

---

[57] A histogram displaying the occupational profile is reproduced in Morton, 'Unionist-Nationalism', chap. 8, Figure 8.1, p. 211.
[58] Ballantyne, *Chronicle of the Hundredth Birthday*, p. 3.
[59] Reported in Ibid., p. 14.

was achieved through the actions of its icons of history. This theme of Burns being fundamental to Scotland's nationhood was echoed at the celebration hosted by the Total Abstinence Society at an event with seating for 400 guests, but where it was estimated that no fewer than 1,500 persons crammed in to all the passageways at the Corn Exchange in Edinburgh. This meeting, it was pointed out, was held not to rival that being held in the Music Hall, but to enable all to honour a man and not be precluded from doing so by the cost of admission. The Rev. Alexander Wallace of Glasgow then addressed the audience:

> What is it that has led to such a national demonstration on the part of a people not easily moved to such meetings as the present? The gatherings in every town and village, from John O' Groats to Maidenkirk, are not sectional or party gatherings, but national. They breathe the spirit of an entire people; for Robert Burns was the most intensely national poet that ever lived. (Cheers; then followed by a rendition of Auld Lang Syne.)[60]

Elsewhere, at six o'clock, noticeably earlier than the middle-class meetings, the Trades' Delegation held a fruit soirée in Queen Street Hall. It was recorded that, when they opened the grave to lay Burns's wife beside the poet, they tried their hats upon the head of Burns, but found that his head was too big. The chairman concluded by 'a comparative sketch of the careers of Burns and James Watt, and the respective influence which each had, on the poetical peasant and the scientific artisan in his own and the present generation'. It was argued that 'Scotland needed a poet to embody in song the life of the nation before a foreign element had weakened and changed its conditions.'[61]

Ballantyne's compilation of the newspaper coverage of the celebrations includes reports on a number of other events. In Dunedin Hall in Edinburgh nearly 2,000 gathered under the auspices of a 'Working Man's Festival'; a fruit soirée run by the Dean and Water of Leith Mutual Improvement Society was held; a students' meeting, and other smaller meetings such as that of the workmen of Younger's Abbey Brewery and the Tam O' Shanter Club, took place. All social classes held their meetings and soirées, both big and small, to celebrate Burns's centenary. All stressed the voice of nationality Burns had given, in contemporary terms, to the Scottish peasantry through, in particular, 'Scots wha hae wi' Wallace bled'. But equally each gathering was an opportunity to express loyalty to Victoria and, as Britain emerged from a period of warfare, a time to bless and celebrate the empire's army and navy, and the contribution of the Scots to them. As the turn of events at the most prestigious Glasgow celebration demonstrated, following the honouring of the military exploits of Burns's own son, the toast was

---

[60] Reported in Ibid., p. 3.
[61] Reported in Ibid., p. 29.

drunk to the strains of 'Rule Britannia' on the organ. In order to demonstrate further this appropriation of Scotland's military achievements to the British cause, Colonel Mellish proposed the toast at the Glasgow celebration with the following:

> that the countrymen of Robert Burns have lately and most brilliantly participated in many gallant achievements of the British navy and army, and have thus shown that they are of the same stamp as those who bled with Wallace, and were led on by Robert Bruce, and whose spirit is still to be found among their descendants, ready with strong hands and stout hearts to do their duty to their country. (Applause.)[62]

In this use of the symbols of Scotland's past, Wallace and Bruce fought gallantly for the British army. Similar sentiments of the complex interchangeability of English and Scottish literary icons was made by Walter Buchanan, MP, in a toast to 'the English poets'. He argued that there was no reason why Shakespeare could not have been born in Scotland, nor any reason why Beattie or Campbell could not have been born in England – but Burns, never. 'He was a concentration of the genius of Scotland. His patriotism is Scotch ... His noble independence was Scotch.' But despite these sentiments to the singular Scottishness of Burns, Buchanan's was a toast to the English poets at one of the peak mid-century celebrations of Scottish nation-hood; and as he sat down, the band played the distinctly non-Scottish refrain, 'The Roast Beef of England'.[63]

But this was a celebration of the life and influence of Robert Burns; it is an important occasion for identifying the straws which are grasped by a society that believes itself independent, but still accepts that it is politically dependent. Mr Bailie Cochrane of Lamington rounded off the Glasgow celebration:

> there was a time, a century ago, when our nationality was endangered, when Scotland had been converted into that battlefield 'where those who conquer do not win, and they must lose who gain' – (Loud cheers.) – the nation felt that a stranger was in the land, and his cold hand was laid on its heart. Ay, at that time there was a danger, not for our national, but for our mental, independence, for a feeling sprung up in the south hostile to our progress; but in spite of all jealousies and antipathies, Scotland marched on England, not in any military way, but in the less dazzling march of mind and of intelligence; this march was preceded by Robert Burns. (Cheers.)[64]

It was Scotland's belief in its independent nationhood which formed the basis of its claims to equal rights with England under the Union. Scott

[62] Reported in Ibid., p. 41.
[63] Reported in Ibid., p. 45.
[64] Reported in Ibid., p. 57.

and Burns were two of the prominent icons to give substance to this belief in an independent civil society. This acceptance of Scottish nationhood was the oxygen that the National Association for the Vindication of Scottish Rights fed off. This belief in an independent Scottish nationhood was premised on a particular interpretation of the Union of 1707. The entire interplay between the symbols of Scottish nationalism and a Scottish identity, a British identity, and that of empire, was that Scotland and England came together under the Union as equals. Scotland, an independent nation, and England, an independent nation, joined together as Great Britain. This very particular interpretation of 1707 was focused on the memory of Sir William Wallace and King Robert Bruce, whose exploits in the fourteenth century, as it was understood in the mid-nineteenth century, forever guaranteed Scotland's independence and, it was believed, *resulted* in the Union of 1707.

The monuments to Wallace and Bruce

There has been, and indeed there still is, a steady stream of literature on the life and adventures of Sir William Wallace.[65] In 1858 one group of enthusiasts attempted to collate a bibliography of works relating to the patriot's life.[66] Most of the early works, especially the chap-books, were versions of (Blind Harry) Henry the Minstrel's poem. However, the number of publications increased, in particular over the nineteenth century when over sixty works published in the period from 1800 to 1858 were identified.

Previous attempts had been made in 1838 and 1846 to build monuments to Wallace at Stirling, partly as a response to an earlier Glasgow effort which 'had fallen through in consequence of the proverbial jealousy which had for so long existed between the Glasgow "folk" and the Edinburgh "people"'.[67] One successfully completed monument had been built overlooking the River Tweed in Dryburgh by the 11th earl of Buchan as early as 1814.[68] Buchan, the founder of the Society of Antiquaries in 1780, was in his later years thought quite mad by his neighbour Sir Walter Scott.[69] In fact Buchan was one of the few voices to argue for an independent Scottish republic at this time.

---

[65] Australian actor Mel Gibson visited Scotland to film *Braveheart*, a Hollywood-produced film with a reputed budget of $40 million, on the life of William Wallace. This interest has spurred on the work of populist historical writers, most notably J. Mackay, *William Wallace: Brave Heart* (Edinburgh, 1995).

[66] *Bibliotheca Wallasiania: List of the Various Works relating to Sir William Wallace from 1488–1858* (1858), Presentation copy, only 50 printed for private circulation.

[67] *Some Records of the Origin and Progress of the National Wallace Monument Movement, initiated at Glasgow in March 1856* (1880) Printed for private circulation, p. 6.

[68] *Glasgow Herald*, 14 Sep. 1991.

[69] R. G. Cant, 'David Steuart Erskine, 11th Earl of Buchan: founder of the Society of Antiquaries of Scotland', in A. S. Bell (ed.), *The Scottish Antiquarian Tradition: Essays to mark the bicentenary of the Society of Antiquaries of Scotland, 1780–1980* (Edinburgh, 1981).

A Wallace statue was constructed for Falkirk in 1820, two statues were on display in Ayr, and another monument in Craigie, Ayrshire, was started in 1837 and completed in 1855. A number of 'heritage sites' – Dunipace wood, waterfalls associated with the patriot hero, and the like, had also been identified.[70] A major publishing industry in cheap biographies, histories, plays and 'lives' of Wallace was in operation.[71] Yet the need was still felt for a national monument, especially to counter comments passed upon the National Association for the Vindication of Scottish Rights in the English press. Thus, in 1856, a movement to build a monument to Wallace at Stirling came into being.

(i) The Stirling monument
The movement to build the Wallace monument was inaugurated on 24 June – the anniversary of Bannockburn. The day was set aside as a holiday in Stirling, and all the corporations and public bodies joined together to form a procession. For the procession, as for other nationalist events throughout the world, 'many ancient and almost forgotten insignia were brought to light'. The band of course played 'Scots wha hae wi' Wallace bled', and upwards of 20,000 spectators gathered to see the earl of Elgin take the chair, and to hear why a monument should be built to Wallace at Stirling Bridge.[72] Elgin, who claimed lineal decent from Robert Bruce, stressed the centrality of Wallace and Bruce to the Union of 1707:

> if the Scottish people have been able to form an intimate union and association with a people more wealthy and more numerous than themselves, without sacrificing one jot of their neutral independence and liberty – these great results are due to the glorious struggle which was commenced on the plain of Stirling and consummated on that of Bannockburn ... And, gentlemen, if time permitted, I would even undertake to show that it is to the successful struggle carried on under Bruce and Wallace that it is showing that the Union between Scotland and England has not only been honourable to the former but profitable to the latter ... [With reference to the troubles in America and Ireland] I believe, therefore, that if the

[70] A former Subscriber for a Wallace Monument, *Traditions, etc., Respecting Sir William Wallace; Collected chiefly from Publications of Recent Date* (Edinburgh, 1856), pp. 6–8.
[71] See, e.g., *The Life of Sir William Wallace, the Scots Patriot* (Edinburgh, 1810); *The Tragedy of the Valiant Knight Sir William Wallace to which is prefixed a brief Historical Account of the Knight, and his Exploits for the Delivery of Scotland, and added a more particular Account of the way in which he was betrayed into the hands of the English* (Edinburgh, 1815?); P. Donaldson, *The Life of Sir William Wallace, the Governor General of Scotland and hero of the Scottish Chiefs. Containing his parentage, adventures, heroic achievements, imprisonment and death; drawn from authentic materials of Scottish History* (Hartford, 1825); J. D. Carrick, *Life of Sir William Wallace of Elderslie* (London, 1840); J. C., *Life of Sir William Wallace* (3rd edn, London, 1849); J. Paterson, *Wallace, the Hero of Scotland* (3rd edn, Edinburgh, 1876).
[72] *Scotsman*, 25 Jun. 1856.

whole truth were to be told in this matter, we might show that England owes to Wallace and Bruce a debt of obligation only second to that which is due to them by Scotland (hear, hear).[73]

Figure 7.2: *J. T. Rochead's winning design for the National Wallace Monument at Abbey Craig, Stirling*[74]

73 Ibid., 25 Jun. 1856. In 1930 the then earl of Elgin helped to raise funds for the purchase of 58 acres of land at Bannockburn to turn the battle ground into a heritage
   site: see D. McCrone, A. E. Morris and R. Kiely, *Scotland – the Brand: The Making of the
   Scottish Heritage Industry* (Edinburgh, 1995), p. 188.
74 *The Builder*, 28 Jan. 1860.

This view of English and Scottish unanimity found common cause with the seconder of the motion, Sheriff H. G. Bell: 'Scotland and England are now one. Any Scotchman who now entertained animosity towards England, or any Englishman who entertained animosity towards Scotland, would be set down as simply insane (hear, hear).'

On the same day, the Wallace Caledonian Institute held its first meeting with the express purpose of overseeing the laying of the foundation stone of the National Wallace Monument. It was also intended, by the raising of a subscription,

> to provide pecuniary aid to cultivate the literature, science, and art, connected with Scotland, in circumstances of indigence; and to provide premiums for compositions of national interest, to be competed for by students attending the Scottish Universities.[75]

As is common in nationalist movements, the focus of a national hero was being used to encourage educational understanding of that particular country, and thus to perpetuate national sentiment.

After this large first meeting, the appeal went out for subscriptions. The acting committee deemed it unnecessary to gave any details why money should be subscribed, because they believed 'he is dear to every Scottish heart':

> The lapse of centuries since our independence was achieved cannot diminish the claims of the patriot through whose valour it was won. The gallantry of our brave countrymen during the recent war ought to increase our veneration for the memory of him who preserved among us the spirit of national heroism.[76]

Scotland was therefore independent within the Union, and it was Wallace who was to be thanked. The laying of the foundation stone took place on 24 June 1861. The procession that day, and the banquet which followed in the evening, attracted nearly two full pages of coverage in *The Scotsman*. It was estimated that upwards of 50,000 people attended, with half of that number appearing in uniform.

Rev. Dr Rodgers, secretary to the organising committee, addressed the gathering:

> Well may the government of Britain recognise the proceedings of this day, for we are celebrating the memory of a chief who made Scotland a nation, placed a new dynasty upon the English throne, and, under Providence, was the means of uniting these kingdoms together on equal terms, and with equal rights.[77]

---

[75] *Scotsman*, 27 Jun. 1861.
[76] *National Monument to Sir William Wallace on the Abbey Craig near Stirling* (n.p., n.d.).
[77] *Scotsman*, 25 Jun. 1861.

Mr James Dunlop then spoke:

> though five hundred years have rolled away, that their social and
> political existence is owing to the victory which was gained here,
> instead of coming here with your peaceful banners, and the insignia
> of social triumph, you would have been engaged in the same awful
> and terrible contest in which Poland, Italy and Hungary are
> engaged at this time. (Cheers.) And never forget that if you are now
> in a fraternal union with England, and have now a great empire to
> defend, that it is to Wallace to whom it must be ascribed. (Cheers.)[78]

It was believed that, by defeating the English, Wallace gained
independence for Scotland and allowed Scotland to join with England as
an equal, which now guaranteed peace between the two nations.
Through warfare there was now peace, was the message. Archibald
Alison reiterated this point in his speech at the banquet which followed
the great public spectacle: 'We would have been unworthy to enter on
equal terms into the English Union if we had not shown ourselves able
to withstand her arms.'[79]

It took thirteen years from start to finish to give Scotland its national
memorial to William Wallace. Archibald Alison was dead by the time of
the inauguration on 11 September 1869, in what was described as a
'quiet' ceremony inside the monument.[80] The day started with the
presentation of a portrait of Dr Rodgers for his 'public work' towards
the venture (accepted by his wife), a dream of his childhood and plan for
thirty years.[81] Because the monument cost just over £13,401, rather than
the original price contracted at £6,500, and because the organising
committee carried a deficit of around £700, it was deemed 'inexpedient
to incur further expenses by organising any procession or demonstration'. Yet a 'considerable' number of people welcomed the 'very small'
inauguration procession on their walk from the Corn Exchange in Stirling to
the Abbey Craig, and afterwards there was a dinner with the 'usual loyal
toasts' as well as a toast to 'The Cause of National Independence'.[82]

This was a rather tame occasion to mark the official opening of the
most explicitly nationalist memorial before or since. Arguably it
coincided with a general lull in nationalist activity before the 1880s and
the question of Home Rule. Indeed, perhaps 1869 marks a shift between
Unionist-nationalism and the parliamentary political nationalism of the
Scottish Home Rule Association and its offshoots (a theme explored in
the final chapter). Nevertheless, the rhetoric behind the appeals to

---

[78] Ibid., 25 Jun. 1861.
[79] Ibid., 25 Jun. 1861.
[80] *Some Records of Origin and Progress of National Wallace Monument Movement*, pp. 25–6.
[81] *Scotsman*, 13 Sep. 1869.
[82] Ibid., 13 Sep. 1869.

subscribers throughout the time it took to complete this monument was that Scotland and England could never have been equals had it not been for the victories of William Wallace and, as we shall see, Robert Bruce. This mid-century interpretation of Scotland's *ethnie* was no more clear than an attempt in Edinburgh to build a monument to Wallace and Bruce in Scotland's capital.

(ii) The Edinburgh attempt

After three years of waiting for subscriptions to accumulate to allow work on the monument to Wallace at Abbey Craig to begin, it was proposed to build a monument to Wallace and King Robert Bruce in Edinburgh in 1859. Although this attempt failed, it is illuminating for the language used by its sponsors to obtain subscriptions to fund its construction. The theme was one of Scotland's two great leaders in her fight for independence from England in the fourteenth century now being used as symbols of support for the Union.[83]

Thus I. Noel Paton RSA put forward: 'A proposal to build a National Memorial of the War of Independence under Wallace and Bruce and of *its results* in the Union of England and Scotland to be erected in the Scottish Metropolis'.[84] Paton himself was to design the monument, and execute it in bronze.

The appeal started off by stating how the Wars of Independence strengthened the Union which now benefits both countries today. Paton played up to the Scots' belief in their own fair-mindedness and good character, of Wallace's 'PATRIOTISM' and Bruce's 'PERSEVERANCE'. Indeed, he proposed that the monument would be regarded as the 'intelligent' answer to peace for both sides, and that Wallace and Bruce added to England:

> The Scottish people cannot be influenced in erecting such a Memorial by anything unbecoming the lesson they seek to perpetuate; nor will England fail to appreciate the endeavour to deepen that love of country and of freedom, which is their own most cherished birthright. Intelligent Englishmen know full well the

---

[83] Compare this with contemporary populist history from Nigel Tranter, who describes Wallace as 'the patriot pure and simple'. He goes on: 'Here is the epic story of a young man of lofty stature but not very lofty birth who, driven to desperation and tears by the savagery and indignities perpetuated upon his fellow countrymen and women, as policy of Edward Plantagenet, Hammer of the Scots, took upon himself to challenge almost single-handed the might of the greatest military machine in Christendom; and who by indomitable courage, shrewd strategy, brilliant tactics, sublime faith and a kind of holy impatience, raised a stricken and leaderless nation to self-respect again and, in the absence of its king, became its acknowledged head as well as its saviour; and then was shamefully betrayed': N. Tranter, *The Wallace* (London, 1975), 'dust-jacket'.

[84] *Proposal to build a National Memorial of the War of Independence under Wallace and Bruce and of its results in the Union of England and Scotland to be erected in the Scottish Metropolis* (1859) [my italics; hereafter all original emphasis, unless otherwise stated].

source of Britain's strength and greatness, and that to the independence achieved under Wallace and Bruce, the UNION of Scotland with her sister kingdom, on terms satisfying to both, owes not only all its practicality, but the greater portion of its success. Intelligent Englishmen also know that their countrymen from Wallace's day, who, in language as in real influence, formed the staple of the English nation, not only had no sympathy with the feudal despotism of the Norman Kings, but mourned for the Scottish patriot as for the forlorn hope against the 'common oppressors of both countries'.[85]

The Wars of Independence were being presented as the success of Scotland which enabled it to obtain equality with England by the time of the enactment of the Union. Paton makes clear just how he sees the contribution of the two great heroes to the Union:

It is not to be a Monument to either Wallace or Bruce – a point as to which it is necessary that the utmost explicitness should exist. *It is the Deliverance and its results, as distinguished from the Deliverers*, that is here sought to be commemorated; and through the Deliverers, in the persons of the two great Chiefs ... its primary idea [is] that of commemorating 'Freedom's Battle' in Scotland.[86]

This is indeed the central passage, conveying explicitly Paton's intended symbolism for the monument. Wallace and Bruce were to be commemorated for their contribution – not to Scotland's independence – but to Scotland's equality with England at the time of Union – an event some 400 years after they departed from this earth. Moreover, by securing independence in the fourteenth century, and thus achieving equality of Union in the eighteenth century, the result was now peace and prosperity in the nineteenth century.

In my design for the projected Monument, while endeavouring to give due expression to the legitimate enthusiasm which we all feel towards our patriot heroes and martyrs, I have been studious to interweave the recognition of the peaceful triumphs of a later and happier day, when the sword of internecine war has been for ever sheathed in these lands, and the Scotch and their 'auld enemies', the English, had become, under the providence of God, one great, free, and united people.[87]

---

[85] Ibid., p. 3.
[86] Ibid., pp. 3–4 [my italics].
[87] Ibid., p. 5.

Figure 7.3: *Proposed design for an Edinburgh monument to Wallace and Bruce,* 1859[88]

This is a wonderful example of the interplay between two apparently opposite symbols of the Scottish past: the Wars of Independence on the one hand and the Union of 1707 on the other. It is the explicit use of pre-modern symbols of the Scottish *ethnie* in the mid-nineteenth century, with the aim of both strengthening the Union and appealing to Scottish notions of independence. It is this sort of discourse in the nineteenth century that has been referred to as Unionist-nationalism.

Edinburgh never got its monument to either Wallace or Bruce until the twentieth century. This was despite Edinburgh Council advertising

[88] *Proposal to build a National Memorial ...*

in 1882 'a public competition for a Wallace and Bruce memorial under the terms of a bequest left by Captain Hugh Reid'. It was remarkably successful in that £2,000 was made available for the construction, yet nothing materialised.[89] It was not until 1929 that statues to the two heroes were unveiled on the esplanade of Edinburgh Castle, by the duke of York, soon to be King George VI.[90]

The National Monument, Calton Hill

To take us from just before our period of study until just after it, the final example in this chapter will emphasise just how clearly the symbolism of national identity is linked to changing definitions of the nation/state axis. The National Monument on Calton Hill is essentially a symbol of England/Britain's 'glorious past' – but an attempt was made to foist it on to Scotland's heritage.

After one year of appealing for subscriptions, which reached 'almost every Scottish nobleman and many Scottish folk home and abroad, besides other sympathisers like the Duke of Wellington', £16,192 was gathered in 1822. It was hoped that £42,000 would be raised, but this was heavily dependent on a claim for a grant from £10,000 from parliament.[91] The amount subscribed was incorporated in an Act of Parliament in 1822, the year George IV came on his jaunt to Edinburgh, and it was for him that construction was started. This was built as a British national monument to be located in Scotland. It was said that 'the carrot' for Scotland was to commemorate the thousands of Scots lives lost during the Napoleonic Wars;[92] it was to celebrate the 'surviving heroes of Trafalgar and Waterloo'.[93] Bearing in mind what has been said earlier about the construction of a common identity, what could be better for the Union than a symbol of a united past for Scotland and England against a third party? 'Scots fighting the battles of their King' was how the duke of Atholl termed it.[94] As an expression of pro-Union loyalty, deliberately coinciding with George IV's visit, it was endorsed by Scotland's leading lights. Not only did the likes of the duke of Buccleuch subscribe, but so too did the then advocates Francis Jeffrey (the co-founder of the *Edinburgh Review*), and Henry Cockburn.[95] The sub-committee appointed to oversee the completion of the monument

89 *Conditions Relative to Proposed Public Competition for the Wallace and Bruce Memorial*, Captain Reid's Bequest, City of Edinburgh (1882).

90 M. T. R. B. Turnbull, *Monuments and Statues of Edinburgh* (Edinburgh, 1989); 'Index to the Inventory of Monuments maintained by the District', *Edinburgh District Council, Department of Architecture*.

91 R. T. Skinner, 'Scotland's Disgrace', *Scotsman*, 3 Dec. 1930 [NLS: MS 639].

92 J. Prebble, *The King's Jaunt: George IV in Scotland, 1822* (London, 1988), p. 153.

93 *Second Report to the adjourned meeting of Directors of the National Monument in Scotland* (1828) [NLS: MS. 352].

94 Prebble, *King's Jaunt*, p. 330.

95 Although being canny fellows their respective 100-guinea donations were made only on condition of completion of the monument.

hoped, in 1822, that it would receive many donations from England and the colonies:

> instead of being regarded as a mere local object, with which Scotchmen only are concerned, it will be looked upon as a splendid addition to the architectural riches of the Empire, in which all its inhabitants are interested.[96]

The point is that a celebrated British victory against France was being offered to, and was endorsed by, sections of the Scottish bourgeoisie as a symbol of not only England's and Scotland's united glorious past, but of Scotland's own glorious past.

By 1828 it was clear that the plans to complete the monument were in trouble. Some argued that the monument should be turned into a church. This idea had always been resisted. Indeed, as far back as 1820 a contributor to the *Scots Magazine* was insistent that an assurance that the National Monument would *not* become a church 'was essential to the success of the proposed measure'.[97] The plan for a church receded, but in an attempt to raise more capital, the idea was hatched to lay out the vaults of the monument into dormitories, consisting of some 100 cells, to create a shrine for the famous dead. Advertisements were published which solicited support for the venture because:

> of the absolute and most peaceful security which it could afford against any attempt to disturb the dead, and the pious desire which many families in Scotland must feel to have the remains of their illustrious ancestors deposited under the spot where their honourable names are to be inserted, and [so have] their noble deeds recorded by grateful posterity.[98]

This proposal collapsed in ignominious ridicule, and by 1846 a petition was raised in Parliament to change the function of the monument once more, and to complete it as a replica of the Parthenon 'for the sake of art'. Equally, by mid-century the failed monument was being seized upon as a symbol of national disgrace, and demands were made more forcibly concerning Scotland's heroic military past. The proposal was to:

> resurrect and keep alive that patriotic independence and martial spirit for which our countrymen were so distinguished, when Scotland was an independent kingdom, but which is apt to die away when united to a larger and richer kingdom like England.[99]

---

[96] *Sub-Committee appointed by a General Committee of Subscribers at Edinburgh, for carrying into execution the design of erecting a National Monument in Scotland in Commemoration of the Triumphs of the late War by Sea and Land* [NLS: MS. 638].

[97] A Traveller, 'Restoration of the Parthenon', *Scots Magazine* (Feb. 1820) [NLS: MS. 638].

[98] G. Gleghorn, 'Essay on the national monument of Scotland', *Transactions of the Architectural Institute of Scotland*, 2nd session (Edinburgh, 1852), pp. 85–6.

[99] Ibid., pp. 113–14.

Figure 7.4: *Title page of the proposal to build a national memorial to Wallace and Bruce in Edinburgh, 1859*[100]

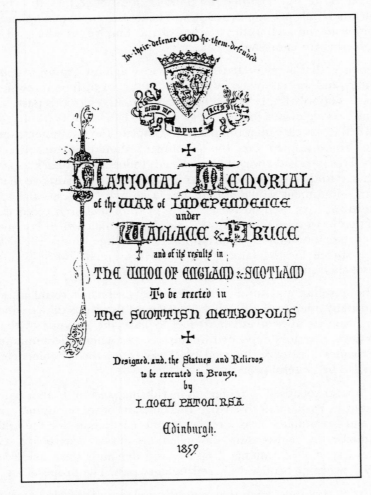

George Gleghorn then quotes from Archibald Alison:

> There are few examples in the history of mankind of any independent kingdom being incorporated with another of greater magnitude without losing, in process of time, the national eminence, whether in arts or arms, to which it had arrived ... Whatever can arrest this lamentable progress, and fix down in a permanent manner the genius of Scotland to its own shores, confers not only an incalculable benefit upon this country, but upon the United

---

100 *Proposal to build a National Memorial ...*

Empire, of which it forms a part. The erection of the National Monument in Edinburgh seems calculated in a remarkable manner to assist this most desirable object.[101]

But Gleghorn insisted that the military achievement was that achieved by Great Britain, who 'fought single handed against bounded Europe for the preservation of her laws, her liberties and her altars'.[102]

The monument has never been completed, although John Grant argued, in the middle of the century, that a practical use should be made of the national monument:

> The thirteen naked columns which rise on the Calton Hill must no longer continue an object of national ridicule. Let us now demand from the Government a share of what we are so rightly entitled to. Let the national monument be finished and occupied as a museum of geology, natural history, antiquities, and sculpture.[103]

From early to mid-century the shift in symbolism has gone from Britain's military achievements, to commemorating Scotland's military dead, to celebrating the arts of Scotland. There was little debate thereafter until 1906, when a publication compiling three articles in the *Evening News* condemned the earlier symbolism of Scotland's contribution to the British army being awarded a national monument.[104] In the argument presented in the *News* the idea of the completed monument retaining its original symbolism was disparaged. No longer was the monument to celebrate Britain's victories against France (and the myth/history of the 'Auld Alliance' is relevant here), but rather it appeared to be incompatible to host such a 'British' monument in Scotland's capital and to term it a national monument. The proposal now was to alter the whole meaning of the building by turning its purpose into a home for the Scottish National Gallery, developing the theme of peaceful progress suggested by John Grant. It was time to celebrate Scotland-as-Scotland, not Scotland as part of the Union with England (i.e. Britain), when national commemoration was called for.

Unionist-nationalism, no more

The very incompleteness of the National Monument is so valuable for our purposes because it allows us to examine for the whole of our period the nationalist rhetoric which surrounded it. The idea of celebrating Scotland's equality with England in the Union, which the National Monument originally symbolised as 'Britishness', and which was

---

[101] Quoted in ibid., p. 114.
[102] Ibid., p. 117.
[103] Ian, 'Neglect of Scotland', *Caledonian Mercury* (n.d., n.p.).
[104] *The National Monument to be completed for the Scottish National Gallery on the model of the Parthenon: An appeal to the Scottish People by William Mitchell, S.S.C.* (1906).

presented as 'Scottishness' in the examples of Scott, Wallace and Bruce, had disappeared by the turn of the century. The meaning of Scotland was no longer within the parameters of Union; it was no longer possible to include Britain and the Union as an unproblematic part of the expression of Scottish national identity. Unionist-nationalism had died out in the 1860s, to be replaced by an identity that was 'more Scottish than British'. Scottish life was to be celebrated, not Scottish death within the British army. It was to be a Scottish national monument, not a British national one – Scottish-nationalistic, not Unionist-nationalistic.

In the period from 1830 to 1860, Scott, Burns, Wallace and Bruce were used as symbols of the Scottish *ethnie* to celebrate Scotland's equality with England. The two nations had joined together as equals in the Union of 1707, and the Scottish past was employed to demand that equality be maintained within the spirit of the Union – hence the term, Unionist-nationalism, applied to the early and mid-nineteenth century, a unique period in the historical construction of Scottish national identity. However, this was an expression of identity that would not see out the century. As has been argued throughout, both the expression of Unionist-nationalism and its demise were linked to the state/civil society axis – that is, linked to the practicalities of 'government'. The governing of civil society could no longer be carried out by a philanthropic bourgeoisie and an empowered local state. The scale of urbanisation and the large amounts of funding and legal and professional expertise involved in all areas from health to sanitation to planning (and all the rest), meant that centralised knowledge and centrally co-ordinated and standardised intervention was increasingly seen as inevitable in society. By the final quarter of the nineteenth century, the focus of government was Westminster, the parliamentary state. Indeed, it was the system of national education post-1870, the creation of the Scottish Office in 1885, and the extension of the franchise to the rural working class in the same year, which had completed the definite shift to a centralised state and fulfilled the fears of the Scottish Rights Society.

The change in symbolism for the national monument expressed a growing split, so evident today, between the Union and Scottish national identity, and it reflected this change in government. Parliamentary nationalism was the inevitable consequence, focusing on Home Rule and bringing the Union into opposition to a new conception of government in Scotland. By the final quarter of the century the Westminster state and the Union were the playing fields of Scottish nationalism, politically relevant like never before, forcing Scottish national identity to change forever. Unionist-nationalism as the pinnacle of Scottishness was a candle in the wind; it was fixed to its own time and to its own place.

CHAPTER EIGHT

Conclusion: Unionist-Nationalism – A 'State' within a State

National identity remains the slipperiest of phenomena. This elusiveness is universal, yet any answer to the question 'who are we?' has, since the age of nationalism, merged ethnic identity with the linearity of history to make the 'nation-state' the means of making sense of other class, familial and religious identities (to name but a few). National identity touches us all, in every period of our lives, although for some the awareness is greater than for others, and some decades are more extreme or political. How we interpret national identity and nationalism is, straightforwardly at least, an examination of content: of the relevance of language, of race, of territory, of lineage, of battles won and battles lost, and of the myriad of other features of what Ernest Renan described as the 'spiritual commonality' underpinning the national soul.[1] Merely listing the composition of nationalism, as building blocks towards political mobilisation, say, can only be of value if we know how to measure its strength. If we care to think about it, we all have some sense of our national identity, but is it relevant to us? Unproblematically (to this author at least), the theory of nationalism in its purest form is, as the modernists would have it, the making congruent of the ethnic and the political. This is first and foremost a theory of self-government. But the strictures of one state for one nation will not allow the measurement of Scottish national identity in the mid-nineteenth century – in the United Kingdom of Great Britain and Ireland – because it fails to account for the duality and even multiplicity in the relationship between the British state and its four civil societies. More importantly, it is a circumscribed reality of self-government at this time. A non-sociological application of the political theory of nationalism ignores the extent to which urban life in Scotland was governed by its own elites, outwith central state administration and outwith central state-created Boards of Control and other bureaucracies.

Mid-century Scottish national identity can only be interpreted wrongly if the state/civil society axis is misconceived. From the evidence presented in Chapters 6 and 7, it is certain that the strength of Scottishness was great and that its coherence was profound. The rhetoric

---

[1] E. Renan, *Qu'est-ce qu'une nation?*, trans I. M. Snyder (Paris, 1882), p. 26.

was straightforward, however strange it may seem to twentieth-century nationalists: Scotland wanted more union, not less. Scotland's mid-nineteenth-century nationalists believed their nation had entered the Union of 1707 as an equal, and that was how they demanded to be treated. Wallace and Bruce, by preserving Scotland's independence in the fourteenth century, made it possible for Scotland to join with England as a partner in the eighteenth century, and enabled Scotland to enhance Great Britain's power over the Empire in the nineteenth century. The icons of Scotland's *ethnie* were used to celebrate both Union with England and Scotland's independent nationhood.

This is not the first piece of research to identify the reluctance of the bourgeoisie of nineteenth-century Scotland to break with the Union. However, what this work has attempted to demonstrate is that this unwillingness should not be seen as failed nationalism or romantic nationalism, but rather that it should be interpreted as a positive and rational response to 'government' in the period between 1830 and 1860. Two notions have been central to the argument presented here. The first has been the state/civil society axis, because it is upon this that national identity is formed. The second is that of 'government'; the state/civil society axis shapes national identity because it is the axis of 'government'.

The ambiguity in the axis between Scottish civil society and its state has been apparent since 1707. Indeed, the very concept of the British 'nation-state' is untenable because of the disparity between a number of civil societies and the one unitary British state (Chapter 1). It has been argued that the resulting form this state/civil society axis took meant that eighteenth-century Scotland was effectively 'managed' on behalf of the British state; after the rebellions of 1715 and 1745, Scotland more or less carried on quietly with its own social and economic development, accepting the role of junior partner with England, and in many ways there was no alternative. Although Scotland, increasingly, became a part of the British body-politic after 1760, the nation enjoyed the absence of the distraction of politics. However anachronistic that management was, it allowed the Scottish elites to be both Scottish and British in their economic, social and political lives – this was acceptable because the state was *their* institution.[2] Dual identities were complementary identities, and no matter what the level of Anglicisation and romanticisation of the symbols of Scotland was, full integration was not apparent, and an all-embracing British civil society failed to materialise. Post-1760 Scottish iconography – in particular that of tartan – was appropriated by the British state, yet it did not break through to cloud the junior partnership of Scotland's dual loyalty.

---

[2] Hall, 'In search of civil society', p. 15.

By the turn of the century the acceptance of Westminster 'management' was challenged by an expanding bourgeoisie, rising from an industrialising society. The state/civil society axis was re-shaped. The Victorian state (Chapter 2) abandoned mercantilism in favour of free trade. In response to urbanisation and industrialisation, this unitary state created a framework whereby Scottish civil society was enshrined on behalf of the bourgeoisie; it was a society tailor-made to the intellectual, moral and practical demands of that group. The concept of infrastructural power explains the link between the formal organs of the state, the legal framework and civil society. The empowerment of the urban bourgeoisie to govern their public world cemented the 'gap' between Scottish civil society and its state: it forged the state/civil society axis.

For theorists of politics with a capital 'P', Scotland was the dog that did not bark: it had nothing but a cultural sub-nationalism that was inevitably inferior (Chapter 3). But such theorists misunderstand the importance of local solutions and resistance to central government. It is a misconception to interpret and judge the symbols of the Scottish *ethnie* in terms of the failure to demand a Westminster-style parliamentary Scottish state, because there was no such demand. As Neil MacCormick has pointed out in a discussion on the idea of divided and limited sovereignty, 'the theorists of the nineteenth century were anxious to argue that nothing which is supreme power can co-exist with a rival supreme power in any stable way within a single legal or political order'.[3] Scottish Whigs, such as Henry Cockburn, regarded Scottish politics as having ended in 1832,[4] and were locked into a British constitutional heritage that was English in origin.[5] Indeed, the idea of 'England's constitutional perfection' was also a part of mid-century French Romanticism.[6]

The strength of English constitutionalism was undoubtedly pushed as the means of political enfranchisement by the bourgeoisie at first, but it was also pushed by the working class: 'the permanent tranquillity of a state must always depend on the honourable and virtuous sentiments of the people'.[7] The Radical Wars of 1820 have been searched by historians for their national content, but although both those involved and the United Scotsman Societies 'wanted to dissolve the Union of Parliaments between England and Scotland of 1707', and intended to 'set up a

---

[3] N. MacCormick, 'Sovereignty: myth and reality', *Scottish Affairs*, xi (1995), p. 7.
[4] M. Fry, 'The Whig interpretation of Scottish History', in Donnachie and Whatley, *Manufacture of Scottish History*, p. 81.
[5] C. Kidd, *Subverting Scotland's Past: Scottish Whig Historians and the Creation of an Anglo-British Identity, 1689–c.1830* (Cambridge, 1993).
[6] J. Barzun, 'Romantic historiography as a political force in France', *Journal of the History of Ideas*, ii (3) (1941), p. 321.
[7] *The Beacon*, i (1), 6 Jan. 1821.

Scottish Assembly or Parliament in Scotland',[8] few seem to have followed up this call.[9] The radical weavers in Renfrewshire in 1819 demanded their rights in line with the Magna Carta[10] while the Lancashire cotton spinners sang *Scots wha hae wi' Wallace bled* to express their freedom as workers and the power of their trades union against tyrants.[11] Smout notes that 15,000 assembled at Bannockburn in 1814 to mark the 500th anniversary of the famous battle, and 1815 witnessed 10,000 'democratic people' following in the footsteps of the Covenanters in Ayrshire.[12] When Edinburgh planned to mark the passing of the 1832 Reform Act, it debated whether to celebrate with an 'illumination' or with a 'Goddess of Liberty' (70 feet high and placed on a 30-foot pedestal). *The Scotsman* reproduced an extract from *The Times* which noted that several correspondents to that paper insisted that 15 June should be the day of celebration, because that was the 'day on which Magna Carta was signed at Runnymede, AD 1215'.[13] At the procession to celebrate reform held in Dalkeith in June, banners displaying the images of Wallace and Bruce as well as St Andrew's flags were displayed alongside the Union Jack, images of Britannia, and Nelson's famous order that 'England expects every man to do his duty!'[14] One of the speakers that day, Mr Hay, thanked the 'patriotic king' for 'helping secure reform'. Then, observing that George IV stayed at Dalkeith in 1822 (as we note in passing the complaints by the NAVSR about the state of repair at Holyrood at this time which precluded his staying there)[15] when George's reception from the crowd was subdued, Hay stated that now the cheers were loud, 'yes – such more the cheers which must have resounded on the fields of Bannockburn, when the battle was won and Scotland was free'.[16] But the cheer of Bannockburn which gave Scotland its freedom was now the cheer of the Hanoverian king, for it was he who was feted as the deliverer of Scotland's latest political freedom: 'To break free from the self-selected magistrates of the towns and paper votes of the county; the king was no longer of a faction, but of the people.'[17]

When Edinburgh finally held its reform jubilee on 10 August – the city deemed it prudent to wait until the Scottish legislation was

8 P. B. Ellis and S. MacA'Ghobhainn, *The Scottish Insurrection of 1820* (London, 1970), pp. 37, 112.

9 Lynch, *Scotland*; J. D. Young, *The Rousing of the Scottish Working Class* (London, 1979) most explicitly links this radicalism with nationalism. This view is carefully contradicted in T. Clarke and T. Dickson, 'The birth of class?', in Devine and Mitchison, *People and Society in Scotland*, i, p. 302.

10 Clark and Dickson, 'Birth of class?', p. 302.

11 Smout, *Century of the Scottish People*, p. 237.

12 Ibid., pp. 236–7.

13 *Scotsman*, 6 Jun. 1832; without a negative comment it can be assumed that *The Scotsman* believed the idea applicable to Scotland.

14 Colley, *Britons*, pp. 338–9. She cites *Order of the Procession* (Edinburgh, 1832).

15 Christie, *Injustice to Scotland Exposed*.

16 *Scotsman* 13 Jun. 1832.

17 Ibid., 13 Jun. 1832.

finalised – this mixture of nationalism, unionism and radicalism was again apparent. The event was opened with (significantly) the 'national anthem' of *Rule Britannia*, sung by fifty professional gentlemen. This was followed by vocalists singing the 'King's anthem', there were a number of addresses, then the singing of *Scots wha hae wi' Wallace bled*. According to the report in *The Scotsman*, upwards of 15,000 took to the streets in a march, with up to 80,000 on the links, and nearly all the shops were closed. The procession included a model of Sir William Wallace in full armour, with closed helmet and huge sword (which preceded the Caledonian Youth Society). Similar patriotic flags and banners were displayed at Leith by the Wallace Youth Society and the Highland Societies, including a large thistle nearly ten feet high.[18]

It had been just ten years since Walter Scott's pageantry of Highland mysticism and romance in which the oversized monarch of German extraction was paraded in front of Scottish society, yet the Stuart symbolism of that day was now downplayed as Scotland celebrated Reform. Now it was Wallace, Bruce and St Andrew – not tartan, clans and Jacobitism – who were intermixed with English monarchical and constitutional history as the popular foci of Scotland's relationship to Westminster.

The argument here, of course, is that this Unionist-nationalism was a product of the 'gap' between Scottish civil society and the British state – a gap which precluded the setting-up of a Scottish state to rival that of Westminster. The ways and means through which the middle classes structured this gap are vital to explaining their administration of civil society. For the middle class in the mid-nineteenth century, claims to status, economic power and statements of identity involved manipulating the institutions and organisations which lay between family and state within the urban environment. Social power was achieved by publicly proclaiming name and influence in the towns and cities. This involved many public acts, and was demonstrated through a wide repertoire of subscriptions and memberships. It was through the associational activity in their public life that the structure was in place to understand the practical nature of 'governing' by the urban middle class (Chapter 4).

Voluntary societies were sometimes philanthropic in objective; but some existed as cultural power and status channels for intra-class conflict within the middle class. The structure of a typical voluntary society was one of status hierarchies inversely related to their day-to-day organisation. A wide range of resources was mobilised by philanthropic societies both to carry out their work and to raise subscriptions and donations. Through its subscriber action the Edinburgh bourgeoisie exercised 'social control' on the working class and the poor, and it was the prime means by which the bourgeoisie responded to a rapidly changing

---

[18] Ibid., 11 Aug. 1832.

society. Such voluntary societies were the focal point of the battle for
hegemonic control in mid-Victorian Edinburgh.

When this use of the concept of 'social control' was extended, and it
was acknowledged that it was a product of bargaining, then analysis of
the political and subscriber activity of the middle class showed it acting
as a coherent class in all that it did. The degree and nature of middle-
class control over urban society was apparent in an analysis of its political
and subscriber profile (Chapter 5). An active elite was identified whose
subscriber activities were spread between a number of societies, and who
supported a number of causes. Led by the Lord Provost or the local
county laird as patron, a certain group of high status individuals exerted
a great deal of influence over Edinburgh's civil society, an influence that
is usually underestimated. Indeed it was the lawyers who were shown to
be over-represented within a number of different societies. It was
postulated that this was indicative of their social power, and that the
legal professions dominated the 'rank and file' membership of the most
active subscribers in Edinburgh's civil society mid-century. In addition,
the occupational groups, 'distribution & processing' and 'craft', were
shown to be numerically important subscribers in most of the societies.
In terms of voting, the subscriber population often followed the general
enfranchised bourgeoisie, although the subscriber population often
produced some strong extremes in their candidate pair choice, and
occasionally subscriber interest outweighed class. The analysis of the
amount subscribed to different causes produced the expected split
between 'low' and 'high' status societies, but stressed the appearance of
pockets of subscriptions. As Chapter 5 concluded, the majority of
subscriptions tended to bunch around favoured amounts, irrespective of
occupation or society. Thus, it was argued, the subscriber population
acted as a class – the culture of subscription across all societies was a
common one, led by the multiple actions of an energetic few.

This was the middle-class action that administered Edinburgh's civil
society. The fear and distrust of 'centralisation' and of the spreading
parliamentary state was fundamental to the rhetoric of the National
Association for the Vindication of Scottish Rights. 'A Scotchman's'
opposition to 'functionaryism' was a prime example of the expression of
Scottish nationalism with an explicit opposition to anything to do with
Westminster.[19] The influence of organisational and associational activity
within civil society was paramount. Bryant has suggested that such an
understanding of civil society would allow the imagining of the 'civil
nation', rather than the 'ethnic nation'.[20] Perhaps we can suggest that
Scotland was, and is, just such a nation, because its *ethnie* was mobilised
to defend its civil society (rather than its civil society being a product of

---

[19] 'Scotchman', *Scottish Rights and Grievances*.
[20] C. G. A. Bryant, 'Civic nation, civil society, civil religion', in Hall, *Civil Society*, pp. 146–7;
see also Hall's introduction to this volume, pp. 26–9.

its *ethnie*). The civil society egg came before the ethnic chicken, as it were, and this was the outcome of a civil society that was enshrined by the state, rather than in opposition to a despotic state. The 'gap' between nation and state was maintained by giving limited powers to the middle classes, and this both ensured stability and produced the Scottish nation's 'state'. Arguably this is what Gellner means by his term the 'modular man' [*sic*] in civil society: the individual who

> can combine into specific-purpose, *ad hoc* limited associations, without binding himself by some blood ritual. He can leave an association without being open to the charge of treason. A properly terminated contract is not an act of treachery, and is not seen as such. A tenant who gives due notice and pays the recognised rent, acquires no stigma if he moves to a new tenancy. Yet these highly specific, unsanctified, instrumental, revocable links or bonds are effective! *This* is civil society: the forging of links which are effective even though they are flexible, specific, instrumental. Society is a structure, it is not atomised, helpless and supine, and yet the structure is readily adjustable and responds to rational criteria of improvement.[21]

Mid-century urban life in Scotland provided this very understanding of civil society. There the middle classes employed the voluntary organisation as a means of association and contract, which allowed participation (class action) within a conception of liberty and decentralisation, and which maintained status and hierarchical divisions, as well as the means to withdraw concerted action at a moment's notice, if so desired.

Unionist-nationalism has been argued to be an expression of Scottishness directly linked to this axis of nation and state. This interpretation of Scotland's *ethnie* does not dismiss its nationalism as romantic, or cranky, or transitory, or just weak because of its failure to stimulate 'real' history. It does not dismiss Scottish nationalism because of its failure to engage in a parliamentary political project[22] – nor does it regard Scotland's support for British politics as being unchallenging.[23] Rather, the rationality of this nationalism as a response to the mid-Victorian state and the independence of Scottish civil society is paramount. We must be sure that we continue to ask 'Scottish questions' of the state and nation in the United Kingdom, rather than compare Scotland with England or with European nations-to-be in the nineteenth

---

[21] Gellner, 'Importance of being modular', p. 42.

[22] As chap. 3 suggests, Breuilly, *Nationalism and the State*, and Hobsbawm, *Nations and Nationalism*, work within the most narrow 'Political' definitions of all the theorists examined in this study.

[23] Harvie used the phrase, 'geological solidity' to highlight the lack of 'political action': C. Harvie, 'Scottish politics', in A. Dickson and J. H. Treble (eds.), *People and Society in Scotland*, vol. III: *1914–1900* (Edinburgh, 1992), p. 242.

century.[24] The fact that the Union of 1707 was agreed peacefully must always be borne in mind. Moreover, despite the Jacobite rising which followed, Protestantism has done much to make notions of Britishness palatable to the mainland nations. When politics is brought in to the equation, our 'Scottish questions' should direct us to the town councils, and when we talk of 'citizen politics', we must look to the £10 ratepayers. It was the urban middle class that ran local government, yet importantly also they exercised a class and social power through a range of voluntary activities in their 'public life'.

After 1860, and after 1870 in particular, this 'government' was changed; at the same time the contemporary interpretation of Scottish national identity was also remade. The working class had gained the vote in 1868 and, more widely, in 1885; 'citizen politics', so essential to the maintenance of state structures, was not now confined only to men of 'worthy character'. The 1872 Education Act opened the new school boards to a property franchise of only £4.[25] By the 1870s the local bourgeoisie lacked the empowered structures that could deal with the extent of the demands made on 'government'. The state was under pressure from the working class, and as industrial society matured in Britain and in the world at large it had to involve itself in areas of society that it had previously avoided. Westminster and the 'quangos' of the state were therefore pushed to the forefront of 'government', as the focus of the state/civil society axis. Both economically and socially a centralised state came to be the norm in Britain.[26]

The Scottish Home Rule Association (SHRA) came into being in 1886, the year after a Scottish Secretaryship (located at Dover House in London) had been established. Although an 'all party' organisation, its weakness was in its very heterogeneity; its romantic notions, and its mixture of socialist and land reforming membership, made uneasy bedfellows. Indeed, as a manifestation of the growing feeling of national identity, which had been so quiet for much of the 1860s and 1870s, it was the impetus for a number of Home Rule Bills which were placed before Parliament following Gladstone's Midlothian speeches of 1885, concern over the balance of public funds between Scotland and England,[27] and the various attempts to solve the question of Irish devolution. Yet, Fry argues, in Scotland there was still the feeling that Westminster was sufficient, if only it would be more sensitive and more

[24] R. J. Morris and G. Morton, 'Where was nineteenth-century Scotland?', *Scottish Historical Review*, lxxiv (1994).

[25] McNeel-Caird, 'Local government and taxation', p. 141.

[26] For this shift, see R. J. Morris and G. Morton, 'The re-making of Scotland: a nation within a nation, 1850–1920'; and R. J. Finlay, 'Scottish nationalism and Scottish politics, 1900–1979', both in M. Lynch (ed.) *Scotland, 1850–1979: Society, Politics and the Union* (London, 1993).

[27] McNeel-Caird, 'Local government and taxation', p. 158.

flexible, and that the SHRA 'saw Home Rule as a step towards greater democracy within a United Kingdom still firmly united'.[28]

Devolutionist or not, separatist or not, the SHRA marked a fundamental shift, whereby the demands for Scottish rights have been about recreating a formal Scottish state on the lines of Westminster. And whether this was to be a devolved state or a separate state, arguments over Scottish rights from the end of the nineteenth century and into the twentieth century have been about the power to legislate, to raise revenue, to manage the economy and the formal actions of the state, rather than the empowerment of informal action. Simply put, the complexity of twentieth-century society and the opening up of 'citizen politics' has precluded the ability of an empowered bourgeoisie to govern their civil society: an elected modern state dominates the axis. This was a change that was recognised by an SHRA pamphleteer reviewing a reprint of W. E. Aytoun's 1853 *Blackwood's Magazine* article, 'Scotland since the Union':

> Almost the only favourable feature of these times [1891], as com-
> pared with those forty years ago, is that 'the great body of the
> people' have now been endowed with the political power that was
> formerly possessed by the classes, whose vested interests render
> them adverse to political changes which, for ought they know, may
> deprive them of the privileges they manipulate.[29]

It was certainly clear that by 1891, citizen politics had altered the axis of 'government'.

To continue this theme, and to speculate a little, perhaps developments in Europe today, especially with respect to the concept of 'regionalism' are the next stage in the axis of government: a way of going beyond nationalism of the unitary nation and the unitary state (as acknowledged by the SNP's slogan 'Independence in Europe'). With the prospect of a federal Europe the state/civil society axis is again shifting, although with what balance it remains unclear; but we can be sure that Scotland's *ethnie* will be dragged with it, and the interpretation of that *ethnie* will subtly, but undoubtedly change.[30]

The use made by nationalists of a nation's *ethnie* is linked to its requirements to govern its own territory at any given time. Because of the developments in the central state after 1870, the dominant version of the Scottish *ethnie* is today not a Unionist-nationalist one, although that

---

28 Fry, *Patronage and Principle*, p. 105.

29 *Scottish Home Rule* [c.1891] 'Pamphlets' [NLS: 3.2850 (5)], p. 7.

30 See C. Harvie, *The Rise of Regional Europe* (London, 1994); and D. Martin, *European Union: The Shattered Dream?* (Broxburn, 1994), both reviewed in D. McCrone, 'Editorial: rhetorics of regionalism', *Scottish Affairs*, vii (1994). This issue is further explored (within the example of Northern Ireland) in J. Anderson and J. Goodman, 'European and Irish integration: contradictions of regionalism and nationalism', *European Urban and Regional Studies*, i (1) (1994).

exists – unattached to the current critical axis of government. Sir Walter Scott remains an ambivalent icon because of his Toryism and his Unionism, but he is now explicitly part of the Scottish *ethnie*, and no longer does he remain the tug-of-war icon between Scotland, England and the wider world.[31] Similarly in the late twentieth century, as the Saltire Society appeals for funds to restore a crumbling statue of Wallace at Lanark, and as the video presentation at the National Wallace Monument explains, the warrior should be commemorated because he defeated the English and enabled Bruce to extract Scotland's independence, 'Separate in all things from England', from the English crown in 1328.[32] At no time are these heroes commemorated today because they helped maintain the Union with England. By 1891, the nationalist and publisher Charles Waddie asked 'how Scotland lost her parliament and what became of it?', not 'how the Union could be made to work better?', which his contemporaries had asked forty years previously.[33] Our understanding of nationalism must be rescued from the ephemeral world of culture and placed firmly within the axis of 'government'. The changes in government, and the social structure that it maintains, is the key underpinning of national identity.

Prior to devolution, only the Conservative and Unionist Party wished to maintain the Treaty of Union in its Westminster focus, offering instead some minor tinkering from its 'taking stock' programme following the 1992 general election.[34] Indeed, even then there followed suggestions that the party should change its name to become the 'Unionist Party' to revive its fortunes in Scotland.[35] The Liberal Democrats and Labour wish to 'break' the Union through devolution, the SNP wishes to break it through independence for Scotland in Europe. In a sense, as McCrone has argued, all four main political parties regard themselves as 'nationalists',[36] because the Scottish versions of the three British national parties and the SNP all claim to put 'Scotland first'. One Scottish Secretary, Ian Lang, had a secret wish to have been a 'fly on the wall' at Bannockburn.[37] Yet, following on from

---

31 Although to understand how in the late 20th century both Tory and nationalist regard Scott as a 'great Scot', see Robertson, 'Walter Scott and the crises of Unionist Patriotism'.

32 The Saltire Society's 1994 Wallace appeal makes no celebration of Union: 'Because of the events in Lanark on a certain Spring day in 1297 [when Wallace slew the Sheriff of Lanark], Sir William Wallace emerged to champion the cause of the Scottish people in their struggle for independence.' The 1994 tourist guide to the national monument, produced by Loch Lomond, Stirling and Trossachs Tourist Board on behalf of Stirling District Council, states that Wallace was acclaimed as 'the hammer and scourge of the English', and that 'Wallace left a legacy: a belief that inspired the whole of Scotland ... In 1314 King Robert the Bruce led the Scots to full nationhood at the Battle of Bannockburn.'

33 C. Waddie, *How Scotland lost her Parliament and what became of it* (Edinburgh, 1891).

34 *Scotland in the Union: A Partnership of Good* (Edinburgh, 1993).

35 *Scotsman*, 26 May 1995.

36 McCrone, 'Editorial: rhetorics of regionalism'.

37 *Scotsman*, 27 Nov. 1993.

his predecessor's insistence in 1988 that the Tories were the oldest party in Scotland and the Union was one of the finest achievements of the Scottish people,[38] Lang's vision of Unionist-nationalism (if it can be so called) fails to find favour in Scotland. Michael Forsyth's emphasis on 'the need to be positive of the benefits of the Union and what it has done for Scotland', and the '300 years of history during which the Westminster parliament has been *our* parliament by the Act of Union',[39] fails to impress the Scottish electorate. The Conservative arguments are now a minority discourse in Scotland. Indeed Lang's Unionist-nationalism was believed by the SNP leader Alex Salmond (perhaps unsurprisingly) to have been the fundamental weakness in the Conservative Party's recent electoral appeal. Salmond proclaimed on the day Roseanna Cunningham (the by-election victor following the death of the tartan-trews-wearing staunch Unionist Sir Nicholas Fairbairn) took her seat at Westminster, that 'the Tories had fought the by-election on "the Union, the Union and the Union", and received their answer resoundingly from the voters of Perth and Kinross'.[40]

Devolution from Westminster or independence within Europe means less Union with England, not more. Popular nationalism in Scotland does not demand to be more like England to be equal with England. Scottishness in the twentieth century is proclaimed in the form of the 'tartan army's' jaunt to the Faroe Islands with 'a banner carrying a salacious message about Jimmy Hill's private life',[41] or the vigil outside the Scottish Parliament House-to-be (but never was), or marches and poetry-reading for democracy and Common Cause, or the Campaign for a Scottish Assembly, or Robbie the Pict's role in the campaign to abolish tolls on the Skye Bridge, or the extremism of Settler Watch, Scottish Watch and *Siol nan Gaidheal*. All see Scotland's *ethnie* as explicitly Scottish – not part of a British identity – and ultimately focused on politics with a capital 'P'. When the SNP turn up each year at Elderslie, the birthplace of William Wallace, they are not there to celebrate the Union. Clearly they are using the memory of the patriot hero to demand independent nation-statehood outwith the Union.[42] 'We're winning with Wallace' proclaimed Alex Salmond to the SNP annual conference in 1995, because 'INDEPENDENCE ... is what Wallace was actually fighting for'.[43]

38 R. J. Morris, 'Victorian values in Scotland and England', in Smout, *Victorian Values*, p. 44. Rifkind was quoted in *The Scotsman*, 12 May 1988, as he attempted to defuse the outcry over Margaret Thatcher's 'Sermon on the Mound', when she addressed the General Assembly of the Church of Scotland.

39 *Scotsman*, 14 Feb. 1995.

40 Ibid., 7 June 1995.

41 Ibid., 7 June 1995.

42 Recent work has doubted whether they have found the correct village: Mackay, *William Wallace*. A report of the SNP's reaction to this revelation that Wallace may have been born in Ellerslie in Ayrshire, rather than Elderslie in Renfrewshire, is found in *The Scotsman*, 12 Apr. 1995.

43 Original emphasis; A. Salmond, 'Winning with Wallace', Address to the 61st Annual

The *Scots Independent* aimed its invective against newspapers who regarded Wallace as their Unionist hero: '[he] led Scotland in awesome battles for liberty and independence not for UNION'.[44] 'Wha's like us? Damn few and they're a' deid!' was a popular cry in 1979, and you can be quite sure that although they may be 'deid', they were not English.[45] Unionist-nationalism is no longer the dominant characteristic of Scottishness.

The meaning given to the symbols of the 'past' changes over time – each set of contemporaries has their own concerns, and their own statements they wish to make. That this past is not 'real' or 'authentic' is irrelevant; the important point for historians is why and how this 'heritage' exerts cultural power.[46] In the mid-nineteenth century, the symbols of Scotland's *ethnie* were linked to the demands of a bourgeoisie governing its civil society. Chapters 4 and 5 outlined the power of this bourgeoisie. Chapters 6 and 7 linked this governing to national identity. Scottish civil society was strongly independent, its organs of government were presided over from within and empowered from without. For the period from 1830 to 1860, Scotland had, essentially, a 'state' within a state. This was to change after 1870, as 'citizen politics' were extended, and the central state was forced to increase its direct intervention in society. But in the mid-nineteenth century, Scottish civil society 'governed' itself, the nation-state axis was self-contained, and this had a particular impact on Scottish national identity. The rational response – the only response – was Unionist-nationalism: nothing more, nothing less.

National Conference, 22 Sep. 1995, Perth City Halls, speech reproduced on the World Wide Web (http://www.snp.org.uk/), 17 Oct. 1995.

[44] Original emphasis; *Scots Independent*, Oct. 1995, p. 2.

[45] The Scottish *ethnie* was used to explain to the 'average Englishman' [*sic*] the contribution of Scottish inventors to the modern world. To quote the postcard version of this popular nationalism: '"Wha's like us?" was created by T. Anderson Cairns, born in Rutherglen, Lanarkshire and G. M. Smith, a Graduate of Glasgow School of Art. "Wha's like us?" first came out in linen Tea Towel form. This souvenir became so rapidly successful (at home and overseas) that the design was launched in Tote Bags, Greeting Cards and Apron forms during the next five years. This postcard was launched in 1986.'

[46] McCrone, Morris and Kiely, *Scotland – the Brand*, p. 207.

Appendix 1

Occupational codes used to classify the occupational titles found in the Edinburgh Pollbook 1852/4, coded by 'organisation' and 'production'

	Organisation		Production
10	Land	01	Agriculture
11	Gardeners	02	Food, drink & tobacco
20	Quarries	03	Mines, quarries & other extractive indust.
30	Distribution & processing	04	Glass & pottery
31	Dealers	05	Chemicals
40	Transport	06	Leather
45	Commerce	07	Metals
46	Bankers	08	General manufacturer
47	Agents & travellers	09	Textiles
48	Clerks & bookkeepers	10	Clothing
50	Manufacturing	11	Timber
51	Managers & employers	12	Paper & printing
55	Craft	13	Construction & repairs
60	Professions (general)	14	Transport
61	Medical men	15	Business & financial services
62	Legal	16	National government
63	Religion	17	Local government
64	Education	18	Defence
65	Miscellaneous services	19	Public utilities
66	Print & publishing	20	Religion
70	Construction	21	Law
90	Independent income	22	Medicine
95	National government	23	General professional services
96	Local government	24	Education
97	Defence	25	Miscellaneous services
99	No occupational title	26	General distribution
		27	Independent income
		28	No occupational title

'Organisation' – nature of the industry within which the work is being carried out.

'Production' – nature of the work, irrespective of industry.

Appendix 2

List of societies and associations in Edinburgh derived from
Oliver and Boyd's New Edinburgh Almanac (1854)

'*Section II Religious Institutions*'

Society for Propagating Christian Knowledge
Lay Association in Support of the Schemes of the Church of Scotland
Scottish Bible Society
Scottish Ladies' Association for the Advancement of female Education in India
Female Association of the Free Church for the Promoting Christian Education among the Females
    of India
Ladies' Association for Promoting Christian Education of Jewish Females
Ladies' Continental Association
Scottish Missionary Society
Society for the support of Gaelic Schools
Ladies' Association for the Support of Gaelic Schools
Baptist Home Mission Society for Scotland
The Friendly Society of Ministers in connection with the U.P. Church
Society in Scotland for Promoting Religious Knowledge among the Poor
Society for the Sons of Clergy
Widows Fund of the Church and the Universities of Scotland
Scottish Monthly Tract Society
Scottish Ladies' Association for Promoting Female Industrial Education in Scotland, especially in
    the Highlands and Islands
Dissenting Minister Widows' Fund
Scottish Anti-State Church Association
The Sabbath Alliance

Miscellaneous Religious and Missionary Societies

Edinburgh Bible Society
Edinburgh Auxiliary to the Irish Evangelical Society
Edinburgh Auxiliary to the London Missionary Society
Edinburgh Auxiliary Bible Society
Edinburgh Mission in aid of the Moravian Missions
Edinburgh Church of England Missionary Association
Edinburgh Auxiliary Naval and Military Society
Edinburgh Ladies' Association
Edinburgh City Mission
Edinburgh Medical Missionary Society
Edinburgh Total Abstinence Society
Edinburgh Continental Association
Scottish Reformation Society
Evangelical Alliance - Edinburgh subdivision
Edinburgh Gratis Sabbath School Society
Edinburgh Religious Tract Society
Edinburgh Sabbath School Teacher's Union
Edinburgh & Leith Seaman's Friend Society
Anti-Oath Association
British League of Juvenile Abstainers
Edinburgh Irish Mission

Scripture Readers in the Old Town
National Protestant Association
Scottish Protestant Alliance
Parochial Mission for the Employment of Scripture Readers
Society for the Due Observance of the Lord's Day

'*Section V Benevolent and Charitable Institutions*'

George Heriot's Hospital
George Watson's Hospital
John Watson's Hospital
Trinity Hospital
The Orphan Hospital
The Maiden Hospital
Cauvin's Hospital, Duddingston
James Gillespie's Hospital and Free School
Fettes' Endowment
Chalmers' Hospital
Donaldson's Hospital
Stewart's Hospital
Edinburgh School for the Blind
The Edinburgh Institution for the Deaf & Blind
Edinburgh Deaf & Benevolent Society
Society for the Industrious Blind
House of Industry and Servant's Home
Edinburgh Ladies' Female Emigrant Association
Edinburgh Association for Improving the Lodgings of the Labouring Classes
Dean Bank Institution
Society for the Relief of the Destitute Sick
House of Refuge and Night Refuge, Queensberry House
Night Asylum for the Houseless Poor
Edinburgh Benevolent & Stranger's Friend Society
Magdalen Asylum
The Shelter
Institution for the Relief of Incurables
Senior Female Society
Charitable or Junior Female Society
Edinburgh Society for the Relief of Indigent Old Men
Mortification by the late Joseph Thomson
Craigrook Mortification
Society in Edinburgh for Clothing the Industrious Poor
Parochial Boards of Managers of the Poor
Fund of Scottish Masonic Benevolence
Edinburgh Aberdeenshire Club
Edinburgh Morayshire Club
Edinburgh Morayshire Mechanic's Society
Edinburgh Caithness Association
Edinburgh Upper-Ward of Lanarkshire Association
Edinburgh Galloway Association
Edinburgh Angus Club
Orkney and Shetland Charitable Society
Social Peeblean Society
Edinburgh Kinross-shire Association
Royal Infirmary
Eye-Dispensary of Edinburgh
Eye Infirmary of Edinburgh
Royal Edinburgh Lunatic Asylum
Royal Public Dispensary
New Town Dispensary

Royal Maternity Hospital
Edinburgh Living-In Institution
Edinburgh General Dispensary and Living-in Institution
Society for the relief of Poor Married Women of Respectable Character when in Childbed
Scottish Register & Home Institution for Domestic Servants
Society for the Relief of Poor Married Women.

'*Section IV Scientific and Literary Societies*'

The Philosophical Institution of Edinburgh
Royal Medical School
Harvein Society
Associated Society of the University of Edinburgh
Scots Law Society
Hunterian Medical Society
Dialectic Society
Edinburgh Obstetrical Society
Medico-Chirurgical Society
Pharmaceutical Society of Great Britain
Edinburgh Geological Society
Juridical Society
Phrenological Society
University Missionary Society
Theological Library College
Theological Society
Speculative Society
The Eclectic Society of the Philosophical Institution
Edinburgh Subscription Library
Edinburgh Select Subscription Library
Edinburgh Mechanics Subscription Library
Iona Club
Ladies' Emancipation Society
Medico-Statistical Society
Scottish Association for Opposing Prevalent Errors
Woodrow Society

'*Section VI Commercial Establishments*'

Merchant Company
Edinburgh Chamber of Commerce and Manufacture
Edinburgh Water Company
Scottish Trade Protection Society
Royal Bank of Scotland
British Linen Bank
Commercial Bank
National Bank
Union Bank of Scotland
Edinburgh & Glasgow Bank
Bank of Scotland

Appendix 3

Decimalised Shillings
12 pence (12d.) = 1 shilling
20 shillings (20/-) = 1 pound
E.g.
Two shillings and six pence (2/6) = 2.5 'decimal' shillings
One pound two shillings and six pence (£1 2/6) = 22.5 'decimal' shillings

Appendix 4

Coded voting pairs: 1852 general election

11	Macaulay	Cowan		19	Cowan	
12	Macaulay	McLaren		20	McLaren	Bruce
13	Macaulay	Bruce		21	McLaren	Campbell
14	Macaulay	Campbell		22	McLaren	
15	Macaulay			23	Bruce	Campbell
16	Cowan	McLaren		24	Bruce	
17	Cowan	Bruce		25	Campbell	
18	Cowan	Campbell		26	No Vote	

Appendix 5

Successful Linkage between Selected Nominal Lists
and the 1852/4 Edinburgh Pollbook
(Showing numbers linked, nominal list size, percentage linked,
and a brief explanation for main causes of failed linkages)

Nominal List (year)	Linked (N)	List (N)	Linked (%)	Explanation of failed linkage to 1852/4 pollbook
Apprentice School (1848)	67	183	36.61	Average fit; low status subs failed to be linked
New Club (c.1854)	90	774	11.62	High country elite; unlinkable to pollbook
Total Abstinence Society (1853)	642	1,589	40.40	Good fit; low subs failed to be linked
Female Delinquency (1857)	49	297	16.50	High female subs; unlinkable to pollbook
Industrial Blind (1857)	232	3,145	7.38	Very high female sub; ditto
Ragged Schools (1857)	437	1,181	37.0	Average fit; low subs failed to linked
Scottish Trade Protection (1858)	332	599	55.43	Good fit; range of subs replicated in pollbook
Philosophical Inst. (1857)	592	2,081	28.45	Average fit; country subs unlinkable
Highland Destitution (1851)	658	2,843	23.14	Average fit; Scotland wide subs unlinkable
NAVSR (1852-4)	110	383	28.7	Ave. fit; Scot-wide & institute subs unlinkable

Bibliography

Manuscript Sources

Edinburgh, National Library of Scotland

'The Abbotsford Subscription' (1833): A.124.c.

'Letter from King intimating pension conferred by him upon the sister of Sir Walter Scott', 24 Nov.(?) 1832: MS. 1631.

'Letter to Skene detailing a Public Meeting in New York to raise subscriptions, with a minimum contribution of $10': MS. 965.

'Membership of the Edinburgh Sub-Committee of the London Abbotsford Subscription': MS. 965.

'Ornate invite, stating the officials at the ceremony': RY.1.1.23 (16).

'Restoration of the Parthenon', by 'A Traveller', *Scots Magazine*, Feb. 1820: MS. 638.

SKENE, J., OF RUBISTLAW, 'Contents of Mr Skene's Reminiscences of Sir Walter Scott, etc.': MS. 965.

SKINNER, R. T., 'Scotland's Disgrace', from *The Scotsman*, 3 Dec. 1930: MS. 639.

Printed Primary Sources

A. PUBLIC REPORTS, ETC.

Association for Promoting Education among Workmen, Apprentices, etc.: Apprentice Schools: Third Annual Report (Edinburgh, 1848).

British League of Juvenile Abstainers: Report for the Twelfth Year, 1857–58, and for the 9th Session of Apprentice School (Edinburgh, 1859).

Central Board for the Relief of Destitution in the Highlands and Islands of Scotland, for 1848 (Edinburgh Section): First Report (Edinburgh, 1848): SRO, HD 6/14; *Reports of the Accounts* (Edinburgh, 1851): [in Edinburgh Public Library].

Clan-Gregor Society: Report Relative to the Objects and Progress of the Society (1830).

Dean Bank and Boroughmuirhead Institution for the Reformation of Juvenile Female Delinquents: Report (Edinburgh, 1857).

Edinburgh Angus Club ...: Reports by the Committee of Management and Minutes of Annual Meetings (Edinburgh, 1868).

Edinburgh Asylum for the Relief of the Indigent and Industrious Blind: Report by the Directors for 1857 (Edinburgh, 1857); *Report ... for 1858* (Edinburgh, 1858).

[Edinburgh] *Committee, appointed at the General Meeting of the Magistrates, and the different public bodies in this city, to consent measures for obtaining a more efficient SYSTEM OF POLICE: Report* (Edinburgh, 1812).

Edinburgh Irish Mission: Missions for the Conversion of Irish Romanists in the Large Towns of England and Scotland explained and recommended, being the Report for the Year 1851, with a list of subscriptions (Edinburgh, 1852).

Edinburgh Original Ragged or Industrial Schools, Ramsay Lane, Castle Hill: Second Annual Report: With a List of Subscribers and Donations (Edinburgh, 1849); *Eleventh Annual Report, for the year ending 31st December 1857* (Edinburgh, 1858).

Edinburgh Total Abstinence Society: Seventeenth Annual Report (Edinburgh, 1853); *Eighteenth Annual Report* (Edinburgh, 1854).

The Foundation for a Civil Society: Report, 1993–4.

High School Club: First Annual Report (Edinburgh, 1850).

Justice to Scotland: Report of the First Public Meeting of the National Association for the Vindication of Scottish Rights, held in the Music Hall, Edinburgh, on the evening of November 2, 1853 (1853).

Justice to Scotland: Report of the Great Public Meeting of the National Association for the Vindication of Scottish Rights, held in the City Hall, Glasgow, December 15, 1853 (1853).

List of the Electors of the City of Edinburgh, arranged according to their residence, Corrected after Appeal Court 1854, showing the voting at the general election, July 1852 (Edinburgh, 1854).

Medico-Statistical Association: First Report, by W. T. Gairdner, M.D., and W. J. Begbie, M.D. (Edinburgh, 1852).

National Monument in Scotland: Second Report to the Adjourned Meeting of Directors (1828): NLS, MS. 352.

Royal Dispensary and Vaccine Institution, for Affording Medical and Surgical Assistance to the Sick Poor of the City and County of Edinburgh: Annual Report for the Year 1854 (Edinburgh, 1855).

Royal Edinburgh Lunatic Asylum: Report by the Managers for the year 1842, presented to the Annual General Meeting, held on Monday 30th January, 1843 (Edinburgh, 1843).

Scottish Association for Opposing Prevalent Errors: Report (Edinburgh, 1848).

Sub-Committee for Erecting a Monument to Sir Walter Scott: Second Report (Edinburgh, 1835); *Third Report* (Edinburgh, 1838).

B. ACTS AND PARLIAMENTARY PAPERS

An Act to Consolidate and Amend the Law Relating to the Public Health in Scotland, 30 & 31 Victoria, Cap. 101 (1867).

An Act to make better Provision for the Removal of Nuisances, Regulations of Lodging Houses, and the Health of Towns in Scotland, 19 & 20 Victoria, cap. 103 (1856).

1852–3, LXXXVI: *Accounts and Papers* (relating to population statistics).

HANSARD, *Parliamentary Debates, House of Commons*.

C. NEWSPAPERS

The Beacon
Caledonian Mercury
Dumfries Courier
The Economist
Edinburgh Advertiser
Edinburgh Evening Courant
Edinburgh Evening Post
Edinburgh Observer and New North Britain
Glasgow Herald
Punch, or the London Charivari
The Schoolmaster and Edinburgh Weekly Magazine
Scots Independent
The Scotsman
The Times
Weekly Journal
The Witness

D. CONTEMPORARY COMMENTARIES AND HISTORIES

'Address by George Godwin on Public Health', Transactions of the National Association for the Promotion of Social Science (1871).

'Address by the Right Hon. the Earl of Shaftesbury, on Public Health', *Transactions of the National Association for the Promotion of the Social Science* (1858).

AYTOUN, W. E., 'Scotland since the Union', *Blackwood's Edinburgh Magazine*, lxxiv (1853).

BALLANTYNE, J. (ed.), *Chronicle of the Hundredth Birthday of Robert Burns* (Edinburgh, 1859).

BENTHAM, J., 'Leading principles of a constitutional code, for any state', *The Pamphleteer*, xliv (1823).

BROUGHAM, H., *Contributions to the Edinburgh Review. By Henry Lord Brougham in three volumes*, vol. II (London, 1856).

CARRICK, J. D., *Life of Sir William Wallace of Elderslie* (London, 1840).

CLEGHORN, G., *Essay on the National Monument of Scotland*, Transactions of the Architectural Institute of Scotland, Second Session (Edinburgh, 1852).

[COCKBURN, HENRY], *Journal of Henry Cockburn, being a continuation of his Memorials of His Time, 1831–1854*: vol. II (Edinburgh, 1854).

DEFOE, DANIEL, *The History of the Union between England and Scotland* (London, 1786 edn).

DOD, C. R., *Electoral Facts from 1832 to 1853: Impartially stated, constituting a complete political gazetteer* (1853), ed. H. J. Hanham (Brighton, 1972).

DUNLOP, G. (ed.), *An Account of the Signet Club with Extracts from the Minutes and a Complete List of Members, 1790–1902* (Edinburgh, 1902).

ENGELS, F., *The Condition of the Working Class in England in 1844* (London, 1950).

[GRANT, JOHN] 'Centralisation', by 'Ian', *Edinburgh Advertiser*, 13 Apr. 1852.

——, 'English Aggression on Scotland', by 'Ian', *Edinburgh News*, 16 Jun. 1854.

HOLE, J., 'Is it desirable that the state or municipality should assist in providing improved dwellings for the lower class; and, if so, to what extent and in what way?', *Transactions of the National Association for the Promotion of Social Science* (1871).

HUME, DAVID, and STAFFORD, W. C., *History of England*: vol. I (London, 1754–62).

JOHNSON, SAMUEL, *A Journey to the Western Isles of Scotland* (London, 1775).

KNOX, R., *The Races of Men: A philosophical enquiry into the influence of race over the destinies of nations* (2nd edn, London, 1862).

LEWIS, G. C., *Essays on the administration of Great Britain from 1783–1830. Contributed to the Edinburgh Review by the Right Hon. Sir George Cornewall Lewis, Bart.* (London, 1864).

MARX, K., 'The crisis in England and the British Constitution' (Mar. 1855), in K. Marx and F. Engles, *On Britain* (London, 1954).

MCNEEL-CAIRD, A., 'Local government and taxation in Scotland', in J. W. Probyn, *Local Government and Taxation, Cobden Club Essays* (London, 1875).

MILL, J. S., *Considerations on Representative Government* (London, 1861).

——, *Principles of Political Economy with some of their Applications to Social Philosophy*, vol. II [from the fifth London edn] (New York, 1923).

——, *Utilitarianism, Liberty and Representative Government* (London, 1910).

PATERSON, J., *Wallace, the Hero of Scotland* (3rd edn, Edinburgh, 1876).

RAMSAY, E. B., *Reminiscences of Scottish Life and Character* (26th edn, Edinburgh, 1892).

STEILL, J., *Scotland and her Union with England* (Edinburgh, 1854).

STUBBS, W., *The Constitutional History of England* (1874–8).

WADDIE, C., *How Scotland lost her Parliament and what became of it* (Edinburgh, 1891).

WORDSWORTH, D., *Recollections of a Tour made in Scotland in AD 1803* (Edinburgh, 1974).

[——], *Historical and Descriptive Sketch of the Scott Monument, Edinburgh* (Edinburgh, 1852).

[——], *History of the Burns Monument* (Edinburgh, 1961).

[——], *Life of Sir William Wallace*, by 'J. C.' (3rd edn, London, 1849).

[——], *The New Club, Edinburgh, from its foundations in 1787* (Edinburgh, 1900).

[——], *Oliver and Boyd's New Edinburgh Almanac and National Repository for the Year 1854* (Edinburgh, 1854).

[——], 'Remarks on Captain Brown's letter to the Lord Provost of Edinburgh', by 'J. C. S.', *Blackwood's Edinburgh Magazine* (1820).

[——], *Scotland in the Union: A partnership of good* (Edinburgh, 1993).

[——], *The Scotsman, the Scottish Clans and their Tartans* (Edinburgh, 1896).

[——], *Some Records of the Origin and Progress of the National Wallace Monument Movement, initiated at Glasgow in March 1856* (1880) Printed for private circulation.

E. OTHER WORKS, PAMPHLETS, ETC.

In National Library of Scotland

BURNS, W., 'Association for the Vindication of Scottish Rights' (1855).

[BURNS, WILLIAM], *A Tract for the Times. Scottish Rights and Honour Vindicated, in letters to Viscount Palmerston, 'The Times', and 'Caledonian Mercury'*, by 'A North Briton' (Glasgow, 1854).

CHRISTIE, R., *Injustice to Scotland Exposed* ... (Edinburgh, n.d.).

EDINBURGH ASSOCIATION FOR THE SUPPRESSION OF DRUNKENNESS, *A Plea, etc.* (n.d.).

EDINBURGH SOCIETY FOR THE RELIEF OF THE INDIGENT AND INDUSTRIOUS BLIND, 'Town Subscriptions, 1856–57' (Edinburgh, 1858).

EDINBURGH TOTAL ABSTINENCE SOCIETY, *Edinburgh Series of Temperance Tracts* (Edinburgh, 1859).

GRANT, JAMES, 'Nemo Me Imusse Lacesset!' (n.p., n.d.).

——, 'Scotland for ever!' (*c.*1853).

GRANT, JOHN, 'Justice to Scotland', 20 Apr. 1852.

——, 'May it Please Your Majesty. The Petition of the undersigned, your Majesty's loyal subjects, inhabiting that part of your Majesty's United Kingdom called Scotland' (n.p., n.d.).

[GRANT, JOHN], 'Neglect of Scotland', by 'Ian', from *Caledonian Mercury* (n.p., n.d.).

[GRANT, JOHN, SEN.], *Scotland and 'The Times': To the Editor of the 'Edinburgh Evening Post' and 'Scottish Record'*, by 'Red Lion' (26 Jul. 1853).

MEMES, J. S., *Letter to John Steele, Esq., S.A., Regarding the Scott Monument* (Edinburgh, 3 Apr. 1838).

New Club, Princes Street, Edinburgh: Rules (Edinburgh, 1923).

SCOTT, MAJOR, OF GALA, Report of his speech to a meeting of the Associates of the National Association for the Vindication of Scottish Rights (n.p., n.d.).

[SCOTT, WALTER], *Hints Addressed to the Inhabitants of Edinburgh and Others, in prospect of His Majesty's Visit*, by 'An Old Edinburgh Citizen' (Edinburgh, 1822).

SCOTTISH ASSOCIATION FOR OPPOSING PREVALENT ERRORS, *Circular* (Mar. 1847).

SCOTTISH RIGHTS ASSOCIATION, *Address to the People* (1853).

[——], *Address to the English and Irish Members of the Honourable the Commons House of Parliament for the United Kingdom and Ireland* (Edinburgh, 1855).

[——], *Agreement between The Phrenological Association and William Henderson's Trustees* (n.p., 1856).

[——], *Alphabetical List of the Members of the New Club corrected to 30th April 1923* (Edinburgh, 1923).

[——], *An Appeal on Behalf of the Proposed Hospital for Sick Children in Edinburgh* (Edinburgh, 1859).

[——], *Apprentice Schools: Plea for Education* (Edinburgh, 1849).

[——], *Banquet in Honour of the Right Honourable the Earl of Eglinton and Winton, K. T., President of the National Association for the Vindication of Scottish Rights to be held at the City Hall, Glasgow, on Wednesday, the 4th October, 1854* (n.p., 1854) [Scottish Rights Association, vol. II).

[——], *Bibliotheca Wallasiania: List of the Various Works relating to Sir William Wallace from 1488–1858* (1858: presentation copy, only 50 printed for private circulation).

[——], *The Edinburgh Academy Bar List – 1824–1894* (n.d.).

[——], *Edinburgh Irish Mission and Protestant Institute* (1852).

[——], *Edinburgh Select Subscription Library. Sketch of the Origin and Progress of the Library* (reprinted from the third appendix to the former catalogue; with postscript in continuation to 1842).

[——], *A Full Account of King George the Fourth's Visit to Scotland in 1822; with a collection of the loyal songs which appeared on that memorable occasion* (Edinburgh, 1838).

[——], *General Meeting of the Scottish Trade Protection Society* (n.p., 1854).

[——], *History of the Speculative Society of Edinburgh from its Inception in 1764* (Edinburgh, 1845).

[——], *House of Refuge for the Destitute, and Asylum for their Children, Morrison's Close, 117 High Street, Edinburgh* (1832).

[——], *An Inquiry into Destitution, Prostitution and Crime in Edinburgh* (Edinburgh, 1851).

[——], *Justice to Scotland; To the Editor of the Times* (Edinburgh, n.d.).

[——], *Laws and Catalogue of the Edinburgh Mechanics' Subscription Library* (Edinburgh, 1859).

[——], *The Laws of the Juridical Society of Edinburgh, Instituted Anno 1773* (Edinburgh, 1830).

[——], *The Life of Sir William Wallace, the Scots Patriot* (Edinburgh, 1810).

[——], 'List of members of the High School Club, March 1851'.

[——], *List of Members of the Scottish Trade Protection Society* (Edinburgh, 1858).

[——], 'The Lyon-King-at-Arms', from *London Morning Post*, 11 Jul. 1856.

[——], *Memorial of the Council of the National Association to the Right Honourable the Lords Commissioners of Her Majesty's Treasury* (1854).

[——], *National Monument to Sir William Wallace on the Abbey Craig near Stirling* (n.p., n.d.).

[——], *Order of the Procession* (Edinburgh, 1832).

[——], *Peacock's Historical Almanac, 1845. Containing Correct Lists of both Houses of Parliament, Great Officers of State, Remarkable Events, etc., etc.* (London, 1845).

[——], *Petition of the National Association for the Vindication of Scottish Rights presented to the House of Lords by its President, the Earl of Eglinton on Thursday last* (1854).

[——], *Public Education: The Original Ragged School and the United Industrial Schools of Edinburgh: Being a Comparative View of their Respective Results* (Edinburgh, 1855).

[——], *Rules and Regulations of the New Club, Edinburgh* (Edinburgh, 1847).

[——], *Rules of the Edinburgh Phrenological Association, Instituted 1855* (Edinburgh, n.d.).

[——], *Scottish Home Rule* (*c*.1891) [Pamphlets].

[——], *Scottish Rights and Grievances: A Letter to the Right Honourable Duncan McLaren, Lord Provost of the City of Edinburgh*, by 'A Scotchman' (Edinburgh, *c*.1854).

[——], *Subscription Paper for Memorial to Sir Walter Scott, to be erected in the Metropolis of Scotland*, broad sheet (*c*.1833).

[——], *Theatre Royal, Edinburgh. In Aid of the Subscription to Erect a Monument to Sir Walter Scott* (Edinburgh, 1841).

[——], *Tracts of the National Association for the Vindication of Scottish Rights*, Nos. 2, 3, 6, 7 (all 1854).

[——], *Traditions, etc., Respecting Sir William Wallace; Collected chiefly from Publications of Recent Date*, by 'A former Subscriber for a Wallace Monument' (Edinburgh, 1856).

[——], *The Tragedy of the Valiant Knight Sir William Wallace to which is prefixed a brief Historical Account of the Knight, and his Exploits for the Delivery of Scotland, and added a more particular Account of the way in which he was betrayed into the hands of the English* (Edinburgh, 1815?).

[——], 'University Debating Societies', part of *History of the Speculative Society of Edinburgh from its Inception in 1764* (Edinburgh, 1845).

[——], *A Vindication of Scottish Rights, Addressed to Both Houses of Parliament*, by 'A Citizen of Edinburgh' (Edinburgh, 1854).

In Edinburgh City Archives

'Bill ordered by the House of Commons for the erection at Edinburgh of a monument to the late Sir Walter Scott', *Council Record*, vol. 234, 30 Mar. 1841.

'Scott Monument', *Council Record*, vol. 212, 3 Oct. 1832.

'Scott Monument', *Council Record*, vol. 233, 7 Jul. 1840.

In Edinburgh Public Library

Conditions Relative to Proposed Public Competition for the Wallace and Bruce Memorial, Captain Reid's Bequest, City of Edinburgh (1882).

'Contributions at St. Petersburg in the aid of the Fund now raising in Great Britain and on the Continent of Europe for Erecting a Monument at Edinburgh to the Memory of the late Sir Walter Scott, Bart.', appeal dated 15 Oct. 1832 from James Skene, Secretary.

Copy Commission of the Peace for the City of Edinburgh and Liberties thereof, printed by order of the Lord Provost, 6 November (Edinburgh, 1848).

The Edinburgh and Leith Post Office Directory (1852/53, 1854/5), Edinburgh.

'Index to the Inventory of Monuments maintained by the District', *Edinburgh District Council, Department of Architecture.*

A Letter to Messrs George Miller, Thomas Allan, and Peter Brown, from Captain Brown, Superintendent of the Edinburgh Police Establishment (Edinburgh, 1821).

Letter to the Right Honourable the Lord Provost; from Captain Brown, Superintendent of the Edinburgh Police, On the subject of the late investigation into the Police Establishment (Edinburgh, 1820).

The National Monument to be completed for the Scottish National Gallery on the model of the Parthenon: An appeal to the Scottish People by William Mitchell, S.S.C. (1906).

The Philosophical Institution: General Syllabus of the Lectures, Session, 1858–59 (Edinburgh, 1859).

Proceedings at the Public Meeting Regarding the Monument to Sir Walter Scott, 5th February 1844 (Edinburgh, 1844).

Proposal to build a National Memorial of the War of Independence under Wallace and Bruce and of its results in the Union of England and Scotland to be erected in the Scottish Metropolis (1859).

Reply to Captain Brown's Letter in Another Letter to the Lord Provost of Edinburgh by a Commissioner of Police [pseud] (Edinburgh, 1820).

Roll of Members of the Philosophical Institution, Edinburgh, 10th February 1857 (Edinburgh, 1857).

'Scott Monument: Foundation Stone of Monument ... to be laid on 15 August, 1840'.

[———], *The Approaching General Election, being the past and present state of the various political parties in Edinburgh and the possible result of the Election* (Edinburgh, 1866).

SECONDARY SOURCES

ADAMS, I., *The Making of Urban Scotland* (London, 1978).

ALTER, P., *Nationalism* (2nd edn, London, 1994).

ANDERSON, B., *Imagined Communities: Reflections on the Origin and Spread of Nationalism* (London, 1983).

ANDERSON, J., and GOODMAN, J., 'European and Irish integration: contradictions of regionalism and nationalism', *European Urban and Regional Studies*, i (1) (1994).

ANSTRUTHER, I., *The Knight and the Umbrella: An Account of the Eglinton Tournament, 1839* (London, 1963).

ARMSTRONG, J. A., *Nations before Nationalism* (North Carolina, 1982).

ASH, M., *The Strange Death of Scottish History* (Edinburgh, 1980).

BAGEHOT, W., *The English Constitution* (London, 1963).

BARKER, E., *National Character and the Factors in its Formation* (London, 1927).

——, *Reflections on Government* (Oxford, 1945).

BARNES, B., and SHAPIN, S. (eds.), *Natural Order* (California, 1979).

BARZUN, J., 'Romantic historiography as a political force in France', *Journal of the History of Ideas*, ii (3) (1941).

BEDARIDA, F., *A Social History of England, 1851–1990*, trans. A. S. Forster (London, 1990).

BELLAMY, C., *Administering Central–Local Relations, 1871–1919* (Manchester, 1988).

BEST, G., 'The Scottish Victorian city', *Victorian Studies*, xi (3) (1968).

BEVERIDGE, C., and TURNBULL, R., *The Eclipse of Scottish Culture* (Edinburgh, 1989).

BLONDEL, J., *Voters, Parties and Leaders: The Social Fabric of British Politics* (London, 1963).

BOBBIO, N., 'Gramsci and the concept of civil society', in J. Keane (ed.), *Civil Society and the State: New European Perspectives* (London, 1988).

BOYLE, A. (ed.), *Scotland's Cultural Heritage*, vol. V: *The Royal Society of Edinburgh: Scientific and Engineering Fellows, elected 1784–1876* (Edinburgh, 1983).

——, et. al. (ed.), *Scotland's Cultural Heritage*, vol. IV: *100 Medical Fellows, 1841–1882* (Edinburgh, 1983).

BRAITHWAITE, J., 'A sociology of modelling and the politics of empowerment', *British Journal of Sociology*, xlv (3) (1994).

BRAND, J., *The National Movement in Scotland* (London, 1978).

BREUILLY, J., *Nationalism and the State* (Manchester, 1982).

BRIGGS, A., *Victorian Cities* (London, 1963).

BROTHERSTON, J. H. F., *Observations on the Early Public Health Movement in Scotland* (Edinburgh, 1952).

BROWN, C. B., 'Religion, class and church growth', in Fraser and Morris, *People and Society*, vol. II.

——, 'Secularisation: a theory in danger?', *Scottish Economic and Social History*, xi (1991).

BROWN, C. G., *Religion and Society in Scotland since 1707* (Edinburgh, 1997).

BRYANT, C. G. A, 'Social self-organisation, civility and sociology: a comment on Kumar's "Civil society"', *British Journal of Sociology*, xliv (3) (1993).

——, 'A further comment on Kumar's "Civil society"', *British Journal of Sociology*, xlv (3) (1994).

——, 'Civic nation, civil society, civil religion', in Hall, *Civil Society*.

BUCKLE, H. T., *History of Civilisation in England* (London, 1857–61).

CALDER, A., *Revolving Culture: Notes from the Scottish Republic* (London, 1994).

CAMPBELL, I., *Kailyard* (Edinburgh, 1981).

CAMPBELL, R. H., *Scotland since 1707: The Rise of an Industrial Society* (2nd edn, Edinburgh, 1985).

CANT, R. G., 'David Steuart Erskine, 11th Earl of Buchan: founder of the Society of Antiquaries of Scotland', in A. S. Bell (ed.), *The Scottish Antiquarian Tradition: Essays to mark the bicentenary of the Society of Antiquaries of Scotland, 1780–1980* (Edinburgh, 1981).

CARTER, I., 'Kailyard: the literature of decline in nineteenth-century Scotland', *Scottish Journal of Sociology*, i (1) (1976).

CHASE, M., 'From millennium to anniversary: the concept of jubilee in late eighteenth- and nineteenth-century England', *Past and Present*, cxxix (1990).

CHECKLAND, O., *Philanthropy in Victorian Scotland: Social Welfare and the Voluntary Principle* (Edinburgh, 1980).

——, and CHECKLAND, S., *Industry and Ethos: Scotland, 1832–1914* (2nd edn, Edinburgh, 1989).

CHECKLAND, S. G., *The Rise of Industrial Society in England, 1815–1885* (London, 1964).

——, and CHECKLAND, E. O. A. (eds.), *The Poor Law Report of 1834* (London, 1974).

CLARKE, T., and DICKSON, T., 'The birth of class?', in Devine and Mitchison, *People and Society*, vol. I.

COCKBURN, H. A., *A History of the New Club, Edinburgh, 1787–1939* (Edinburgh, 1938).

COHEN, A. P., and RAPPORT, N., 'Introduction: consciousness in anthropology', in A. P. Cohen and N. Rapport (eds.), *Questions of Consciousness* (London, 1995).

COHEN, J. L., *Class and Civil Society* (Oxford, 1982).

COLLEY, L., *Britons: Forging the Nation, 1707–1837* (New Haven and London, 1992).

COLLS, R., and DODD, P., *Englishness: Politics and Culture, 1880–1920* (London, 1986).

CORRIGAN, P., and SAYER, D., *The Great Arch: English State Formation as Cultural Revolution* (Oxford, 1985).

COWAN, R. M. W., *The Newspaper in Scotland: A Study of its First Expansion* (Glasgow, 1946).

CRICK, B., 'An Englishman considers his passport', in N. Evans (ed.), *National Identity in the British Isles* (Coleg Harlech, 1989).

——, 'The English and the British', in B. Crick (ed.) *National Identities: The Constitution of the United Kingdom* (Oxford, 1992).

——, 'Essay on Britishness', *Scottish Affairs* (2) (1992).

CROUZET, F., *The Victorian Economy*, trans. A. S. Forster (London, 1982).

CROWTHER, M. A., 'Poverty, health and welfare', in Fraser and Morris, *People and Society*, vol. II.

CUNNINGHAM, H., 'The language of patriotism', in Samuel, *Patriotism*, vol. I.

DAICHES, D., 'Scott and Scotland', in A. Bell (ed.), *Scott: Bicentenary Essays* (Edinburgh, 1972).

DALE, R., ESLAND, G., and MCDONALD, M. (eds.), *Schooling and Capitalism: A Sociological Reader* (London, 1976).

DAUNTON, M. J., *Progress and Poverty: An Economic and Social History of Britain, 1700–1850* (Oxford, 1995).

DAVIDOFF, L., and HALL, C., *Family Fortunes: Men and Women of the English Middle Class, 1780–1850* (London, 1987).

DAVIES, J., *A History of Wales* (London, 1993).

DEANE, P., *The First Industrial Revolution* (Cambridge, 1965).

DEUTSCH, K., *Nationalism and Social Communication* (2nd edn, Massachusetts, 1966).

DEVINE, T. M., and MITCHISON, R. (eds.), *People and Society in Scotland*, vol. I: *1760–1830* (Edinburgh, 1988).

DEVLIN-THORP, S. (ed.), Scotland's Cultural Heritage, vol. I: *One hundred medical and scientific fellows of the Royal Society of Edinburgh, elected from 1783–1832* (Edinburgh, 1981); vol. II: *100 Literary Fellows, 1783–1812* (Edinburgh, 1981); vol. III: *100 Medical Fellows, 1783–1844* (Edinburgh, 1982).

DICKSON, T., and CLARKE, T., 'Social control: Paisley, 1841–1843', *Scottish Historical Review*, lxv (1986).

DINWIDDY, J., *Bentham* (Oxford, 1989).

DONALDSON, G., *et al.*, 'Scottish devolution: the historical background', in J. N. Wolfe (ed.), *Government and Nationalism in Scotland* (Edinburgh, 1969).

DONALDSON, P., *The Life of Sir William Wallace, the Governor General of Scotland and hero of the Scottish Chiefs. Containing his parentage, adventures, heroic achievements, imprisonment and death; drawn from authentic materials of Scottish History* (Hartford, 1825).

DONALDSON, W., *Popular Literature in Victorian Scotland* (Aberdeen, 1986).

——, *The Language of the People* (Aberdeen, 1989).

DONNACHIE, I., and WHATLEY, C. (eds.), *The Manufacture of Scottish History* (Edinburgh, 1992).

DUNDAS, W. C., *Development of Local Government in Counties in Scotland* (London, 1942).

DYER, M., *Men of Property and Intelligence: The Scottish Electoral System prior to 1884* (Aberdeen, 1996).

ELLIS, P. B., and MACA'GHOBHAINN, S., *The Scottish Insurrection of 1820* (London, 1970).

ENGERMAN, S. L., 'Mercantilism and overseas trade, 1700–1800', in Floud and McCloskey, *Economic History of Britain*, vol. I.

ERIKSON, T. H., *Ethnicity and Nationalism: Anthropological Perspectives* (London, 1993).

EVANS, E. J., 'Englishness and Britishness: national identities, *c*.1790–*c*.1870', in Grant and Stringer, *Uniting the Kingdom?*

EVANS, N., 'Cogs, cardis and hwentws: regions, nation and state in Wales, 1840–1940' (paper presented to the Social History Society Conference, 'National Identity', 4–6 Jan. 1992).

FINLAY, R. J., 'Scottish nationalism and Scottish politics, 1900–1979', in Lynch, *Scotland, 1850–1979*.

——, *Independent and Free: Scottish Politics and the Origins of the Scottish National Party, 1918–1945* (Edinburgh, 1994).

FLINN, M. W. (ed.), *Report on the Sanitary Condition of the Labouring Population of Great Britain by Edwin Chadwick, 1842* (Edinburgh, 1965).

FLOUD, R., and MCCLOSKEY, D. (eds.), *The Economic History of Britain since 1700*, vol. I: *1700–1860* (2nd edn, Cambridge, 1994).

FLOURNOY, F. R., 'British Liberal theories of international relations, 1848–1898', *Journal of the History of Ideas*, ii (2) (1946).

FRASER, D., *Urban Politics in Victorian England: The Structure of Politics in Victorian Cities* (Leicester, 1976).

——, 'Joseph Chamberlain and the municipal ideal', in Marsden, *Victorian Values*.

FRASER, W. H., and MORRIS, R. J. (eds.), *People and Society in Scotland*, vol. II: *1830–1914* (Edinburgh, 1990).

FRY, M., *Patronage and Principle: A Political History of Modern Scotland* (Aberdeen, 1987).

——, *The Dundas Despotism* (Edinburgh, 1992).

——, 'The Whig interpretation of Scottish History', in Donnachie and Whatley, *Manufacture of Scottish History*.

GARRARD, J., *Leadership and Power in Victorian Industrial Towns, 1830–80* (Manchester, 1983).

GELLNER, E., *Nations and Nationalism* (London, 1983).

——, 'The importance of being modular', in Hall, *Civil Society*.

GIDDENS, A., *The Nation-State and Violence: Volume II of a Contemporary Critique of Historical Materialism* (London, 1985).

——, *Sociology* (Cambridge, 1989).

GIROUARD, M., *The Return to Camelot: Chivalry and the English Gentleman* (New Haven, 1981).

GOMME, G. L., *Lectures on the Principals of Local Government. Delivered to the London School of Economics, Lent Term, 1897* (London, 1897).

GORDON, G., 'The changing city', in G. Gordon (ed.), *Perspectives of the Scottish City* (Aberdeen 1985).

GOSDEN, P. H. J. H., *Self-Help: Voluntary Associations in Nineteenth-Century Britain* (London, 1973).

GRANT, A., and STRINGER, K. J. (eds.), *Uniting the Kingdom? The Making of British History* (London, 1995).

GRAY, R. Q., *The Labour Aristocracy in Victorian Edinburgh* (Edinburgh, 1976).

GREENFELD, L., *Nationalism: Five Roads to Modernity* (Massachusetts, 1992).

GRIERSON, A., *Reconstruction Problems: Local Government in Edinburgh and District. Report by the Town Clerk of Edinburgh* (Edinburgh, 1919).

GRIMBLE, I., *Clans and Chiefs* (London, 1980).

GUTCHEN, R. M., 'Local improvements and centralisation in nineteenth-century England', *Historical Journal*, iv (1961).

GUTHRIE, D., *A Short History of the Royal Society Club of Edinburgh, 1820–1962, Published privately by the Royal Society Club* (Edinburgh, 1962).

HALL, J. A., 'Nationalisms: classified and explained', *Daedalus*, cxxii (3) (1993).

—— (ed.), *Civil Society: Theory, History, Comparison* (Cambridge, 1995).

HANHAM, H. J., 'Mid-century Scottish nationalism: romantic and radical', in R. Robson (ed.), *Ideas and Institutions of Victorian Britain: Essays in Honour of George Kitson Clark* (London, 1967).

——, *The Nineteenth-Century Constitution: Documents and Commentary* (Cambridge, 1969).

——, *Scottish Nationalism* (London, 1969).

HARRISON, B., *Drink and the Victorians: The Temperance Question in England, 1815–1872* (London, 1970).

HART, T., 'Urban growth and municipal government: Glasgow in comparative context, 1864–1914', in A. Slaven and D. H. Aldcroft (eds.), *Business, Banking and Urban History* (Edinburgh, 1982).

HARVIE, C., 'Scottish politics', in A. Dickson and J. H. Treble (eds.), *People and Society in Scotland*, vol. III: *1914–1900* (Edinburgh, 1992).

——, *The Rise of Regional Europe* (London, 1994).

——, *Scotland and Nationalism* (2nd edn, London, 1994).

HECHTER, M., *Internal Colonialism: The Celtic Fringe in British National Development, 1536–1966* (London, 1975).

——, 'Internal colonialism revisited', *Cencrastus*, x (1982).

HENNOCK, E. P., 'Centre/local government relations in England: an outline, 1800–1950', *Urban History Yearbook*, xl (1982).

HOBSBAWM, E. J., *Industry and Empire* (London, 1968).

——, *Nations and Nationalism since 1780: Programme, Myth, Reality* (Cambridge, 1990).

——, and RANGER, T. (eds.), *The Invention of Tradition* (Cambridge, 1983).

HUDSON, P., *The Industrial Revolution* (London, 1992).

HUTCHINSON, J., *The Dynamics of Cultural Nationalism* (London, 1987).

——, *Modern Nationalism* (London, 1994).

——, 'Back from the dead? The rediscovery of cultural nationalism', *The Association for the Study of Ethnicity Bulletin*, viii (1994–5).

——, and SMITH, A. D. (eds.), *Nationalism* (Oxford, 1994).

HUTCHISON, I. G. C., *A Political History of Scotland, 1832–1914: Parties, Elections and Issues* (Edinburgh, 1986).

KEARNEY, H., *The British Isles: A History of Four Nations* (Cambridge, 1989).

KEATING, M., *Labour and Scottish Nationalism* (London, 1979).

KELLAS, J. G., *The Scottish Political System* (3rd edn, Cambridge, 1984).

——, *The Politics of Nationalism and Ethnicity* (London, 1991).

KELTIE, J. S. (ed.), *A History of the Scottish Highlands, Highland Clans and Highland Regiments with an account of the Gaelic language, literature and music and an essay on Highland scenery*, vol. II (Edinburgh, 1881).

KERMACK, W. R., *The Clan Macgregor* (3rd edn, Edinburgh, 1979).

KIDD, C., *Subverting Scotland's Past: Scottish Whig Historians and the Creation of an Anglo-British Identity, 1689–c.1830* (Cambridge, 1993).

KING, R., *The State in Modern Society: New Directions in Political Sociology* (London, 1986).

KITSON-CLARK, G. S. R., *An Expanding Society: Britain, 1830–1900* (Cambridge, 1967).

KODITSCHEK, T., *Class Formation and Urban Industrial Society: Bradford, 1750–1850* (Cambridge, 1990).

KOHN, H., *Prophets and Peoples: Studies in Nineteenth-Century Nationalism* (New York, 1946).

KUMAR, K., 'Civil society: an enquiry into the usefulness of an historical term', *British Journal of Sociology*, xliv (3) (1993).

LASKI, H. J., *Political Thought in England: Locke to Bentham* (London, 1920).

LEE, C. H., *Scotland and the United Kingdom: The Economy and the Union in the Twentieth Century* (Manchester, 1995).

LEVITT, I., *Poverty and Welfare in Scotland, 1890–1948* (Edinburgh, 1988).

—— (ed.), *Government and Social Conditions in Scotland, 1845–1919* (Edinburgh, 1988).

LEWIS, R. A., *Edwin Chadwick and the Public Health Movement, 1832–1854* (London, 1952).

LIPMAN, V. D., *Local Government Areas, 1834–1945* (Oxford, 1949).

LUBENOW, W. C., *The Politics of Government Growth: Early Victorian attitudes towards State Intervention, 1833–1848* (Devon, 1971).

LYNCH, M., *Scotland: A New History* (London, 1991).

—— (ed.), *Scotland, 1850–1979: Society, Politics and the Union* (London, 1993).

LYON, J. M., 'The Herder syndrome: a comparative study of cultural nationalism', in *Ethnic and Racial Studies*, xvii (2) (1994).

MACAULAY, T. B., *History of England* (London, 1855–61).

——, *The Works of Lord Macaulay: Complete*, vol. VIII (London, 1866).

MACCORMICK, N., 'Sovereignty: myth and reality', *Scottish Affairs*, xi (1995).

MCCRONE, D., *Understanding Scotland: The Sociology of a Stateless Nation* (London, 1992).

——, 'Editorial: rhetorics of regionalism', *Scottish Affairs*, vii (1994).

——, and ELLIOTT, B., *Property and Power in a City: The Sociological Significance of Landlordism* (Basingstoke, 1989).

MCCRONE, D., MORRIS, A., and KIELY, R., *Scotland – the Brand: The Making of the Scottish Heritage Industry* (Edinburgh, 1995).

MACDONAGH, O., *A Pattern of Government Growth: The Passenger Acts and their Enforcement* (London, 1961).

MACDONALD, H., 'Public Health Legislation and Problems in Victorian Edinburgh, with special reference to the work of Dr Littlejohn as Medical Officer of Health' (Edinburgh University Ph.D. thesis, 1972).

MACGREGOR, F., *Clan Gregor* (Edinburgh, 1977).

MACKAY, J., *William Wallace: Brave Heart* (Edinburgh, 1995).

MACKENZIE, W. J. M., *Political Identity* (Middlesex, 1978).

MACKIE, J. D., and PRYDE, G. S., *Local Government in Scotland* (Dunfermline, 1932).

MACKINNON, J., *The Union of England and Scotland: A Study of International History* (London, 1896).

MACKINTOSH, J. P., 'The new appeal of nationalism', *New Statesman*, 27 Sep. 1974.

MANN, M., 'The autonomous power of the state', *Archives Européenes de Sociologie*, xxv (1984).

MARSDEN, G. (ed.), *Victorian Values: Personalities and Perspectives in Nineteenth-Century Society* (London, 1990).

MARSTON, M., *Sir Edwin Chadwick (1800–1890)* (London and Boston, 1925).

MARTIN, D., *European Union: The Shattered Dream?* (Broxburn, 1994).

MILLER, W. A., *The 'Philosophical': A Short History of the Edinburgh Philosophical Institution and its Famous Members and Lectures, 1846–1948* (Edinburgh, 1949).

MORE, C., *The Industrial Age: Economy and Society in Britain, 1750–1985* (London, 1989).

MORGAN, N., and TRAINOR, R., 'The dominant classes', in Fraser and Morris, *People and Society*, vol. II.

MORGAN, P., *The Eighteenth-Century Renaissance* (Dyfed, 1981).

MORRIS, A., 'Patrimony and Power: A Study of Lairds and Landownership in the Scottish Borders' (Edinburgh University Ph.D. thesis, 1989).

——, and MORTON, G., *Locality, Community and Nation* (London, 1998).

MORRIS, R. J., 'The middle class and British towns in the Industrial Revolution', in D. Fraser and A. Sutcliffe (eds.), *The Pursuit of Urban History* (London, 1983).

——, 'Voluntary societies and British urban elites, 1780–1850: an analysis', *Historical Journal*, xxvi (1983).

——, 'The state, the elite and the market: the "visible hand" in the British Industrial City System' (paper for the International Group for Urban History Colloquium, Leiden, 1988).

——, *Class, Sect and Party: The Making of the British Middle Class. Leeds, 1820–1850* (Manchester, 1990).

——, 'Clubs, societies and associations', in F. M. L. Thompson (ed.), *The Cambridge Social History of Britain, 1750–1950*, vol. III (Cambridge 1990).

——, 'Petitions, meetings and class formation amongst the urban middle classes in Britain in the 1830s', *Tijdschrift voor Geschiedenis*, cii (1990).

——, 'Scotland, 1830–1914: the making of a nation within a nation', in Fraser and Morris, *People and Society*, vol. II.

MORRIS, R. J., 'Urbanisation in Scotland', in Fraser and Morris, *People and Society*, vol. II.

——, 'Victorian values in Scotland and England', in Smout, *Victorian Values*.

——, and MORTON, G., 'The re-making of Scotland: a nation within a nation, 1850–1920', in Lynch, *Scotland, 1850–1979*.

——, and ——, 'Where was nineteenth-century Scotland?', *Scottish Historical Review*, lxxiv (1994).

MORSE, D., *High Victorian Culture* (London, 1993).

MORTON, G., 'Unionist-Nationalism: The Historical Construction of Scottish National Identity. Edinburgh, 1830–1860' (Edinburgh University Ph.D. thesis, 1993).

——, 'Presenting the self: record linkage and referring to ordinary historical persons', *History and Computing*, vi (1) (1994).

——, 'Scottish rights and "centralisation" in the mid-nineteenth century', *Nations and Nationalism*, ii (2) (1996).

——, 'What if? The significance of Scotland's missing nationalism in the nineteenth century', in D. Broun, R. Finlay and M. Lynch (eds.), *Image and Identity: The Making and Remaking of Scotland through the Ages* (Edinburgh, 1998).

——, 'Civil society, municipal government and the state: enshrinement, empowerment and legitimacy. Scotland, 1800–1929', *Urban History*, xxv (3) (1998).

——, 'The most efficacious patriot: the heritage of William Wallace in nineteenth-century Scotland', *Scottish Historical Review*, lxxvii (1998).

MURDOCH, A., *'The People Above': Politics and Administration in Mid-Eighteenth-Century Scotland* (Edinburgh, 1980).

——, and SHER, R. B., 'Literacy and learned culture', in Devine and Mitchison, *People and Society*, vol. I.

NAIRN, T., *The Break-Up of Britain* (2nd edn, London, 1981).

——, *The Enchanted Glass: Britain and its Monarchy* (London, 1988).

——, 'Internationalism and the second coming', *Daedalus*, cxxii (3) (1993).

——, 'Upper and lower cases', *London Review of Books*, xvii (16) (1995).

NENADIC, S., 'The rise of the urban middle class', in Devine and Mitchison, *People and Society*, vol. I.

NEWMAN, G., *The Rise of English Nationalism, 1740–1830* (London, 1987).

NYE, J. V., 'The myth of free trade Britain and fortress France: tariffs and trade in the nineteenth century', *Journal of Economic History*, li (1) (1991).

O'BRIEN, P., 'Central government and the economy, 1688–1815', in Floud and McCloskey, *Economic History of Britain*, vol. I.

OSMOND, J., *The Divided Kingdom* (London, 1988).

PATERSON, L., *The Autonomy of Modern Scotland* (Edinburgh, 1994).

PATON, D. W., 'Drink and the Temperance Movement in Nineteenth-Century Scotland' (Edinburgh University Ph.D. thesis, 1977).

PEARCE, R., and STEARN, R., *Government and Reform, 1815–1918* (London, 1994).

PEARSON, R., *The Longman Companion to European Nationalism, 1789–1920* (London, 1994).

PENROSE, J., 'Reification in the name of change: the impact of nationalism on social constructions of nation, people and place in Scotland and the United Kingdom', in P. Jackson and J. Penrose (eds.), *Constructions of Race, Place and Nation* (London, 1993).

PHILLIPS, J. A., *The Great Reform Bill in the Boroughs: English Electoral Behaviour, 1818–1841* (Oxford, 1992).

PHILLIPSON, N. T., 'Nationalism and ideology', in J. N. Wolfe (ed.), *Government and Nationalism in Scotland* (Edinburgh, 1969).

PITTOCK, M. G. H., *The Invention of Scotland: The Stuart Myth and the Scottish Identity, 1638 to the Present* (London, 1991).

POCOCK, J. G. A., 'The limits and divisions of British History: in search of an unknown subject', *American Historical Review*, lxxxvii (2) (1982).

PORTER, R. (ed.), *Myths of the English* (Oxford, 1993).

POTTINGER, G., *The Secretaries of State for Scotland, 1926–76. Fifty Years of the Scottish Office* (Edinburgh, 1979).

PREBBLE, J., *The King's Jaunt: George IV in Scotland, 1822* (London, 1988).

PRYDE, G. S. (ed.), *The Treaty of Union of Scotland and England, 1707* (London, 1950).

QUINAULT, R., '1848 and parliamentary reform', *Historical Journal*, xxxi (1988).

RENAN, E., *Qu'est-ce qu'une nation?*, trans. I. M. Snyder (Paris, 1882).

ROBBINS, K., *Nineteenth-Century Britain: England, Scotland and Wales. The Making of a Nation* (Oxford, 1988).

——, 'An imperial and multinational polity: the "scene from the centre", 1832–1922', in Grant and Stringer, *Uniting the Kingdom?*

ROBERTSON, J., 'Walter Scott and the crises of unionist patriotism', *Radical Scotland*, xlvi (1990).

ROSE, R., *Understanding the United Kingdom: The Territorial Dimension in Government* (London, 1982).

SALMOND, A., 'Winning with Wallace', Address to the 61st Annual National Conference, 22 Sep. 1995, Perth City Halls, speech reproduced on the World Wide Web (http://www.snp.org.uk/), 17 Oct. 1995.

SAMUEL, R. (ed.), *Patriotism: The Making and Unmaking of British National Identity*, vols. I–III (London, 1987).

SCOTT, J., *A Matter of Record: Documentary Sources in Social Research* (Cambridge, 1990).

SCOTT, P. H., *Scott and Scotland* (Edinburgh, 1981).

SEED, J., 'Unitarianism, political economy and the antinomies of liberal culture in Manchester, 1830–1850', *Social History*, vii (1) (1982).

SETON-WATSON, H., *Nations and States: An Enquiry into the Origins of Nations and the Politics of Nationalism* (London, 1977).

SHANNON, R., 'David Urquhart and the Foreign Affairs Committees', in P. Hollis (ed.), *Pressure from without in Early Victorian England* (London, 1974).

SHAPIN, S., and BARNES, B., 'Science, nature and control: interpreting Mechanics' Institutes', in Dale, Esland and McDonald, *Schooling and Capitalism*.

SHAW, J. E., *Local Government in Scotland: Past, Present and Future* (Edinburgh, 1942).

SHILS, E., 'Nation, nationality, nationalism and civil society', *Nations and Nationalism*, i (1) (1995).

SMITH, A., *A Summer in Skye* (London, 1865).

SMITH, A. D., *The Ethnic Origin of Nations* (Oxford, 1986).

——, 'The myth of the "modern nation" and the myths of nation', *Ethnic and Racial Studies*, xi (1) (1988).

——, *National Identity* (London, 1991).

——, 'The problem of national identity: ancient, medieval and modern?', *Ethnic and Racial Studies*, xvii (3) (1994).

——, 'Gastronomy or geology? The role of nationalism in the reconstruction of nations, *Nations and Nationalism*, i (1) (1995).

SMITH, D. (ed.), *A People and a Proletariat: Essays in the History of Wales, 1780–1980* (London, 1980).

SMITH, G., 'Karl Marx and St George', *Journal of the History of Ideas*, ii (4) (1941).

SMOUT, T. C., *A History of the Scottish People, 1560–1830* (London, 1969).

——, 'Centre and periphery in history', *Journal of Common Market Studies*, xviii (3) (1980).

——, 'Scotland and England: is dependency a symptom or a cause of underdevelopment?', *Review*, iii (4) (1980).

——, *A Century of the Scottish People, 1830–1950* (London, 1986).

——, 'Problems of nationalism, identity and improvement in later eighteenth-century Scotland', in T. M. Devine (ed.), *Improvement and Enlightenment* (Edinburgh, 1989).

——, 'Scotland, 1750–1950', in F. M. L. Thompson (ed.), *The Cambridge Social History of Britain, 1750–1950*, vol. I: *Regions and Communities* (Cambridge, 1990).

——, 'Perspectives on the Scottish identity', *Scottish Affairs*, vi (1994).

—— (ed.), *Victorian Values: A Joint Symposium of the Royal Society of Edinburgh and the British Academy, December 1990, Proceedings of the British Academy*, lxxviii (Oxford, 1992).

STAPLETON, J., *Englishness and the Study of Politics: The Social and Political Thought of Ernest Barker* (Cambridge, 1994).

SUTCLIFFE, A., 'The growth of public intervention in the British urban environment during the nineteenth century: a structural approach', in J. H. Johnston and C. G. Pooley (eds.), *The Structure of Nineteenth-Century Cities* (London, 1982).

TAYLOR, A. J., *Laissez-faire and State Intervention in Nineteenth-Century Britain* (London, 1972).

TAYLOR, P. J., 'The English and their Englishness: "a curious, mysterious, elusive and little understood people"', *Scottish Geographical Magazine*, cvii (3) (1991).

TAYLOR, T., 'On central and local action in relation to town improvement', *Transactions of the National Association for the Promotion of the Social Science* (1857).

THOMPSON, F. M. L., *The Rise of Respectable Society: A Social History of Victorian Britain, 1830–1900* (London, 1988).

TILLY, C., 'National self-determination as a problem for all of us', *Daedalus*, cxxii (3) (1993).

TRANTER, N., *The Wallace* (London, 1975).

TREBLE, J. H., *Urban Poverty in Britain, 1830–1914* (London, 1979).

TURNBULL, M. T. R. B., *Monuments and Statues of Edinburgh* (Edinburgh, 1989).

WATTS, D., *Whigs, Radicals and Liberals, 1815–1914* (London, 1995).

WEBB, K., *The Growth of Nationalism in Scotland* (Glasgow, 1977).

WEBB, S., and WEBB, B., *English Poor Law History, Part II: The Last Hundred Years*: vol. I (London, 1929).

WHATLEY, C., 'An uninflammable people?', in Donnachie and Whatley, *Manufacture of Scottish History*.

WHETSTONE, A. E., *Scottish County Government in the Eighteenth and Nineteenth Centuries* (Edinburgh, 1981).

WHYTE, W. E., *Local Government in Scotland, with complete statutory references* (2nd edn, London, 1936).

WILLIAMS, J. C., 'Edinburgh Politics: 1832–1852' (Edinburgh University Ph.D. thesis, 1972).

WILLIAMS, R., *The Long Revolution* (London, 1961).

WITHERS, C., 'The historical creation of the Scottish Highlands', in Donnachie and Whatley, *Manufacture of Scottish History*.

YOUNG, J. D., *The Rousing of the Scottish Working Class* (London, 1979).

YOUNGSON, A. J., *The Making of Classical Edinburgh* (Edinburgh, 1966).

ZELDIN, T., *France, 1848–1945* (Oxford, 1980).

ZUBIADA, S., 'Nations: old and new. Comments on Anthony D. Smith's "The myth of the 'modern nation' and the myths of nations"', *Ethnic and Racial Studies*, xii (3) (1989).

Index